THE PREMARITAL COUNSELING HANDBOOK

THE
PREMARITAL
COUNSELING
HANDBOOK

H. NORMAN WRIGHT

MOODY PRESS
CHICAGO

Contents

CHAPTER

1

Marriage Today

T he wedding service is about to begin. Three hundred people are crowded into the sanctuary with an air of expectancy. A popular couple from the church is about to commit themselves to one another for the rest of their lives. They have gone together for the past three years and seem so ideally suited for each other. Ever since they were in their early teens many people have said this couple seem destined to be together. They are intelligent, expressive, capable, involved in the activities of the church, and each has a stable family background.

Who would think that just four years later this couple would meet in a courtroom to finalize the details of the dissolution of their marriage?

Divorce happens. It has happened to a couple you know. Perhaps you even officiated at their wedding ceremony. It's painful for everyone involved. The loss of dreams, hopes, and expectations has a lasting effect not only upon the couple, but on their families and everyone involved in their initial coming together.

Marriage is the closest bond that can occur between two people. That was God's original intent. But who is really prepared for the demands of living together in such a way that needs are met, dreams are fulfilled, harmony is attained, and God is glorified through their relationship? Very few. Someone needs to help couples of all ages enter marriage with a greater opportunity for it to last and for each partner to be fulfilled. It is safe to say that the church and its pastoral staff is the last agency to make an impact upon marriage and divorce today.

Marital breakup is so frequent, even among Christian couples, that it appears to be an accepted part of our society. Even cartoons reflect this attitude.

The attitude toward marriage today was revealed in the office of a marriage counselor when a young woman said, "When I got married I was looking for an ideal, but I married an ordeal, and now I want a new deal!" A recent cartoon in the *Los Angeles Times* pictured a pastor performing a wedding. Instead of the usual "till death do you part," he said, "till divorce do you part." This is not entirely unreal.

Another cartoon shows a minister performing the wedding ceremony for a couple and he is saying, "And do you, Mary, take Jim to be your husband, to have and hold, love and cherish, until things get a little tough, you get burned out, and split?" Still another recent cartoon shows a couple in a pastor's office working out the wedding vows and the woman is saying, "And finally, we'd like to change the 'until death do you part' section of our vows to 'substantial penalty for early withdrawal.'"

This past year a Los Angeles paper ran an advertisement for a wedding chapel in Reno, Nevada. The ad read, "Marriage Discount $22.00, includes wedding service, music, witness, cassette recording of ceremony, marriage scroll, parking." Unfortunately this reflects how little thought and preparation are given to one of the most important events in a person's life.

What is happening today with marriage and divorce? Family life is changing. Only 25 percent of the households are "traditional" anymore —two parents with children. There are as many single-person households as there are traditional. The age for first marriages is significantly higher than it once was—26 for men, 24 for women. This last fact is healthy for marriages since marrying too young contributes to divorce. The divorce rate for our country has leveled off and, because of the delay of age of marriage, the rate may actually drop during the nineties.

Within California, the divorce rate varies radically from county to county. In Los Angeles County there were 41,326 licensed marriages and

32,011 confidential marriages in 1989 for a total of 73,392 marriages. There were 42,088 divorces that year. But in Orange County 3,888 licensed marriages and 6,079 confidential marriages took place, totaling 9,967. There were 16,123 divorces for the same year.[1]

Confidential marriages may take place when a man and woman have been living together and marry without first procuring a marriage license or obtaining and filing health certificates. This means they do not have to take a blood test and AIDS test, and the woman does not undergo the test for rubella. To be married, they are required to go through a ceremony of solemnization by a person authorized to solemnize marriages and to complete a special marriage certificate. The certificate is mailed to the county clerk and kept there as a permanent confidential record.

The original purpose of this law was to encourage persons living together, perhaps having had children, to legalize their relationship by allowing them to do so with a minimum of publicity and embarrassment. But it appears that many see it as a short cut to having a public ceremony. And it runs counter to the purpose of the physical exam and blood testing, which were originally instituted for the protection of the couple.

The concern over the status of marriage and the family has been with us for many years. A pioneer in the field of counseling, Carl Rogers made the statement:

> To me it seems that we are living in an important and uncertain age, and the institution of marriage is most assuredly in an uncertain state. If 50-75 percent of Ford or General Motors cars completely fell apart within the early part of their lifetimes as automobiles, drastic steps would be taken. We have no such well organized way of dealing with our social institutions, so people are groping, more or less blindly, to find alternatives to marriage (which is certainly less than 50 percent successful). Living together without marriage, living in communes, extensive child care centers, serial monogamy (with one divorce after another), the women's liberation movement to establish the woman as a person in her own right, new divorce laws which do away with the concept of guilt—these are all groping toward some new form of man-woman relationship for the future. It would take a bolder man than I to predict what will emerge.[2]

MARRIAGE AS SCHOOL, AS SPACE VOYAGE

Marriage is one of God's greatest schools of learning—it can be a place where a husband and wife are refined. The rough edges are gradually filed away until there is a deeper, smoother, and more fulfilling working and blending together that is satisfying to both individuals. But this takes an incredible amount of time, energy, and effort.

In his book *The Mystery of Marriage,* Mike Mason describes the marital journey in a unique way:

> Marriage partners may be thought of as the astronauts of society—the daring explorers who do all the test flying in a sort of ongoing experiment in the most radical fringes of human relations. Naturally there are many crashes, many casualties in this stratosphere of intimacy. It is a most dangerous profession, and one with a high rate of burnout. It is demanding, draining, and often dreary work, and unlike space exploration the rewards it offers do not seem very glamorous. There will be no ticker tape parades for the good wife or husband, and most couples actually have a tendency to avoid the very aspects of their work which do offer the greatest rewards. Particularly are they prone to resent all the time that they must "waste" with one another, and after the first year or so of marriage they begin to have great difficulty believing that the lavish interpersonal extravagance which characterized their courtship might actually still be allowed, let alone be a necessary or glorious thing. Accordingly, great amounts of energy are channeled into other concerns, into friendships and social life, into careers, into the raising of offspring (godly or otherwise), into every conceivable cause except the cause of marriage itself. For what possible practical use could there be in continuing that systematic and unrelenting invasion of privacy which is the heart and soul, the rocket fuel, of a loving relationship? Everywhere else, throughout society, there are fences, walls, burglar alarms, unlisted numbers, the most elaborate precautions for keeping people at a safe distance. But in marriage all of that is reversed. In marriage the walls are down, and not only do the man and woman live under the same roof, but they sleep under the same covers. Their lives are wide open, and as each studies the life of the other and attempts to make some response to it, there are no set procedures to follow, no formalities to stand on. A man and a woman face each other across the breakfast table, and somehow through a haze of crumbs and curlers and mortgage payments they must encounter one another. That is the whole purpose and mandate of marriage. All sorts of other purposes have been dreamed up and millions of excuses invented for avoiding this central and indispensable task. But the fact is that marriage is grounded in nothing else but the pure wild grappling of soul with soul, no holds barred. There is no rulebook for this, no law to invoke except the law of love.

So while marriage may present the appearance of being a highly structured, formalized, and tradition-bound institution, in fact it is the most free and raw and unpredictable of all human associations. It is the outer space of society, the wild frontier.[3]

DREAMS VERSUS REALITY

As most couples move toward marriage, their sense of reality is distorted by wishfulness and fantasy. Once they are husband and wife, this intense romantic illusion can neutralize positive developments in their marriage. Unrealistic expectations and fantasies create a gulf between the partners and cause disappointments. Each person in the relationship can create such detailed fantasies that neither the other partner nor the relationship has any chance for survival.

Many marriages today are like the house built upon sand—they have been built upon a weak foundation of dreams. When we dream our minds do not have to distinguish between reality or fantasy, so we are able to create without restraint. Often, therefore, our dreams are starting points for successful endeavor. However, dreams that are not followed by adequate planning usually do not come true.

Marriages built on dreams are risky because dreams do not consider the disappointments and changes that are inevitable in every marriage. When the season changes and the rains of reality and the winds of stress blow upon such marriages, the relationship that should hold them together crumbles. Much more is involved in fulfilling dreams than merely expecting them to come true. Mason describes marriage's blunt reality in this manner:

> To be married is not to be taken off the front lines of love, but rather to be plunged into the thick of things. It is to be faced, day in and day out, with the necessity of making over and over again, and at deeper and deeper levels, that same terrifying momentous and impossible decision which one could only have made when one was head-over heels in love and out of one's mind with trust and faith. This is not resignation to a fate, but the free and spontaneous embracing of a gift, of a challenge and a destiny.
>
> Is it any wonder if people cannot take the pressure? It is a pressure that can only be handled by love, and in ever-increasing doses. Marriage involves a continuous daily renewal of a decision which, since it is of such a staggering order as to be humanly impossible to make, can only be made through the grace of God.[4]

Building a good marriage means a person must take time to redefine roles, beliefs, and behaviors and negotiate the differences with his/her partner. Money, time, power, family traditions, friends, vocations, and use of space in the home are just a few of the issues that need to be negotiated.

A newly married couple needs a spirit of adventure, because getting married to a "stranger" means that there are going to be a lot of discoveries. What if one is a night person and the other is a morning person? One is talkative in the morning and one at night? Perhaps one likes to be babied when he or she is sick while the other hides illness and wants to be left alone. Or one likes the room at 78 degrees and the other at 68 degrees. Maybe one wears a set of underwear for three days; the other changes it twice a day. One uses a towel once and discards it; the other uses it for a week. These are just a few of the practical day-to-day items that can drive a couple crazy. The spirit of adventure will help the couple realize, "We're different and that's OK."

Perhaps this dilemma is best expressed this way: "A marriage is not a joining of two worlds, but an abandoning of two worlds in order that a new one might be formed."[5]

WHY MARRIAGES FAIL

Here are four usually unidentified reasons that marriages dissolve. First, one or both persons fail to understand the stages and changes of individual development—the seasons of their lives—and how these affect their marriage. Many women experience an identity transition around thirty and experience a mid-life transition in their late thirties or early forties, as do men.

Second, people have an inadequate basis upon which they build their personal identity and security. Too many build their identity on performance, perfectionism, or appearance, and these eventually fade. The best basis for marriage comes from the one who instituted marriage in the first place; but for too many, the teachings of God's Word have not been incorporated in depth into their lives, transforming both their identity and their security.

Third, people come to marriage with either unresolved issues between them and their parents, or they come from dysfunctional families, and this intrudes upon their marriage.

Fourth, some marriages dissolve because the partners were never prepared for marriage and because their expectations about marriage were totally unrealistic. David Mace, a pioneer in the field of marriage enrichment, describes this lack of preparation:

When I try to reconstruct, in counseling with couples, their concepts of the making of a marriage, I find that it adds up to a most confused hodgepodge of starry-eyed romanticism, superstition, superficial concepts, and laissez-faire. Seldom do I find any real understanding of the complexity of the task of bringing two separate individuals into a delicately balanced coordination of each other's thoughts, feelings, wishes, beliefs, and habit patterns.[6]

What happens if a couple marries at the start of their transition from adolescence to adult? They find themselves learning to separate from their parents, trying out the new adult world, and adapting to a spouse all at the same time. Sometimes early marriage (ages seventeen to twenty-two) contributes to difficulties with parents, and the partners end up retaining some of their childish qualities. The new husband and wife may both feel extra strain at this time because they are both emerging. This is why early marriages have such a high risk.

These young adults may have had little experience in forming peer relationships with members of the opposite sex. One mate may become a tool to help the other relinquish the relationship with his/her parents and become an adult.

GROWTH AND DEVELOPMENT

No matter at what stage a couple enters marriage, they will have issues and conflicts to resolve. Both the man and woman must continue to develop personally as well as together. They can no longer rely upon their society, culture, family, or even their commitment to their faith to keep their marriage together. Marriages receive less outside support today than they used to because of the change in values, culture, divorce laws, and an emphasis upon selfishness and individualism. Greater effort and commitment on the part of each are needed. Couples also must develop a strong commitment to two primary marriage concepts in Scripture: fidelity and permanency.

A lasting relationship is more possible if both partners continue to grow and develop. If the husband uses his wife to further the attainment of his dream and in the process she loses her own dream, her growth will be stifled and eventually both will be disappointed. For example, a medical student marries and his wife supports him for years in the pursuit of his dream. She forgoes her own advancement, education, and intellectual development. Soon children arrive. He is into his eighty-hour-a-week practice and becomes acquainted with a woman who is freer, less restricted, and more intellectually stimulating than his wife. He decides to change partners.

Or a man may choose to marry only because in his profession a family man is more acceptable. In this case he may see wife and children as necessary accessories.

Sometimes a marriage relationship hinders the pursuit of a man's dream. His wife may have no interest in his dream and may even prevent him from attaining it. Her own dream may be complementary, different, or antagonistic. Any of these conditions can affect the success of the marriage.

If a woman sees herself exclusively in the traditional roles of wife and mother, she may derive her identity from her husband and what he does. She sees her husband as her protector and turns her whole being over to him. She continues to support his dream as long as he gives sufficient attention to her and their family, and as long as she feels needed by him and their children. She probably believes that men are attracted primarily to physical beauty and helplessness. But as she ages, her physical attractiveness may fade and her husband may grow weary of her "helplessness." By her thirties and forties she may be needed less and less by her husband and family, and she may be forced to seek out her own identity.

If a woman has been overly dependent on her husband and decides to change, her husband may feel threatened, especially if the change costs him something. He accepts it better if it benefits him. She could begin to believe that her husband is the obstacle to her growth. Actually, it may just be that he is not giving her the encouragement she desires from him.

It is not uncommon for a woman in her late thirties or early forties to experience an identity crisis. She may become disillusioned with her traditional role; she may resent her caretaker husband. If she decides to develop some independence and pursue a career, she may face a number of obstacles. Job availability may be limited. Or if she finds a job, she may find the role of both career woman and homemaker a strain. Some women are fearful of the feelings of competition and power within them that have lain dormant for so many years. Accepting these and using them in creative ways, both within the home and in a career, can be a freeing experience.[7]

But no matter what age a person marries, he or she will find certain difficulties—as well as a great many advantages—in adjusting to married life. It is our task in premarital counseling to help people in advance.

In the midst of developing their own personal lives, a man and a woman marry. The romantic idealism eventually turns to the question, "Will we make it together?" Great expectations and hopes are mixed with fears, anxieties, and surprises. A host of new and unexpected events come into their lives. Those that are expected or anticipated will be handled fairly smoothly, but the surprises can be disruptive. This is why extensive and thorough premarital preparation with a minister or counselor is a necessity. As there are stages and phases to work through in one's own life, there are also important stages and phases to work through in the first few years of marriage. Too many couples are unaware of these, and such premarital counseling can help them anticipate these adjustments.

TWO TASKS IN MARRIAGE

The first task is to define what a *wife* is and what a *husband* is. In marriage, each must retain his/her individual identity while drawing close together as a couple. A marriage relationship is meant to be a freeing-up relationship, never a confinement. Each person is freed to develop uniqueness and spiritual giftedness in his or her own way, and join these to give the marital relationship strength and greater potential.

This may mean breaking loose from preconceived images each one has of what a spouse should be. If couples cannot allow each other to develop, grow, and be creative in defining new roles, the conflict will be intense. As one person vividly put it, "Both of you will wind up drilling holes in your own marriage before it has left the shore."

A second task is to develop the romantic love of courtship into a love based upon steady commitment. Before people marry, they may be drawn to their friend because of a specific character trait that they see as a strength. But when they marry they may find that this "strength" begins to bother them. They begin to view it as a weakness rather than a strength and soon want the person to change. This character trait, however, is an expression of their mate's personality. If it bothers a person it needs to be discussed but not attacked as a weakness. Labeling a behavior as a weakness does little to bring about change.

The love that is needed to stabilize a marriage is the type of love God displays to each of us—an unconditional commitment to an imperfect person. This takes energy and effort. It means caring about the other as much as you care about yourself. Krantzler describes what marital love actually means:

15

Marital love requires the ability to put yourself in your partner's place, to understand that the differences that divide you are the differences of two unique personalities, rather than betrayals of your hopes and dreams. The unconditional willingness of each of you to understand and resolve these differences through the sharing of your deepest feelings, concerns, attitudes and ideas is a fundamental component of marital love. Postponement of your need for instant gratification when your partner feels no such need; sharing the struggle to triumph over adversities as well as sharing the joys and delights of being together; nurturing each other in defeat caused by forces beyond our control and renewing each other's courage to prevail in the face of despair; carrying necessary obligations and responsibilities as a flower rather than as a hundred-pound knapsack; acknowledging the everyday value of your partner in a look, a smile, a touch of the hand, a voiced appreciation of a meal or a new hair style, a spontaneous trip to a movie or a restaurant; trusting your partner always to be there when needed; knowing that he or she always has your best interests at heart even when criticism is given; loyalty and dedication to each other in the face of sacrifices that may have to be made—all of these are additional components of marital love that courtship knows little about.[8]

WHAT KEEPS A MARRIAGE?

One way in which the premarital counselor can assist couples is by telling them the facts of other successful marriages. One survey studied couples with enduring marriages to discover how marriages both survive and satisfy those involved. In a survey of 351 couples, 300 said they were happily married; nineteen were unhappily married but were staying together for various reasons. The remaining thirty-two couples contained one person in the marriage who was unhappy. Each husband and wife responded individually to a questionnaire that included thirty-nine statements and questions about marriage.

The couples were asked to select from the list those statements that best reflected their own marriage. The results are shown below.[9] Interestingly, the top seven reasons for what makes a good marriage were the same for men as for the women.

Here are the top reasons respondents gave, listed in the order of frequency:

MARRIAGE TODAY

Men	Women
My spouse is my best friend.	My spouse is my best friend.
I like my spouse as a person.	I like my spouse as a person.
Marriage is a long-term commitment.	Marriage is a long-term commitment.
Marriage is sacred.	Marriage is sacred.
We agree on aims and goals.	We agree on aims and goals.
My spouse has grown more interesting.	My spouse has grown more interesting.
I want the relationship to succeed.	I want the relationship to succeed.
An enduring marriage is important to social stability.	We laugh together.
We laugh together.	We agree on the philosophy of life.
I am proud of my spouse's achievements.	We agree on how and how often to show affection.
We agree on a philosophy of life.	An enduring marriage is important to social stability.
We agree about our sex life.	We have a stimulating exchange of ideas.
We agree on how and how often to show affection.	We discuss things calmly.
I confide in my spouse.	We agree about our sex life.
We share outside hobbies and interests.	I am proud of my spouse's achievements.

The emphasis that partners place on friendship can lead to a helpful discussion with your couples. I encourage you to share this chart with them. List the characteristics in any order on a piece of paper and have them select what they think would be the most important. Then present the results.

The First Year of Marriage, by Miriam Arond and Samuel Parker, is a significant resource for both counseling and teaching. One author is a psychiatrist and the other is a former editor of a bridal magazine. The authors write:

In researching this book, we contacted hundreds of men and women who shared with us their experiences of adjusting to marriage. We spoke with newlyweds in their teens, newlyweds who are almost senior citizens, newlyweds who married interracially and interreligiously, newlyweds who married people much younger and older than themselves, newlyweds who have children from a previous marriage and newlyweds gaining stepchildren.

We found that regardless of age, reason for marrying, cultural and family background, or previous marital history, there are issues that newlyweds universally face. Inherent in the intimacy of marriage are practical, everyday questions of handling money and dividing household chores, as well as such complex emotional matters as trying to balance the need for closeness with the desire to maintain one's individuality. It is, in fact, in addressing and resolving these and other issues that you establish and solidify your identity as a married couple.[10]

The authors discovered that people who enter marriage unprepared for any problems, adjustments, or disappointments often panic when their marriage is not as it should be and end up feeling they made a big mistake. The basic difference between couples who split up early in marriage and those who stay together is often their attitudes toward their problems. A realistic, prepared, firm biblical attitude toward life and difficulties is a foundation.

Is there a future for family life and marriage as we know it today? Definitely. The vast majority of people in our society want a stable marriage and family life. But we are competing with non-Christian values that are reflected in every phase of our society. Thus, encouraging fidelity and commitment must be our continual message. What people desire and what they end up with are not always the same. In any endeavor, having dreams and goals without concrete plans and preparation will bring failure.

That is where counselors in the church have an opportunity. Imagine what would happen if each couple who married in the next ten years experienced six to eight hours of premarital counseling in their local church, as well as spending sixty to seventy hours on outside preparation through books and tapes. This is the concept of this book. And it is already happening in many churches today.

NOTES

1. Telephone conversation, Bureau of County Records, 227 N. Broadway, Los Angeles, CA 90012; and Bureau of County Records, 630 N. Broadway, Santa Ana, CA 92701.

2. Carl Rogers, *Becoming Partners: Marriage and Its Alternatives* (New York: Delacorte, 1972), p. 11.

3. Mike Mason, *The Mystery of Marriage* (Portland, Ore.: Multnomah, 1985), pp. 73-74.

4. Ibid., pp. 55-56.

5. Ibid., p. 91.

6. David Mace and Mera Mace. *We Can Have Better Marriages If We Really Want Them* (Nashville: Abingdon, 1974), p. 98.

7. Material in this section was adapted from Maggie Scarf, *Unfinished Business* (N.Y.: Doubleday, 1980) and Daniel Levinson, *The Seasons of a Man's Life* (N.Y.: Ballantine, 1979).

8. Mel Krantzler. *Creative Marriages*, (New York: McGraw-Hill, 1988), p. 50.

9. Jeanette Lauer and Robert Lauer, "Marriages Are Made to Last," *Psychology Today*, June 1985, pp. 22-27.

10. Miriam Arond and Samuel L. Pauker, *The First Year of Marriage* (New York: Warner, 1987), pp. 3-4.

2

A Survey
of Premarital Programs

Twenty-five years ago the concept of marital preparation and individual premarital counseling was in its infancy. Today it has moved to a level of maturity as church ministers realize their calling is not to perform weddings but to nurture marriages so that they will become fulfilling and permanent and reflect the presence of Jesus Christ.

For too many years it has been too easy to get married. Unfortunately, in many cases the church has contributed to the divorce problem of our nation by promoting easy weddings. People have spent more time preparing to obtain their driver's license than in preparing for their marriage.

THE COMMUNITY MARRIAGE POLICY

The situation is changing. A growing number of programs are designed to prepare couples for marriage. One with great promise is the

Community Marriage Policy. The policy apparently originated in the central California community of Modesto, where church pastors adopted a community-wide marriage policy in 1986 to make it tougher to get married. A covenant was signed by seventy-three ministers representing more than thirty Protestant, Catholic, and Greek Orthodox churches and Modesto's only Jewish synagogue.

The policy mandated a four-month minimum waiting period before couples could be married. During that time they are required to complete at least two premarital counseling sessions, evaluation testing, biblical teaching on morality, marriage and divorce, and—as needed—marital instruction from "a mature married couple."

Three key changes were made in Modesto. First, Protestant churches agreed with Catholic churches to have a minimum preparation period for engaged couples of at least four months. Second, they added more counseling. Churches with no requirements began demanding two or three sessions. Others already at that level required six sessions. Third, churches began cooperating across the denominational lines for the first time. When a Baptist church told an engaged couple that they had to stop cohabiting if they wanted to be married there, the couple went across town to another church, which they thought would be more liberal. They found the second church's marriage instruction required more sessions than the first.

"We have already had three sessions elsewhere," the couple said. But when the second pastor learned why they had left First Baptist, he informed them. "We also require couples living together to separate. I suggest you separate and go back to First Baptist." The couple did so, and now undoubtedly they have a much better chance for success in their marriage. Modesto demonstrates that churches can raise their standards for marriage preparation with a uniform community policy.

The policy statement, as used in Modesto, California, is shown below. Each counselor who agrees to the policy signs the covenant in section IV.

Community Marriage Policy

I. CONCERN: "Marriage is holy."

One concern as ministers of the Gospel is to foster marital unions under God and to establish successful spiritual families. Almost 90% of all marriages are performed by pastors, and we are troubled by the nearly 50% divorce rate. Our hope is to radically reduce the divorce rate among those married in area churches.

It is the responsibility of pastors to set minimal requirements to raise the quality of commitment in those we marry. We believe that couples who seriously participate in premarital testing and counseling will have a better understanding of what the marriage commitment involves. As agents of God, acting on his behalf, we feel it is our responsibility to encourage couples to set aside time for marriage preparation, instead of concentrating only on wedding plans. We acknowledge that a wedding is but a day; a marriage is for a lifetime.

II. SCRIPTURE: "What God hath joined together, let no man put asunder" (Matt. 19:6).

God has established and sanctified marriage for the welfare and happiness of the human family. For this reason, our Savior has declared that a man shall leave his father and mother and be joined to his wife, and the two shall become one. By his apostles he has instructed those who enter into this relationship to cherish a mutual esteem and love; to share in each other's affirmities and weaknesses; to comfort each other in sickness, trouble and sorrow; to provide for each other and for their household; to pray for and encourage each other; to live together as heirs of the grace of life; and to raise children, if there are any, in the knowledge and love of the Lord. In Malachi 2:13-16 it says that God hates divorce, and in Ephesians 5 the image of marriage is that of Christ and his church.

III. IMPLEMENTATION: These are the minimum expectations:

A. Waiting Period: A minimum of four months from the initial appointment until the wedding date.

B. Premarital Counseling: A minimum of two sessions that would include a relational instrument, inventory or test (e.g., Myers/Briggs or T-JTA) to help the couple evaluate the maturity of their relationship objectively.

C. Scripture: Teach biblical doctrines on morality, marriage and divorce. Encourage them to memorize key verses on marriage.

D. Engagement Seminar: Encourage the couple to participate in a concentrated period of joint introspection.

E. Helping Couples: Provide, as needed, a mature married couple to meet with them to assist in the concept of marital "bonding."

F. Postmarital: Commit ourselves to counseling the couple, as needed.

IV. COVENANT:

    A. I covenant to build successful spiritual families.

    B. I covenant to follow Scripture and to implement these minimum preparations for the couples that I marry to substantially reduce the divorce rate in our area.

    C. I covenant to join with other spiritual leaders to encourage couples to seriously participate in premarital preparation.[1]

The results of this policy are still in process. The number of marriages has remained constant in the Modesto area. In 1988, two years after the community marriage policy was adopted, the number of divorces dropped for the first time. But the numbers went back to previous levels in 1989 and higher in 1990.[2] Why? We are not entirely sure at this point. And there has not been enough time for the community marriage policy to have an effect. The average marriage ending in divorce takes seven years. The better bonding of couples married in 1987 to 1990 should be seen during 1994 to 1997.

The development of community marriage policies has been embraced nationally by the news media and other communities. Most major national Christian magazines have written about Modesto's innovation. *Christian Herald* reported:

> The ministers of Modesto have signed a pact not to perform hurry-up weddings. Whereas individual clergy across the nation have long insisted on a period of preparation with at least some premarital counseling, a couple in a hurry could always go down the road and find a willing pastor. Now the Greater Modesto Ministerial Association has all but shut the door.[3]

Christianity Today devoted a page to the Community Marriage Policy in its September 8, 1989, issue.[4] *Charisma & Christian Life* headlined its April 1990 story with an important result of the covenant: "Divorce Rate Down in California Town." The article reported that "statistics gathered by the *Modesto Bee* suggest the 1986 pact is already having a citywide effect." In summer 1990, *Equipping For Ministry* became the fifth national magazine calling attention to the community marriage policy in Modesto, publishing Modesto's entire text.

Meanwhile, pastors in at least a dozen other cities have transplanted the idea to their own communities. They range from Fresno, California, where 105 pastors have made this commitment, to Beaver, Pennsylvania, with 9 pastors. Fairbanks, Alaska; Kokomo, Indiana; Washington, Pennsl-vania; and Cuyahoga Falls, Ohio all started a similar policy after news columnist Michael McManus made speeches there urging the step.

The community marriage policy has been refined and improved by some second-generation communities. The pastors in Beaver resisted what they thought was an overly rigid formula by saying the "general standards may be applied faithfully, yet flexibly" and they speak of a "normal minimum of four months" preparation period. They hold one event per year "with attendant community publicity to encourage youth to consider the importance of marriage preparation earlier than the few months before an intended marriage." They pledge to "communicate in writing and/or in person with couples in the first months and years of their marriage, offering resources of counsel and encouragement." In Fairbanks, where many weddings involve military personnel stationed there a short time, the minimum preparation period is three months, not four. But instead of requiring a minimum of two counseling sessions, as in Modesto, they ask for at least six counseling sessions, and ask the couple to attend at least one session of post-marital counseling.

The Fairbanks Community Marriage Policy was lavishly praised in an editorial by the *Fairbanks News-Miner,* appearing March 4, 1990:

> The high divorce rate is a troubling phenomenon that creates havoc in the lives of the adults and children who go through it.
>
> Anyone can walk into the state courthouse and get a marriage license in four days.... With such an effective civil system in place, there is no reason for churches to be marriage factories. After all, religious institutions have different responsibilities.... If people want to get married in a church, then it seems appropriate that the churches should do something to increase the chances that those people will stay married. Training and discussion of spiritual princi-ples, morality and marriage are vital if the union is to work.
>
> The key to this policy is that the churches have a way to make people aware of what life is like after the honeymoon.... In the in-terest of stronger marriages and a reduction in the divorce rate, we hope that more of the 100-plus churches in the Fairbanks and North Pole areas embrace this policy.

Four Illinois cities have expanded the community marriage policy to include marital enrichment. Pastors of thirty-eight churches in Peoria, Quincy, Rock Island, and Moline in fall 1991 signed an enlarged commu-nity church policy that insists on premarital counseling and also requires

(1) a minimum of two postmarital counseling sessions with a mentor couple, (2) a "marriage ministry" of mentoring couples whose marriages once nearly failed to work with troubled marriages, (3) encouraging all married couples to attend a couples retreat such as Marriage Encounter or Marriage Enrichment, and (4) ratification of the policy by each pastor's local church board, to assure church-wide support.[5] McManus says the new policy is stronger than the original Modesto statement due to its "emphasis on how the church can deepen and refresh existing marriages, and restore those that are breaking."[6]

"RELATIONSHIP INSTRUCTION"

In addition to this program, Rev. Jim Talley of First Baptist in Modesto began many years ago to convince "seriously dating couples" to take "Relationship Instruction" before even talking about engagement. The sessions include the study of Scripture on marriage and divorce, learning communication skills, and signing a "contract" in which the couples agree to remain chaste and to limit their time together to only four hours a week. Of 1,000 people who have taken "Relationship Instruction" for more than fifteen years, half did not marry. But of those who did, *only 5 percent divorced.*[7]

GROUP AND PRIVATE COUNSELING

At another church in Escondido, California, any couple desiring to be married must contact one of the several ministers of the church. After the initial screening interview with the minister, the couple is then recommended to an eight-week premarital counseling class. At the end of the fourth session of the class the couple resumes their individual counseling of two to six weeks with the pastor. At the conclusion of the counseling and with the approval of the minister, the couple can then put their wedding date on the church calendar. All couples need to begin the counseling and instruction a minimum of six months before their desired wedding date.

The total number of couples who have completed this program over a period of ten years is approximately 400. Of the 400, information is available on approximately 300. The couples had been married between one and ten years and were distributed evenly across the years (about thirty marriages per year). Of the 300 couples, fourteen had divorced— 4.66 percent. About 15 percent had chosen not to marry. The rest had married and were married at the time of follow-up.[8]

We must observe one caution in interpreting these findings. Not all the couples have been married a full ten years, so we must assume additional divorces will occur. If we average out the divorces with the amount of years married, we could anticipate that the divorce rate would not exceed 15 percent. This is still significantly below the national average.

OTHER CHURCH PROGRAMS

A Variety of Approaches

Many churches today have developed extensive ministries for couples seeking to be married. A wide variety of approaches, policies, and resources is in use. Here is a portion of a brochure couples receive at a Midwest evangelical church when planning marriage:

> Marriage is a marvelous experience. It is a union which is compared by Christ to that which exists between our Lord and the Church. There is no union more intimate than this. Next to the union we have with Jesus Christ, marriage can be the happiest relationship one can find. This happiness will be built upon a mutual love for Jesus Christ and for each other, giving oneself away unselfishly in loyalty, consideration and service. The blessings of the Lord will be apportioned to you according to the measure in which you follow His will, as revealed in Scripture.
>
> We are interested in being of help to those who are looking to God for His blessings in marriage. Our pastors...desire to meet with you and share with you the true meaning of the marriage relationship.
>
> The following is our policy for the use of any of our facilities for a wedding:
>
> 1. The pastor performing the wedding should be contacted first, generally 6 to 12 months before the desired marriage date. Reservations for church facilities will be made through him before the date and time are placed on the church calendar or announced.
>
> 2. Normally we expect at least four premarital preparation and enrichment sessions. The couple will be asked to purchase and read books, listen to tapes (loaned) and evaluate themselves and their relationship by the use of certain "tools." Some sessions may be with another pastor rather than the one who will perform ceremony.[9]

Here is the letter given to couples seeking counseling at a large Baptist church in Southern California by one of the staff pastors:

27

Dear Engaged Couple:

Thank you for considering First Baptist Church as the place where you wish to seal your marriage vows. We are honored by your interest, and want to let you know what is involved in preparing for your wedding so you can come to a more informed decision.

The marriage preparation and counseling process at First Baptist Church, which is outlined below, is both intensive and extensive. Considerable time, effort, and commitment will be required of you . . .which is good training for marriage!

1. *Premarital Counseling:*

   a. Duration: minimum of 6 2- to 3-hour sessions over a 4-5 month period. Special needs/circumstances/problems may require more sessions with the minister or a professional counselor, as the minister deems necessary.

   b. Normal schedule of counseling sessions:

      1.) "Getting to know you." Extensive Q & A about individual histories, spiritual backgrounds/status, reasons for marrying, etc. Establishing relationships, explaining requirements. Homework: "Expectations/Relationship Survey" to be completed and brought to next meeting.

      2.) More relationship building and exploring of issues; updates on spiritual progress, wedding preparations. Discuss at length "Expectations/Relationship Survey." Homework: "Family History Analysis," to be completed and mailed back 2 weeks prior to next meeting.

      3.) Evaluate progress and preparations; spend most of the session discussing the "Family History Analysis." Homework: "Taylor-Johnson Temperament Analysis," to be completed and mailed back 2 weeks prior to next meeting.

      4.) Evaluate progress and preparations; spend most of the session explaining/discussing "TJTA." No homework!

      5.) Preliminary read-through of standard wedding service. Discuss options and essentials. Send copy home for further review. Begin to view video series "Before You Say I Do" with video #1, "Communication" (each video is 2 hours long).

      6.) Settle final details on wedding service. Go through checklist of things that need to be finished before wedding can take place. View video #2, "Finances"; schedule video #3, "Intimacy." (Note: this final meeting will be about 1 month prior to wedding. Couples should call back 1 week before the wedding just to "touch base," so we can make sure all essential preliminaries have been completed.)

   c. Cost: Premarital counseling is included in the package price you pay to the church for the wedding. Costs for professional testing/counseling, if required by the minister, must be borne by the engaged couple.

   d. Priority of counseling: The importance of premarital counseling cannot be overstated. You will be acquiring knowledge and skills to help you the rest of your lives. Therefore, please assign the meetings your highest priority, and be willing to adjust your regular agenda if necessary to schedule and attend them. (This may involve, for example, taking time off work.) If you must cancel a meeting, please do so at least one day in advance.

2. *Marriage Preparation:*

   a. Approval of wedding: The minister will tentatively inform you by the end of the first counseling session whether he can officiate at your wedding. This will be based on his knowledge at that point. Should he agree to officiate, then later become aware of matters that could have a significant negative impact on your relationship; or if either of you fail to meet the agreed-upon requirements of the marriage preparation/counseling process, the minister may have to rescind his approval.

   b. Church attendance: A church wedding is a service of worship to Almighty God. The significance of such a service can best be appreciated by those who regularly participate in church. Therefore, for couples who have no present church relationship, the minister will require attendance at this church's services of worship for a certain number of weeks before the wedding; and will also want to discuss your religious beliefs.

   c. Church relationships: Since we work so closely with the people we marry, and invest so much time and effort in their lives, it is our normal policy to perform weddings only for couples who are involved in the life of our church. If you are active in and committed to another church, and plan to continue that involvement after your marriage, it is recommended that you arrange to have your wedding there. If that church is too small, we recommend using a larger church of the same denomination, or securing the use of a private hall, as we cannot rent our facilities for weddings.

   d. Difficult issues: If any of the following is a past or ongoing issue in your lives or relationship, it must be resolved to the minister's satisfaction before the wedding can take place: couples living together; history of divorce; lack of openness to spiritual counsel; emotional instability, immaturity or incompatibility; substance, spousal, or child abuse; financial mismanagement; history/practice of immorality; Christians marrying non-Christians; and any other matter which the minister considers a significant barrier to a happy, lasting marriage.

If you have any questions concerning any of the above issues, or disagree with any of the stated positions, please mention it to the minister at your first meeting. We are here to understand and help you, not to judge you. If we can agree with you on reasons why any of our standards and requirements should be waived in your case, we will do it.

May God bless you as you continue to prepare for your marriage![10]

Refusal to Marry a Couple

As noted above under "Difficult Issues," a minister may choose not to marry a couple. When it comes to a believer and an unbeliever's seeking marriage, the Scriptures clearly forbid the uniting of such a couple (see 2 Cor. 6:14); this would be the standard for refusing to perform the ceremony.

Nonetheless, many pastors in evangelical churches have stated that they do perform weddings joining believer and unbeliever. Their reasons include pressure from parents who are members, board-member pressure, fear of offending long-standing friends, and doubt that the non-Christian would respond to any proclamation at this time. A pastor may weigh in his mind what his congregation will think about what he does. His feeling of the approval or disapproval of the church figures in his decision. A common, final reason is that if the couple is allowed to marry, the unbeliever may eventually respond to the church and its message through this contact. Too often, though, the opposite occurs: because of the influence of the one, both individuals are lost to the church, and the faith of the believer begins to wane. I discuss the issue of marrying unbelievers further in chapter 6.

Group and Individual Counseling

At Grace Community Church in Sun Valley, California, about 200 couples are involved in marriage preparation each year. The church uses a combination of group and individual counseling. Each couple will have two to four individual sessions with a contact lay couple. The group classes are held every Sunday afternoon from 12:30 to 5:00. Here is their course content:

Session	Topic
1	Understanding yourself
	Improper reasons for marriage
2	Purpose of engagement
	The sufficiency of Christ
	Expectations
	How to minister to your spouse
3	Male/female differences
	Biblical headship/submission
4	Dysfunctional communication
5	Biblical communication
6	Conflict resolution
7	Birth control
	Inlaws
8	Physical Intimacy

Each couple is counseled as well, using the results of their weekly homework and the T-JTA. Thirty percent of those counseled choose not to pursue marriage. Of those thirty percent, 85 percent have dated for longer than a year.

In a letter from a staff minister from this church came this comment: "Our premarital ministry here continues to be a great source of blessing as we see God glorified by both the dissolution of some engagements and the lasting marriages of others."

Elmbrook Church in Brookfield, Wisconsin, also uses group and individual counseling, while requiring four conditions for marriage in the church: (1) attendance at church for at least thirteen weeks prior to signing up for a wedding date, (2) completion of a premarital class, (3) premarital counseling with a pastor, and (4) a signed statement from the pastor stating that he is satisfied that the couple will bring the necessary spiritual commitment to the marriage.

Couples must demonstrate their commitment to the church through attendance for at least three months prior to signing up for a wedding date. Since couples usually are anticipating their wedding dates six months or more after their engagement announcement, this gives the church members contact with the couple for at least nine months.

The premarital class runs for eight consecutive Sunday mornings for one and one-fourth hours each Sunday. Sessions combine large group lecture and small group discussion, with topics ranging from "What Is Love—God's Way" and "What Is a Christian Marriage?" to "Satisfying Sexuality" and "The Couple's Devotional Life." For strong interaction, the small groups usually have a maximum of four couples. These small groups are also required to meet once in the small group leaders' home for a less formal time of interaction.

The couple is also required to write two book reports. One book is specifically assigned, and the second may be chosen from an approved list. The required book is *So You're Getting Married* (Regal Books).

After completing the class, couples meet with their officiating pastor for premarital counseling. Pastors usually spend four one-hour sessions with each couple. Dave Seemuth, director of premarital counseling, reports that many Elmbrook ministers use *Premarital Counseling* (Moody), and a diagnostic tool, either T-JTA or the PREPARE instrument. A couple does not have a confirmed wedding date until after they have met with the pastor. As Seemuth explains,

> That pastor must be satisfied with the spiritual commitment the couple has, their lifestyle, and their previous marriage issues (if necessary). Once the pastor and couple have thoroughly discussed these things to the pastor's satisfaction, the couple may be married at Elmbrook Church. . . .
>
> Once the couple completes the process and is married, we seek to integrate the couple into the couples ministry. We especially seek to involve them in one of our small groups. In this way we can track their progress. We also run marriage enrichment programs and retreats.[11]

Couples Counseling

Dove Christian Fellowship International in Ephrata, Pennsylvania, operates a strong premarital program that includes a counseling couple who work one-to-one with the counselee couple. The trained lay couple lessen the counseling load of the busy pastor; thirty-five couples are trained to give pre- and postmarital counseling in the church of 2,300.

A detailed and extensive workbook/manual is used by both the couple conducting the counseling and the premarital couple. The engaged couple attends six hours of meetings; the lay couples conducting the counseling usually have been through some deep waters in their own marriages and have recovered. Trained by the church staff, the lay couples are supervised by a staff pastor during their first counseling sessions. Half-way through the counseling experience, the engaged couple begins consultations with a staff pastor in regard to their future marriage. Approximately 85 percent of the counseled couples marry.

A couple planning to be married at the Church of the Saviour in Wayne, Pennsylvania, must complete the premarital seminar and present a certificate of successful completion to the pastor performing the marriage ceremony. The pastors and elders view this as a practical demonstration of their commitment to establish a sound marriage. After the premarital seminar, the couple attends at least five counseling sessions (one after the wedding) with the seminar staff. In addition, each couple is matched with counselors, usually a couple, best suited for them.

If either person has been previously married, he or she must submit the form "Information From The Previously Married," which is reviewed and approved by the counselor and the elder supervising the seminar. In addition, both persons must complete a "Fresh Start" seminar—a four-week Bible study—prior to attending the premarital seminar, or, in any event, prior to the wedding.

The premarital seminar consists of ten classroom sessions covering (1) the biblical view of marriage, (2) the biblical roles of husband and wife, (3) building up one another, (4) communications in marriage, (5) financial stability, (6) preparing for parenting, (7) sexual anatomy and response, and (8) growing in the Lord together.

At Church of the Saviour, each couple must supply background information and take a Taylor-Johnson Temperament Analysis prior to the beginning of classes. Each couple receives a notebook to hold homework, information, and notes, and they must read *So You're Getting Married* and listen to an album of tapes. Graduates advise that couples complete the seminar at least two months before the wedding.

PREMARITAL COUNSELING AND MINISTRY

Whatever program of premarital counseling you use, good counseling is a ministry, helping couples move toward marriages that honor God and one another—and in some cases to postpone or avoid marriage altogether. Recently a young pastor from a small church completed one of my training seminars in premarital counseling and began to implement premarital counseling in his own church. In a letter, he wrote about his experience:

> What a revolution! Little did I know that this church has had a long reputation of marrying anybody. The current pastor had been

concerned about the situation since his coming two years ago, but didn't know what to do to change it. I began as associate pastor four months ago, shortly after taking your pre-marital course at Grace Graduate School.

We are a small community of about 2,000 and have about 200 in services Sunday morning. The policy has been handed out to six couples in four months. Attached is a copy of the policy which I proposed and which was accepted by our church board. Of the six who have received the policy, two went elsewhere to be married, one began and quit after one session (he left town when she couldn't think of one reason why she should marry him), two couples we haven't heard from again, and one couple just has the fifth session to complete. Obviously they are the ones I counseled for the assignment for your class.

People are beginning to realize that our church takes marrying seriously. They're seeing that we're not as concerned with pretty weddings as with establishing solid homes where God is honored and people are growing in love. We've seen the results of the former lack of policy, and it is high time for this change. The mother of the girl whose fiance left town approached me and said, "Thanks for not just marrying them. You saved Mary and us a lot of heartache." I could go on, but just let me say thanks. The premarital program is a giant leap in a positive direction.

In thousands of churches throughout the Western Hemisphere, marriage is being taken seriously. Those of us involved in the ministry of the local church have the greatest opportunity of any group to minister to couples. Eighty percent of couples are married in religious ceremonies. Even those couples who give little thought to the church at any other time want to be married in a church.

In my experience, the most effective style of premarital counseling is the individual approach in which you meet with the couple. Group premarital is a supplement to the individual approach but it is only about 30 percent as effective by itself. I recommend both approaches, but if you have to make a choice, meet with each couple on their own.

If possible, use both approaches together. A well-developed model of this combined approach is found at Emmanuel Faith Community Church in Escondido, California. The material this church uses for the group sessions is available in a teacher's manual including the content handouts and transparency patterns. It is called "The Integrated Approach to Premarital Counseling." For information, contact Mr. Dave Ferreira at 127 E. 3d Ave., Suite 201, Escondido, CA 92025.

Some people believe that little change can be accomplished with a couple in their engaged state and thus the counseling should occur during the initial year of marriage. We have not found this to be true. Thousands of ministers and counselors are making an impact on couples through their premarital ministry. Couples need their assistance in advance of, not after, potentially devastating disruptions. Since a significant number of couples have made a decision not to marry through their premarital counseling experience, that in itself has an effect upon the divorce rate. During a year-and-a-half period, I conducted the premarital sessions for twenty-eight couples. Fourteen were married, and the other fourteen decided not to marry.

A study of five primary PREPARE categories (conducted by David Olson, the developer of PREPARE, and Blaine Flowers) found that couples who decided not to marry most highly resembled couples who divorced. What the counselor learns prior to marriage should be applied then; waiting until after the marriage to give assistance is courting disaster.

Couples *will* change in their attitudes, beliefs, behaviors, and skills. We have seen this occur for more than twenty years. What will bring about this change? Three factors. The first is the ability, knowledge, and skill the counselor brings to the sessions. Who you are and the manner in which you carefully and sensitively orchestrate the sessions will be vital. Your own marriage (if you are married) needs to be strong since each couple will have the freedom to ask about your own marriage.

A second factor is a commitment to creating some unrest or dissonance in the counselees. Premarital is different from other counseling approaches. How? I would like to see the couple leave my office a bit troubled or concerned, pondering the weight of this step they are about to take. I want them to leave at times with questions and concerns rather than with everything tied up in a neat package. When they return and show that they spent hours in deep discussion and application of what they were struggling with in the last session, I feel the counseling is going well. In a sense, the counselor should create a sense of crisis in a positive way with each couple. This brings about the ideal conditions for growth. It can be accomplished in the individual approach but is quite difficult to accomplish in the group process.

The third element is our own reliance upon our Lord Jesus Christ to guide our thoughts and words in each counseling encounter. Inviting the Holy Spirit to be present as our own guide is essential.

NOTES

1. The policy was written by journalist Michael J. McManus. Used by permission of Michael J. McManus, 9500 Michael's Court, Bethesda, MD 20817.

2. Michael J. McManus, "Ethics and Religion." *The Modesto Bee,* October 5, 1985.

3. "No More Quickie Weddings," *Christian Herald,* June 1987, p. 23.

4. Jeffrey Williams, "Churches Unite, Take a Stand to Prevent Divorce," *Christianity Today*, September 8, 1989, p. 65.

5. For a copy of the Peoria Community Marriage Policy, write Michael J. McManus at the Bethesda, Maryland, address shown in endnote 1.

6. Michael McManus, personal correspondence, October 31, 1991.

7. Telephone interview with Jim Talley, January, 1990. The survey spans couples receiving counseling during the fifteen years ending in 1989.

8. Letter from Dave Ferriera, marriage, family, and child counselor; Emmanuel Faith Community Church, Escondido, California, n.d.

9. Premarital and wedding preparations by an evangelical Protestant church.

10. Steven Mitchell, "Normal Standards and Requirements for Premarital Counseling and Marriage Preparation"; letter to couples, First Baptist Church, Downey, California. Used by permission.

11. Letter from Dave Seemuth; Elmbrook Church, Brookfield, Wisconsin, n.d.

CHAPTER
3

*Helping to Take the Risk
Out of Mate Selection*

A young man came into my office one morning and said, "It's not worth it! I see so many of my friends' marriages breaking up, I'm never getting married. Marriage appears to be such a gamble— and it's the only game in town where both players can lose. There's too much risk involved in getting married. I don't want to end up a statistic." Perhaps he was running scared and being a bit overly cautious. Yet his concern is echoed by many young people. In some cases this attitude lends itself to the move toward simply living together.

There is risk involved in the marriage process, but the essential element is not so much finding the right person as it is becoming the right person. Both individuals can lose in the game of marriage, but it is just as possible for both to win.

Most couples are not fully aware of the complexities and dimensions of the marital relationship. Marriage means sharing in many areas of life such as:

- *Emotional.* Sharing the emotional and fantasy levels of life.
- *Economic.* Sharing the accumulation, use, and distribution of money.
- *Recreational.* Sharing recreation and pleasure. This involves not only recreation together but allowing your spouse to enjoy recreation with his or her own set of companions.
- *Social.* Sharing of social and interpersonal activities. Some will be enjoyed together, some separately.
- *Geographical.* Sharing space, time, and geographical proximity.
- *Sexual.* A unique sharing of the physical, sensual, and sexual aspects of two people.
- *Legal.* A couple's involvement in the civil and legal process of a society.
- *Religious.* Sharing beliefs, values, and traditions.

What is involved in the process of selecting a mate? What factors, conscious and unconscious (some have said that all couples in love are unconscious!), move people toward one another? What does the evangelical church have to say to a young person about his or her choice of a life partner? Do we say that God has one person that He has selected to be your mate, or is there an unlimited stockpile that you can select from and still be within God's will? Often the church says only that a believer must marry a believer. That is scripturally true, but there are more factors involved in the selection of a mate than spiritual oneness.

REASONS FOR MARRIAGE

There are numerous reasons for marriage apart from being in love. *Pregnancy* is still a reason for marriage. In fact, about one-fourth of all marriages occur when the bride is pregnant. Probably many of these marriages would not have occurred had the woman not been pregnant. Research on these marriages shows a relationship between a premarital pregnancy and unhappiness in marriage.[1] In God's grace, these marriages do not have to end in a higher divorce rate or have a greater rate of unhappiness than others; the forgiveness of Jesus Christ that each person experiences and gives to his or her partner can affect this situation as well as any other.

Rebound is a reason for marriage when a person attempts to find a marriage partner immediately after a relationship terminates. In a sense it is a frantic attempt to establish desirability in the eyes of the person who terminated the relationship. Marriage on the rebound is questionable because the marriage occurs in reference to the previous man or woman and not in reference to the new person.

Rebellion is a motivation for marriage and occurs in both secular and Christian homes. This is a situation in which the parents say no and the young person says yes. It is a demonstration of one's control over one's own life, and possibly an attempt to demonstrate independence. Unfortunately, the person uses the marriage partner to get back at his or her parents.

Escape from an unhappy home environment is another reason for marriage. Some of the reasons given are fighting, drinking, and molestation. This type of marriage is risky, as the knot-tying is often accomplished before genuine feelings of mutual trust, respect, and mature love have had any opportunity to develop.

Loneliness is a reason that stands by itself. Some cannot bear the thought of remaining alone for the rest of their days; they do not realize that a person can be married and still feel terribly lonely. Instantaneous intimacy does not occur at the altar, but must be developed over months and years of sharing and involvement. The flight from loneliness may place a strain upon the relationship. One person may be saying, "I'm so lonely. Be with me all the time and make me happy." The problems stemming from this attitude are apparent.

Physical appearance is a factor that probably influences everyone to some degree. Our society is highly influenced by the cult of youth and beauty. Often the standards for a partner's physical appearance are set not so much to satisfy one's needs but simply to gain the approval and admiration of others. Some build their self-concept upon their partner's physical attributes.

Social pressure may be direct or indirect and can come from many sources. Friends, parents, churches, and schools convey the message "It is normal to be married; to fit the norm you should get with it." On some college campuses a malady known as "senior panic" still exists, and in some areas it occurs on the high school level. Engagement and marriage may be a means of gaining status; fears of being left behind are reinforced by others. In some churches when a young unmarried pastor arrives, matchmaking becomes the order of the day. Some churches will not hire a minister unless he is married; thus a young minister must either marry before he is ready or spend many months looking for a church.

Guilt and pity are still involved in some marriages. Marrying a person because one feels sorry for him or her because of physical defects, illness, or having a poor lot in life does not make a stable marital relationship.[2]

What about *romance*? Aren't love and romance a factor? Yes, but it is important to distinguish between genuine love and romantic love. Romantic love has been labeled cardiac-respiratory love. This is love with an emphasis on excitement, thrills, and palpitations of the heart. Some people react as though there were a lack of oxygen in the area. Ecstasy, daydreaming, and a deep physical yearning are all indications of this malady. Not only is this type of love blind, it is also destructive. Neither the past nor the future is taken into consideration in evaluating the potential of the relationship. James Peterson aptly describes the dangers of marrying for this reason:

> First, romance results in such distortions of personality that after marriage the two people can never fulfill the roles that they expect of each other. Second, romance so idealizes marriage and even sex that when the day-to-day experiences of marriage are encountered there must be disillusionment involved. Third, the romantic complex is so short-sighted that the premarital relationship is conducted almost entirely on the emotional level and consequently such problems as temperamental or value differences, religious or cultural differences, financial, occupational, or health problems are never considered. Fourth, romance develops such a false ecstasy that there is implied in courtship a promise of a kind of happiness which could never be maintained during the realities of married life. Fifth, romance is such an escape from the negative aspects of personality to the extent that their repression obscures the real person. Later in marriage these negative factors to martial adjustment are bound to appear, and they do so in far greater detail and far more importantly simply because they were not evident earlier. Sixth, people engrossed in romance seem to be prohibited from wise planning for the basic needs of the future even to the point of failing to discuss the significant problems of early marriage.
>
> It is difficult to know how pervasive the romantic fallacy really is. I suspect that it creates the greatest havoc with high school seniors or that half of the population who are married before they are twenty years old. Nevertheless, even in a college or young adult population one constantly finds as a final criterion for marriage the question of being in love. This is due to the distortion of the meaning of a true companionship in marriage by the press, by the magazines, and by cultural impact upon the last two or three generations. The result is that more serious and sober aspects of marital choice and marital expectations are not only neglected but sometimes ridiculed.[3]

MATE SELECTION

Ask college students why most people get married and one usually still receives the answer: because of romantic love. "We are destined to marry each other," or, "We just have this attraction for one another and marriage is the logical step," couples say. Such couples often overlook the fact that marriage partners need to fulfill certain qualifications to be suited to each other. In reality, more couples are thrown together by factors other than romance or the logic of intelligence.

There are many limits on mate selection. Physical location is the most significant limitation, a fact that seems highly unromantic.[4] The farther two people live apart, the more intervening opportunities there are to choose someone else. There is a limit to how much time and money a man will spend traveling to see a woman when there are other women nearby. Occasionally romantic love breaks all barriers, but those cases are the exception.

Research studies regarding marriage indicate that persons marry with greater than chance frequency within their own social class.[5] Any overall tendency for people to marry either "up" or "down" in a social class is negligible.

Contradictory Versus Complementary Traits

When a person marries, does he choose a person just the opposite of himself? For years the statement "opposites attract" has been used to explain part of the attraction process. And yet the results of hundreds of studies of married couples indicate that, almost without exception, in physical, social, and psychological characteristics the mates are more alike than different. The exceptions, or those that appear to be exceptions, do not alter this overall tendency.

Within the framework of like marrying like, however, some characteristics appear to be quite opposite in each spouse. Since the fulfillment of needs is at the heart of such mate selection, one will find that some needs in couples are complementary whereas some are contradictory.

It is in the area of complementary characteristics and needs that the concept "opposites attract" is seen to be somewhat accurate. The most important complementary needs involve dominance and submissiveness. If a person has a need to dominate he will tend to marry and be gratified by a person who needs to be submissive. If a man marries a woman who has the need to be dominant and he is submissive, there will be some conflict because the social expectations of our society call for the male to be dominant and the female to be submissive. In spite of social pressures, many couples choose to go against the expectation. If one has a need to nurture others, such as giving sympathy, love, protection, and indulgence, he would be happy with a partner who has the need to be nurtured. (Most people, fortunately, are capable of both, and that is healthier.) A person who needs to admire and praise others would enjoy being married to a person who needs to receive respect and admiration. If the needs of one spouse change years later, the relationship could be disrupted. Complementary needs help determine how two people treat each other.

It is important to keep in mind the distinction between complement and contradiction. Unfortunately, some couples label any difference between themselves as complementary. Complementary needs fit so well together that no compromise is required, whereas contradictory needs require a compromise on some middle ground, but not usually on a happy medium. For example, if one is extremely thrifty and the other is a big spender, the needs will clash head-on. If one enjoys social contacts and the other is a recluse, conflict is almost inevitable.[6]

In our American culture people choose a partner whom they expect to be gratifying to them. It is interesting to note that both engaged and married couples see things in each other that cannot be found through testing. What an individual sees in another person is what pleases him. "What would ever attract him to that girl?" we ask, because we cannot see in her the things he sees. A couple's choice of each other is based upon a set of relationships pleasing to themselves, which they attribute to one another.

Basic Needs

As people date and are attracted to one another, basic needs are met. Much of a couple's relationship is based upon the meeting of those needs. This means that there are literally thousands of people of the opposite sex who could fulfill those needs if the person has appropriate status qualities. Being held in esteem in someone else's eye confirms our worth in our own eyes. The need to fall in love and to have someone else fall in love with us does not require a particular person. The first step is having those basic needs met. Then the details of "personality meshing" can be filled in imaginatively. This personality meshing probably determines the future of the relationship established by a couple.

Couples who marry for healthy reasons and those who marry for unhealthy reasons have basically the same motivating forces propelling them toward marriage, but their intensity varies.

Most individuals are attracted to one another by dependency needs. We all have these needs, no matter how healthy we are. Healthy dependency needs reflect a desire to experience a sense of completion. However, when a person has exaggerated dependency needs, there is a desire for completion *and* for possession.

Self-esteem and its potential for enhancement propel people toward marriage. Everyone wants to receive affirmation of worth and value from another person. Some have the excessive need for their spouses to make them feel worthy, good, attractive, wanted, desired, and so on. Gradually the excessive need can exact a strain upon the relationship.

The normal desire for affirmation, however, is also a strong attracting and maintaining force of marriage. The desire of increased self-esteem and dependency needs both build commitment, which has been called the glue of marriage. That glue is in the process of setting when a couple arrives for premarital instruction.

Assessing Dependency Needs

It is important to carefully assess the amount of dependency needs and need for self-esteem of each person during the process of the counseling. Asking the man and woman about the extent of each of these in their desire to marry has been both helpful and revealing with a number of couples.

Helpful questions include: In what way do you see yourself dependent upon your partner? and, How are you expecting your future spouse to enhance your self-esteem?

Marriage and mate selection is not a matter of chance. Mate selection is very purposeful, and people choose the persons they need at that point in time. On a conscious and subconscious level people do know what they are getting when they marry. In their research of hundreds of couples Robert F. Stahmann and William J. Hiebert state:

> Our assumption that marriage is neither accidental nor dichotomous has been influenced by our clinical practice with the hundreds of couples we have seen both in marital counseling and in premarital counseling. In thinking about these couples and the manner in which they chose each other, we have discovered that the couples were apparently performing a task and involved in a process. It has

struck us that many couples were involved in the task of finding some way to initiate growth. The growth could be in many areas. Perhaps it was in becoming more outgoing, more self-confident, more intimate, or some other dimension of their personality that they felt needed expansion. The mate they chose, therefore, from the millions of individuals available was exactly the person who could provide them with the kind of growth they needed. Some women, for example, seek out a particular man who can teach them to be tough, just as some men seek out a woman who can teach them to be soft. It almost seems to us that couples in some way find each other and choose each other on the basis of their potential to induce change. It is as if couples are in a strange way performing the task of therapy. Perhaps we could say that marriage is an amateur attempt at psychotherapy.

All of this is a way of saying that we believe that marriage is purposeful and that couples choose each other on the basis of the ability of the other person to help them initiate growth. We think that couples are involved in a task of healing. It is as if many individuals at the point of dating and moving to marriage find themselves to be incomplete in some way. Their search for a mate is not haphazard but rather based on some kind of deeply intuitive homing device that relentlessly and purposely pursues exactly the kind of person who will provide them with the stimulation for the growth they are seeking.[7]

Cultural Influences

Further complicating the selection of a mate is the factor of the cultural "ideal mate" image, depending upon what marriage means in a particular society. If, for example, marriage is primarily a division of labor and child-rearing, the ideal wife would be one who is physically strong with broad shoulders and broad hips. Descriptions of masculine and feminine characteristics provided by a culture influence the ideal mate images. In one society the ideal woman is sweet and delicate, in another she is extroverted and sexually provocative. Culture defines it; we fit into the pattern.

Cultural definitions of the ideal mate can influence mate selection in two ways. Because this definition identifies what is desirable in a mate, it almost labels the desirability of each person. The closer a person gets to this cultural ideal, the more attractive he or she becomes to a greater number of people. And if the person realized that he is approaching the ideal, he can be more selective in his own choice of a mate and hold out for the one closest to the ideal.

The second way in which this cultural definition of the ideal mate can influence mate selection is called "idealization of the mate." It means that, even if your choice does not meet the cultural standard of idealization, you attribute those characteristics to the person with whom you have fallen in love.

The choice of the partner is complicated by this human penchant for wishful thinking. Unfortunately, the more insecure a person is, the greater is his need for idealizing his partner.

Most people do not think about mate selection in a logical, analytical manner, but we are unconsciously influenced by these factors and in subtle ways we probably do adhere to them. Yet many people would vehemently deny these ideas, protesting that "it is our love that brought us together"

If cultural images influence one's selection of a mate, what about the images that parents have of their offspring's future mate? Parents exert considerable indirect control over the associations of their children; this in turn limits the field of possibilities for mate selection. College students feel this pressure less than those who remain at home. Parents help determine an acceptable grouping of eligibles from which their child may choose a mate.[8] Interestingly, one study shows that when a woman's parents disapproved of her relationship with a young man, more than twice as many relationships ended in broken engagements or early divorce as when both parents approved. The approval of the man's parents does not seem to be nearly as important.[9]

An interesting theory of who marries whom and why has been suggested by Bert Adams in "Mate Selection in the United States: A Theoretical Summarization." He describes mate choice as a process and isolates a series of factors that are involved. Adams found that it is more likely that individuals will marry if the following occurs:

(1) A person is dating someone who is near and available in time and space rather than a person who is not.

(2) Physical attractiveness and similar interests also assist in early attraction.

(3) Early attraction is perpetuated and reinforced by favorable reaction by other significant people. If that does not come, the relationship may be weakened.

(4) Self-disclosure is another necessary ingredient so that rapport can develop. It is a matter of learning to feel comfortable in one another's presence. If the conditions of favorable response and rapport are established, then deeper attraction can develop.[10]

A deeper attraction will develop, according to Adams, if the couple's values are similar, there is a similarity in physical attractiveness, or there is a personality similarity. An alternate attraction, however, can intrude and hinder the developing relationship. The alternate attraction could be another person, education, involvement at work, a job change, even a new hobby. The stronger the attraction, the more possible the current relationship could be terminated.

At this point the relationship can move even deeper. The reasons can be either healthy or unhealthy. For example, a person with low self-esteem tends to hang onto a relationship rather than run the risk of developing a new relationship.[11]

ROMANCE, TRUE LOVE, AND THE COUNSELOR

All of this sounds very unromantic. Most people, however, still come back to "we married because we loved one another." So what constitutes love? Many of the elements involved in mate selection discussed earlier are behind what we call love. But the emotional element of love lingers with us. One romanticist describes love this way: "Love is a feeling you feel when you feel that you're going to get a feeling that you never felt before." This is about the only way some people know how to describe their relationship.

What does all this have to do with the pastor and premarital counseling? It has everything to do with the potential success of the marriage relationship. If the pastor is the one conducting the premarital counseling, all the previously mentioned information should be etched upon his mind as he evaluates the motivation for a marriage. One should look for apparent and not-so-apparent reasons for marriage. Through skillful questioning, some of those before-mentioned factors may emerge. It is important to remember that the courtship and engagement period can be a deceptive time when fogged by romance.

MARRIAGE AND GOD'S WILL

Just where does the will of God enter into all this? How does one determine God's will for a mate? What guidelines can the counselor use?

Many people seem to rely upon inner impressions or feelings. Others say that the Lord revealed to them what they should do, and yet they are a bit fuzzy as to the means of this revelation. Many have the leading or impression that they should marry a certain person. What principles could a person follow? James Dobson has suggested four basic principles for recognizing God's will for any area of one's life. Those principles should be applied to any impressions that a person might have regarding marriage.

Is the impression scriptural? Guidance from God is always in accordance with His Word. If a Christian is considering marrying a non-Christian, there is no use in praying for God's will; the Scripture is clear concerning this situation. In searching the Scriptures, verses should be taken within context, not in a random sampling.

Is the impression right? The expression of God's will should conform to God's universal principles of morality and decency. If human worth is depreciated or the integrity of the family is undermined by some "special leading," then it is probably not a leading from God.

Is it providential? Every impression ought to be considered in the light of providential circumstances. Are necessary doors opening or closing? Is God speaking through events?

Is the impression reasonable? Does the impression make sense? Is it consistent with the character of God to require it?

If a person has numerous mixed feelings about marrying the other individual, if there is no peace over the upcoming event, and if the majority of friends and relatives are opposed to the wedding, the decision ought to be reconsidered.[12]

MARRIAGEABILITY TRAITS

As most people eventually get married, it is important to be aware of the traits that make an individual a better partner and give him or her more potential to make a marriage work. Eight basic factors have been called marriageability traits: adaptability and flexibility, empathy, ability to work through problems, ability to give and receive love, emotional stability, similar family backgrounds, similarities between the couple themselves, and communication. If those elements are present, there is a greater likelihood of marital satisfaction and stability. As the counseling proceeds, one should be evaluating the couple in light of those factors.

Perhaps all these factors could be considered as some of the elements of compatibility. Many couples ask, "Are we compatible?" Compatibility can mean how well the intrinsic characteristics of two people fit. Compatibility between individuals can also determine how easily a relationship can be established. However, this provides only the potential for a good marriage; it is necessary, but not sufficient. The more compatible the better, but the potential must be activated and used. Compatibility is a matter of becoming and developing as well as being.

No two people are ever entirely compatible. My answer to the question, "Are we compatible?" is, "No. No couple marrying is compatible. It's a matter of your becoming compatible during your early years of marriage."

Adaptability and Flexibility

Adaptability and flexibility are necessary ingredients. This means the person must be able to adjust to change with a minimum of rigidity. He must be able to accept the differences in his partner, adapt, and work toward a different lifestyle if necessary,

In his book *Letters to Philip,* Charles Shedd tells the story of two rivers flowing smoothly and quietly along until they came together and joined. When this happened, they clashed and hurled themselves at one another. But as the newly formed river flowed downstream, it gradually quieted down and flowed smoothly again. Now it was broader and more majestic and had much more power. Shedd suggested that a good marriage is often like that. When two independent streams of existence come together, there will probably be some dashing of life against life at the junction. Personalities rush against one another, preferences clash, ideas contend for power, and habits vie for position. Sometimes, like the waves, they throw up a spray that leaves you breathless and makes you wonder where the loveliness has gone. But that's all right. Like the two rivers, what comes out of this struggle may be something deeper, more powerful than each river was on its own.

This is what occurs in the adaptability process. Ephesians 4:2 says, "Because we love one another, we are willing to make allowances for one another" (Amp).* It is vital that one learn to look at the interests of the other person, to consider the other's needs and ideas, and, because of love, to be willing to allow the other to think and do things differently. It means that a person evaluates his or her spouse's differences as being only differences—not marks of inferiority.

Empathy

Empathy is a positive characteristic necessary for all interpersonal relationships, and especially for those who are married. It is the ability to be sensitive to the needs, hurts, and desires of others, feeling with them and experiencing their world from their perspective. If they hurt, we

Amplified New Testament.

hurt. If they are excited, we can be excited with them and understand and perceive their feeling response. Romans 12:15 tells us that we are to rejoice with those who rejoice and to weep with those who weep. This passage from the Word of God seems to reflect the idea of empathy.

Judson Landis, one of the foremost family sociologists, has said that the most marriageable people are those whose ability to empathize is high. They are able to use their empathetic ability in a very positive manner. They can control their words and actions so they do not say the wrong things that will hurt the other individual.

Working Toward Solutions

A third marriageability trait is the ability to work through problems. Problems, conflicts, and differences are part and parcel of marriage. Some couples run from and ignore problems or give each other the silent treatment. Couples who accept and properly dispel and control their emotional reactions, clarify and define their problems, and work together toward solutions will probably remain married.

The counselor can alert engaged couples to the fact that their lives soon fill with unanticipated and unplanned-for changes. Often changes in our lives come upon us without warning. We are not prepared for them and have not planned what we will do in the event they occur. But much of the time we can anticipate and control changes. Ignoring the inevitable and refusing to think about and plan for these changes will make adjustment to them even more difficult. Ask the couple what major changes they will undergo during the first ten years of marriage.

There are some potential changes that most couples would rather not face. They can choose not to plan for them in their marriage.

Some couples react to changes in their relationship by creating distance; they separate or divorce. Often this response comes when each partner believes that the other person is responsible for the trouble in the marriage. Both of these solutions—refusing to plan for changes and creating distances from the marital partner—are the result of believing that change occurs outside of themselves. This belief will hinder growth and positive changes that can take place in marital relationships.

Everyone needs to expect change in marriage, say David and Vera Mace:

> We need to see marriage in new terms, as a continually growing, continually changing, interaction between a man and woman who are seeking the warmth and richness of the shared life. Marriage has

too often been portrayed as two people frozen together side by side, as immobile as marble statues. More accurately, it is the intricate and graceful cooperation of two dancers who through long practice have learned to match each other's movements and moods in response to the music of the spheres.[13]

All changes, whether predictable or intrusive, hold the potential for growth; they are also risky. Untimely or unexpected events upset our plans, their sequence, and fulfillment. They bother us because they are thrust upon us, leaving us feeling powerless. No one likes to feel out of control and thus a person resists, reacts negatively, or feels overwhelmed instead of seeking creative possibilities in this inevitable situation.

Robert Mason, Jr., and Caroline L. Jacobs put it this way:

> Unfortunately, many marriages die prematurely because too many husbands and wives choose to ignore the inescapable fact that people do change.
>
> People can grow apart even when they truly love and care for each other. For some the resistance to change is so deeply ingrained that acceptance of change, even in someone they dearly love, is almost impossible. However, since it is an indisputable fact of life that people do change, and since this is one of the major reasons listed by couples as the source of problems in marriage, couples would do well to explore in depth their ability to adjust to the many changes which are inevitable in the years after marriage.
>
> Difficulties might be anticipated if:
>
> 1. Either person seems locked into a way of thinking or behaving which allows for no difference of opinion or new ideas.
> 2. Either has communicated to the other what he or she wants in a husband or wife and gives the impression that he or she will not tolerate any deviation from this rigid stance, now or in the future.
> 3. One of the individuals demonstrates a desire to grow and improve while the other seems determined to maintain the status quo.
> 4. One or both show a noticeable lack of curiosity or interest in the changes which are occurring around him or her from day to day.
> 5. Either gets upset easily or acts as if the whole day is ruined if things do not go according to schedule or plans are changed. The individual who is unable to adjust to change before marriage is not likely to be able to adjust to change after marriage.[14]

Any new change carries a time of risk, insecurity, and vulnerability. But many of life's events can be planned for in advance—such as having a baby—and can bring security and satisfaction. Some aspects of the various seasons of a marriage are fairly predictable in the changes they bring. These also can be anticipated. As a person moves from his twenties to his thirties, to his forties and fifties, he will display characteristics that most people have in common. Becoming parents, having adolescents, the empty nest, the midyears, becoming grandparents, and retirement are seasons we are aware of; we know when they are upon us for the most part. Some events, however, come as a surprise and bring tension, pain, and unexpected circumstances.

Giving and Receiving Love

The ability to give and receive love is a trait that needs both elements for success. The giving of love involves more than just verbalizing it. It must also be evident in tangible ways that are identifiable and recognizable to both parties. Behavior, actions, and attitudes convey this in a meaningful manner. But just as important is the ability to accept love from another. Some people have such a need to be needed that they feel fulfilled by giving. To receive and accept love threatens them and lowers their sense of self-worth. If this non-acceptance response is continued, usually the other partner will give up or find someone else who will accept his love.

Emotional Stability

Emotional stability—accepting one's emotions and controlling them —lends balance to a relationship. We depend upon a person who has a consistent, dependable emotional response. Extreme flare-ups and decisions based upon emotional responses do not lend themselves to stable relationships.

The more similar the family backgrounds, the more contributions each can make to the marriage relationship. The greater the differences —economic, cultural, religious, being an only child compared to having several siblings—the more adjustments must be made. Those adjustments can add even more pressures to learning to live together. Naturally, the more mature the couple, the more easily the adjustments can be made.

Similarities

Another trait, closely tied to similarity in family background, is similarities between the couple themselves. Earlier it was mentioned that like tends to marry like more than the opposite. If a couple has similar interests, likes and dislikes, friends, educational level, and religion, the marriage relationship is greatly enhanced.

Communication

The final trait that is necessary for a love relationship to develop is communication. There are differences in ability, styles, and beliefs about communication. Free interchange of ideas is essential. Communication is the ability to share in such a way that the other person can understand and accept what is being said. But listening is also involved. True listening means not thinking about what you are going to say when the other person stops talking. It means not making value judgments as to how the other person expressed himself and the words he used. It means that if you are really listening you can reflect back both the meaning and feeling of what was expressed. The tendency in our culture is for men not to communicate on a feeling response level, to verbalize less, and to be more solution-oriented instead of talking about the problem. This puts a great strain upon the marriage relationship.

One of the most important elements in the communication process is the couple's ability to learn to speak one another's language. Learning to discover the meaning of words of one another as well as the ability to speak their style will create a very close, intimate relationship. More will be said about this in chapter 9, but do keep in mind there are significant differences in male-female communication. This will affect your own style of responding to a couple and could hinder the establishment of rapport and the level of understanding if you are not aware of it.

Consider for a moment some of the differences in male-female communication styles. Generally speaking:

- Women use intensifiers when they talk such as, "That movie was so enjoyable," whereas a man avoids emphasis and intensity and in response to the same movie might say, "It's fine."
- In communication, women tend to be cooperative whereas men tend to be competitive.
- Women tend to regard questions as a way to maintain a conversation while men view them as a request for information.

- Women are more likely to share feelings and secrets whereas men like to discuss less intimate topics, such as sports and politics.
- When men talk, they want a purpose and an agenda.
- When men initiate a conversation with a woman, there is a 96 percent chance it will continue, but when a woman initiates a conversation with a man, there is a 36 percent chance it will continue.[15]

Men and women also listen in different ways. Men generally express listening sounds comparatively infrequently and when they do, it is usually meant to indicate "I agree with you." A man may tend to listen impassively without giving his wife feedback like nodding, gesturing, changing facial expression or making sounds. One of the books the counselor can recommend for the woman to read during the premarital counseling is *Understanding the Man in Your Life* (Word).

Other Factors

Numerous studies during the past two decades provide additional indicators of marital success. Those who differ radically from the norm in these characteristics often believe that they will be the exceptions and will make their marriage work in spite of gross differences. For a few it may work.

Various studies point out the importance of significant relationships with other people. If a person has experienced warm and satisfying relationships with both his father and mother, his marriage will be influenced positively. If the parents were affectionate, firm, consistent, and fairly well adjusted in their own marriage, this contributes to the new marriage relationship. Another interesting factor centers on friends of both sexes: if each person has friends, and these become and remain mutual friends after marriage, the marriage relationship will be enhanced.

Environmental conditions in the person's background, both social and physical, can influence the marriage somewhat. A happy childhood, lack of poverty, and completion of extensive formal education can contribute to success in marriage.

The socioeconomic level of a man's parents seems to affect the economic status of his own marriage. Research has indicated that stability and adjustment of the marriage are directly related to the income of the husband. The lower the husband's income, the greater the possibility that the marriage will be more unstable and maladjusted.

Another factor affecting marital success centers on particular events in the person's past and the timing of those events. Marriage at an early age is not favorable to a healthy adjustment nor to marital longevity. A brief whirlwind romance or a premarital pregnancy is an additional adverse condition. A good work record, definite and reasonable occupational plans, and a low residence-mobility factor contribute positively.

The most difficult factors to measure are the psychological attributes of the individuals. Yet they are important. A strong interest in family life, just as strong a commitment to make it succeed, and a willingness to work together are the positive points. Even if one person within a relationship will exert effort there is more chance of that marriage succeeding than if both just coast along.[16]

EMOTIONAL INDEPENDENCE

A very interesting finding for marital success is the level of emotional independence. Those who adapt well to marriage have been able to leave home emotionally or psychologically. They are no longer dependent upon their parents to take responsibility for their lives. They function as an adult. Second, they have had an opportunity to live alone after they have left home and before marriage. This involves surviving on their own. They have assumed adult responsibilities such as buying groceries, cooking, laundry, and budgeting. Again and again these findings emerge in the literature on families.

Why is it that those who leave home psychologically adapt better?

Let's answer that question by considering the problems of those who haven't left home. They keep getting involved in family problems. They bring their family problems into the marriage and they become a marital problem. Because they have not yet left home psychologically, they tend to look for spouses who will continue the parenting of their parents. They also tend to have more physical ailments than others. And finally, those who have not left home psychologically tend to come from homes where the parents hang onto them.[17] In other words, they don't want their children to grow up and separate from them. This is why using the Family History Analysis as one of your major tools in premarital counseling is essential.

As you work with a couple, discover whether they have left home psychologically. If they have never had an opportunity to live away from home (and this means being on their own and not having someone else take care of their needs), encourage them to either live on their own for a while or begin functioning as an independent adult while living at home. I have suggested both and sometimes it is an easier transition to have them live on their own even though financially it could be a hardship. If they are still at home, parents may resist letting them purchase food, cook meals, do laundry, or make their own decisions, and so forth. But it's a necessary transitional step in their development and for the health of their upcoming marriage.

Couples who have reported happy marriages appear to concentrate their energy on their relationship. Those who seem less happy concentrate on situational aspects of marriage such as home, children, and social life as sources of their marital happiness. Feelings of happiness in marriage have a direct correlation to the way the partners are relating to one another.

Other studies reveal that in the area of communication, happily married couples differ from unhappily married couples in the following ways: They (1) talk more to each other; (2) convey the feeling that they understand what is being said to them; (3) are able to discuss a wider range of subjects; (4) preserve their communication channels and work on keeping them open; (5) show more sensitivity to each other's feelings; (6) personalize their language symbols; and (7) make more use of additional nonverbal techniques of communication.[18]

LIVING TOGETHER BEFORE MARRIAGE

In the past several years, an unexpected factor has developed concerning the success of a marriage—whether a couple has lived together prior to marriage. When the trend of cohabiting prior to marriage started, the assumption was that this would be healthy for a marriage relationship. The startling results have shown just the opposite effect.

Several studies have found that couples who live together first tend also to get divorces first. University of Wisconsin researchers report that 38 percent of couples who lived together before they married were divorced within ten years, compared with 27 percent of couples who married without cohabiting first. The finding—which follows a smaller 1987 study that found a 30 percent higher divorce rate among couples who had lived together compared to those who hadn't—surprised many experts who assumed that living together helped iron out potential marital problems and thus lessened the chances of eventual divorce.[19]

In an article entitled "Marriage: The First Years, What Holds You Together..." the author writes, "If a couple lived together before marriage, they were twice as likely to have trouble later on. A little over one-third of the couples in the study had lived together before marrying. Of those marriages, more than one-quarter—27%—were found to be "distressed" after 30 months." Of the 64 percent who did not live together beforehand, only 13% reported later distress.[20]

A recent study of 17,000 couples who completed the PREPARE inventory found that cohabiting couples had significantly lower premarital satisfaction compared to couples where the two people lived alone before marriage. Almost two-thirds (64 percent) of the cohabiting couples fell into the low satisfaction group, whereas almost two-thirds (64 percent) of the couples where both partners lived alone fell into the very satisfied group. Premarital satisfaction was measured by an average Positive Couple Agreement (PCA) score summed across all the PREPARE categories. The high satisfaction group represented those who scored in the upper third of the sample, whereas the lower satisfaction group were those who scored in the lower third.[21]

COMMITMENT

One final element that must be present for any possibility of success is commitment. Robert Blood has summarized it best:

> Commitment is dangerous. It can be exploited. If my wife takes my commitment for granted, she may rest too easily on her laurels. Perhaps commitment should be not simply to each other as we are but to the highest potentialities we can achieve together. Commitment then would be to marriage not simply as a status but as a dynamic process. Let me commit myself to a lifelong adventure, the adventure of living with this woman. The route of this adventure has been only dimly charted by those who have gone before. Because I am unique and my partner is unique, our marriage will also be unique. We commit ourselves to undertaking this adventure together, and to following wherever it may lead. Part of the excitement of marriage is not knowing in advance what either the joys or the sorrows will be. We can be sure, however, that we will be confronted with countless challenges. Commitment provides the momentum for going forward in the face of those challenges.[22]

All these facts, then, should be part of the pastor's filtering system as he works with the couple. The counseling session will give him an opportunity to determine the potential qualities of the future relationship as well as family and individual differences. And if the minister or counselor doesn't assist the couple with this process, who will?

NOTES

1. David Knox. *Marriage: Who? When? Why?* (Englewood Cliffs, N.J.: Prentice-Hall, 1974), n.p.

2. Ibid., pp. 36-42.

3. Lyle B. Gangsei, ed., *Manual for Group Premarital Counseling* (New York: Association, 1971), pp. 56-57.

4. J. Richard Udry. *The Social Context of Marriage,* 3d ed. (New York: Lippincott, 1974), p. 157.

5. Ibid.

6. Robert Blood, Jr. *Marriage* (New York: Free Press, 1969), pp. 38-43, adapted.

7. Robert F. Stahmann and William J. Hiebert. *Premarital Counseling* (Lexington, Mass.: Lexington Books, 1980), p. 18.

8. Udry. *The Social Context of Marriage,* p. 187.

9. Ibid.

10. Bert Adams, "Mate Selection in the United States: A Theoretical Summarization," ed. Wesley Burr, Reuben Hill, F. Ivan Nye, and Ira Reiss, vol. 1, *Contemporary Theories About the Family* (New York: Free Press, n.d), pp. 259-63.

11. Ibid., pp. 264-67.

12. James Dobson. *Dr. James Dobson Talks About God's Will* (Glendale, Calif.: Regal, 1974), pp. 13-21, adapted.

13. David and Vera Mace. *We Can Have Better Marriages If We Really Want Them* (Nashville: Abingdon, 1974), p. 9.

14. Robert Mason, Jr., and Caroline L. Jacobs, *How to Choose the Wrong Marriage Partner and Live Unhappily Ever After* (Atlanta: John Knox, 1979), p. 40.

15. Steven Naifeh and Gregory White Smith, *Why Can't Men Open Up?* (New York: Clarkson B. Potter, 1984), pp.70-71, adapted.

16. Udry, *The Social Context of Marriage,* p. 236.

17. Robert E. Stahmann and William J. Hiebert. *Premarital Counseling* (Lexington, Mass.: Lexington Books, 1987) pp. 85-86.

18. Carlfred B. Broderick, ed., *A Decade of Family Research and Action* (Minneapolis: National Council on Family Relations, 1972), p. 66.

19. "Heartbreak of Cohabitation Ends in Divorce," *Los Angeles Times*, November 16, 1989.

20. Mary Ellen Schoonmeker, "Marriage: The First Years, What Holds You Together . . ." *Family Circle,* September 1, 1988, p. 99.

21. Stewart, Kenneth and David H. Olson, "Cohabiting Couples and Premarital Satisfaction," PREPARE/Enrich newsletter, November 1988.

22. Blood, *Marriage*, pp. 10-11.

Dysfunctional Family Background and the Engaged Couple

A new vocabulary exists in today's counseling that includes words and phrases such as *codependent, dysfunctional,* and *adult child*. The vocabulary reflects counseling developments in the past two decades that can help in predicting the future patterns—and problems—in a marriage. It is vital for anyone conducting premarital counseling to understand dysfunctional characteristics and roles in order to identify the effects of these upon a person's life and any subsequent marital relationship.

Consider two single women, Susan and Mary. (All names in this book are changed to protect the identities of the counselees.) Each is engaged and each finds that her family ties bind her to the past and make her question the future.

This chapter is based on and quotes largely from chapters 8 and 9 of *Always Daddy's Girl* (Ventura, Calif.: Regal, 1989). Used by permission of Gospel Light/Regal Books.

Susan is a twenty-year-old junior, attending a college 2,000 miles from home. She is planning to be married in eight months. "Dad calls me every other day to get advice or to complain about Mother," she told me. "He tells me things he should have shared with Mother over the years. I've probably received more attention from him than from my mother or any of the other kids. I thought that when I went away to school I wouldn't have to be this involved with my family. But it hasn't changed. Why has this happened? And how is it going to affect my marriage? Will he do this after I'm married?"

What is Susan saying about her family of origin?

Mary is a perfectionist. Her dress is impeccable and everything about her is precise. It's difficult for her to relax because she feels that she is always on display. Her fiance is more laid back and accepting. He keeps encouraging her not to be so structured and uptight. She told me that her parents were divorced when she was four. When her mother remarried several years later, Mary found out that her stepfather saw her as a "necessary nuisance"—that's what he called her. He was a cold, rigid workaholic.

"Do you know why I am such a perfectionist?" Mary asked me. "It's true there are some benefits to perfectionism, but at times I wonder if there isn't a better way to live. Why am I this way? And John and I are so different! How will this affect our marriage?"

THE HOME THAT SHAPED YOU

Many factors combine to make us who we are. A person is the product of his family birth order, his neurological structure, and interactions with his mother, father, siblings, and so on. But the atmosphere of a home, and especially the relationship with parents, has a significant impact on shaping identity and behavior.

The Functional Family

If a person was reared in a healthy home, he or she is fortunate. These families are called functional families because they function effectively and productively. Functional families display many of the following positive qualities:

- The climate of the home is positive. The atmosphere is basically nonjudgmental.
- Each member of the family is valued and accepted for who he or she is. There is regard for individual characteristics.

- Each person is allowed to operate within his or her proper role. A child is allowed to be a child and an adult is an adult.
- Members of the family care for one another, and they verbalize their caring and affirmation.
- The communication process is healthy, open, and direct. There are no double messages.
- Children are reared in such a way that they can mature and become individuals in their own right. They separate from Mom and Dad in a healthy manner.
- The family enjoys being together. They do not get together out of a sense of obligation.
- Family members can laugh together, and they enjoy life together.
- Family members can share their hopes, dreams, fears, and concerns with one another and still be accepted. A healthy level of intimacy exists within the home.

The Dysfunctional Family

The characteristics of a healthy, functional family are just opposite those of a dysfunctional family. Dysfunctional families lack much of the acceptance, openness, affirmation, communication, love, and togetherness of healthy families. In many cases, a dysfunctional family is the product of a dysfunctional husband-father, one who has failed to fill a healthy, positive role due to noninvolvement, domination, illness/death, or perhaps desertion/divorce.

Several times a year I travel on airplanes. So far I've always arrived at my intended destination, mainly because the plane stayed on course. If a plane were to stray off course just a few degrees, I might end up in Cuba instead of Washington, D.C. The longer a plane travels off course, the farther it wanders from its destination.

A dysfunctional family is a family that has strayed off course. Though they probably don't think of it in these terms, every newly married couple wants to build a functional family. Their "destination" is a loving, healthy, happy relationship between husband and wife, parents and children. But many little things can go wrong in families: feelings get hurt, needs and expectations go unmet. If these minor midcourse errors are not corrected, greater problems arise: love and acceptance are withheld, "me" and "mine" take priority over "us" and "ours." Soon the prospective "happy family" is far off course and exhibiting many other characteristics.

Many children from dysfunctional families are thrust into adulthood feeling empty and incomplete, afraid and unable to trust because their needs went unmet. And when they don't feel secure in themselves, they look for some type of security outside of themselves. They're always trying to fill up the empty space inside. It's this constant quest to have needs met that leads people to create or adopt compulsive or addictive behavior patterns, and to make poor choices for marital partners or place impossible demands upon their spouses.

Any family can become dysfunctional for a period of time, especially during a crisis when people don't function at their normal levels. Often someone else—such as a pastor or a counselor—must step in and help them function until they get back to normal. But in a dysfunctional family the crisis is perpetual and the roles of the family members are usually constant.

One of the best descriptions of a dysfunctional family comes from author Sara Hines Martin:

> It can be a home where a parent or grandparent is chronically ill or mentally ill or a home where a parent is emotionally ill, including chronically depressed. It could also be a home where one parent dies and the surviving parent is so overcome by grief he or she is unable to cope with the parenting tasks; a home where physical and/ or sexual abuse takes place; a home where suicide has taken place; a home where a child was adopted; and the rigidly religious home. (This last category surprises many people because nothing is specifically done, as in the other categories. This type of home produces similar dynamics because children are not valued for themselves but are raised by rigid rules. The father, if a minister, may neglect his family while carrying out his work. The children can get the feeling they must make the parents look good in the eyes of the community.) In summary, these families focus on a problem, addiction, trauma, or some "secret" rather than on the child. The home is shame-and-blame based.[1]

The phrase "shame-and-blame based" is one of the best descriptions for this type of home. It is totally contrary to the pattern of love and acceptance presented in the Scriptures. Some of the people you counsel during premarital sessions come from such a home.

CHARACTERISTICS OF THE DYSFUNCTIONAL FAMILY

Families that stray off course display several telltale traits. How many of these exist in a family and how often they occur reflect how far the family has strayed from healthy family norms. The counselor should look for these during the conversations with the couple or on the information provided on the Family History Analysis.

Abuse

Abuses that characterize the dysfunctional family can include physical, emotional, or sexual injury or neglect. Abuse may be blatant, such as some family member striking or screaming at another. It can be subtle, as when one person ignores another. Abuse can also be vicarious, such as the inner pain the individual suffers when observing the abuse experienced by his mother, brother, or sister.

One form of abuse that is often overlooked because it leaves no visible scars is emotional mistreatment. Here are some examples:

- Giving a child choices that are only negative, such as saying, "Either eat every bite of your dinner or get a spanking"
- Constantly projecting blame onto a child
- Distorting a child's sense of reality, such as saying, "Your father doesn't have a drinking problem, he just works too hard and he's tired"
- Overprotecting a child
- Blaming others for the child's problem
- Communicating double messages to the child, such as saying, "Yes, I love you" while glaring hatefully at the child (the child will believe the nonverbal message and be confused by the words)

Perfectionism

Perfectionism is rarely considered an unhealthy symptom, but it is a common source of many family problems, especially in Christian homes. After all, isn't the challenge of the Christian life to be perfect as God is perfect? Not really. Christians are called to live a life of excellence. Excellence is attainable, perfectionism is not. Expecting perfect behavior from spouse or children, even in a Christian family, is living in a world of unreality.

A perfectionistic parent conveys his or her standards and expectations through verbal rebukes and corrections, frowns, penetrating glances, smirks, and so on, which continually imply, "It's not good enough." He lives and leads by oughts, shoulds, and musts. These are "torture words" that elevate guilt and lower self-esteem.

Rigidity

Dysfunctional families are characterized by unbending rules and strict lifestyles and belief systems. Life is full of compulsions, routines, controlled situations and relationships, and unrealistic and unchallenged beliefs. Joy? There is none. Surprises? There are none. Spontaneity? There will be none—unless it is planned! The PREPARE Inventory will give the counselor indications of this characteristic.

Silence

Dysfunctional families operate by a gag rule: no talking outside these walls. Don't share family secrets with anyone. Don't ask anyone else for help if you're having a problem. Keep it in the family.

If the gag rule existed at home, a person probably grew up thinking that he had to handle all of his problems by himself. It's difficult for him to ask for assistance or advice. Openness in relationship with his or her fiance may be lacking or there could be a low level of trust. This may come out on the communication category of PREPARE or the Expressive/ Inhibited category on the Taylor-Johnson Temperament Analysis.®

Repression

A man or woman may have grown up in a family where emotions were controlled and repressed instead of identified and expressed. Emotional repression has been called the death sentence of a marriage. Anger, sadness, joy, and pain that should be expressed among family members are buried. The name of the game is to express the feelings that are appropriate instead of what you really feel. Deny reality and disguise your true identity by wearing a mask is the lesson learned.

Emotions are a very important part of life. Like a pressure valve, they help us interpret and respond to the joys and sorrows of life. Clogging the valve by repressing or denying feelings leads to physical problems such as ulcers, depression, high blood pressure, headaches, and a susceptibility to many other physical ailments. Repressing feelings can trigger overeating, anorexia and bulimia, substance abuse, and compulsions of all types. And in a marriage, it kills the relationship. Once again the Expressive/Inhibited trait on the Taylor-Johnson Temperament Analysis® will be an important factor to discuss in your premarital counseling.

Triangulation

Some individuals you see will bear the effects of triangulation. This refers to the communication process in the family. In triangulation, one family member uses another family member as a go-between. Father tells his daughter Jean, "Go see if your mother is still angry at me. Tell her I love her." Jean complies with his request. But Mother retorts, "Tell your father to get lost!" How does Jean feel about getting caught in the middle? Perhaps she feels like a failure. She let her father down. Perhaps she fears that her mother is angry at her.

If triangulation is a regular pattern in a family, the child feels used and becomes involved in problems of which she should not be a part. She becomes a guilt collector, experiencing feelings she doesn't need and cannot handle. Throughout her life she tries to be a "fixer" and could easily carry this tendency into her marriage.

Double Messages

A wife asks her husband if he loves her. "Of course I do," he says as he gulps his food while reading the newspaper. Then he spends four hours in front of the TV and goes to bed without saying one more word to her. His words say, "I love you, " but his actions say, "I don't care about you at all." It's a double message.

A young girl puts her arms around her father and feels his back stiffen as he subtly tries to pull away. Both say, "I love you," but she also hears his body language saying he doesn't like being close to her. It's a double message.

Double messages abound: "I love you"/"Don't bother me now"; "I love you"/"Get lost"; "I need you"/"You're in my way"; "Yes, I accept you"/"Why can't you be more like Susan?" Double messages are confusing, especially to a child. Ask your couple if either experienced this in their homes. If so, how did they feel when this happened? How will it affect their marriage?

Lack of Fun

Dysfunctional families are typically unable to loosen up, play, and have fun. They are overbalanced to the serious side of life. Their mottos are: "Be Serious;" "Work Hard;" "You Are What You Do." When members of a dysfunctional family engage in play, it usually ends up with someone getting hurt. They don't know when to stop. And humor is used as much to hurt as to have fun. There can be a major conflict in a new marriage if one person comes from this background. Their partner knows how to have fun, but they don't.

Martyrdom

Dysfunctional families display a high tolerance for personal abuse and pain. Children hear their parents preaching that others come first, no matter what the personal cost. Children see their parents punish themselves through excessive behaviors such as drinking too much, overworking, overeating, or exercising too hard. Children are challenged: "Tough it out, son; big boys don't cry"; "You aren't hurt, Jane, so quit that whimpering—or else!" They see themselves as victims, pleasers, or martyrs.

As adults, these people learn to brace themselves against weakness by denying themselves pleasure, advantage, or by suppressing their true feelings. Some martyrs actually pride themselves on how much they can bear before the pain becomes intolerable. What impact will this have on a marriage? In your counseling look for this tendency on the Family History Analysis and the Dominant/Submissive trait on the Taylor-Johnson Temperament Analysis.

Entanglement

The members of a dysfunctional family are emotionally and relationally entangled in each other's lives. Individual identities are enmeshed. There are no clear-cut boundaries between each member. Everybody is poking his nose into everybody else's business. Mom makes Dad's problems her problems, Dad makes the kids' problems his problems, and so on. If one family member is unhappy, the whole family is blue, and everybody blames everybody else for the state they're in. It's as though the whole family is sitting together on a giant swing. When one goes up, the others go up. When one goes down, the others go down. Nobody thinks or feels for himself. The lack of proper boundaries can be very destructive in a new marriage. Look at the Family History Analysis and PREPARE for indications.

ROLES WITHIN A DYSFUNCTIONAL FAMILY

Often those who come from a dysfunctional family develop an obvious role. As a child grew up he probably played a role or combination of roles in his interaction with his family. The role was not his true self, but an identity he took on, or was forced to play, in order to get along in the dysfunctional family. People usually continue to play their roles as they move through adult life.

Often the role is a mask, a way of coping with the pain of not having needs fully met by a father or mother or other family members. If a person didn't receive recognition or affirmation for who he was, he may have tended to take on a role that garnered him the attention he needed. Consider these ten roles:[3]

The Doer

The doer is a very busy individual who provides most of the maintenance functions in a family. Also called the responsible one, he or she makes sure that the bills are paid and that people are fed, clothed, and chauffeured. These tasks need to be completed even in a functional home, but the doer uses almost all his time and energy to do them. The family's motto is: "Give it to him and it will get done."

The doer has an overdeveloped sense of responsibility that drives him. The person receives satisfaction from his accomplishments because family members like what he does and, in one way or another, they encourage the person to "keep it up." Often the doer feels tired, isolated, ignored, and used. But the recognition received for what is done keeps him going. Sometimes the doer is also the enabler in the family.

The doer in most families is one of the parents, often the mother. In any way is one of your premarital clients a doer?

The Enabler

The enabler provides the family with emotional and relational nurture and a sense of belonging. She or he is the peacemaker, preserving family unity at all costs. The main goal is to avoid conflicts and help everyone get along. Actions are driven by two fears: the fear that family members cannot survive without each other and the fear of being abandoned.

Enabling behavior usually happens so gradually that the enabler is often unaware of it. The person is constrained to do whatever is necessary to keep the family on an even keel. Unfortunately, the enabler will even excuse or defend a family member's dysfunctional behavior in order to keep peace. For example, the wife of an alcoholic may cover for him and deny that he has a problem in an attempt to hold the family together. But, sadly, enabling behavior also allows the enabled family member to continue his dysfunctional behavior.

Sometimes the enabler can be unpleasant, resorting to anger, nagging, or sarcasm to get the family to do what is wanted. Some Christian enablers misuse their faith in family crises. Instead of doing something constructive about a problem, they sit around waiting for God to intervene with a miracle. Look for behavior or responses in your session as well as submissive scores on the Taylor-Johnson Temperament Analysis to indicate this pattern.

The Loner

This person copes with family pressures by physically or emotionally withdrawing from others. He or she avoids intimate contact with family members, preferring to stay out of sight, either in his room or away from the home. When they are with others they don't enter in much. In a sense the withdrawal fills the need other family members have for autonomy and separateness. But the way it's done is unhealthy for everyone.

A loner probably doesn't feel close to either parent. Notice the responses on the first three pages of the Family History Analysis. Usually the person's personality is quite passive, and he shows very little anger. The loner rarely distinguishes himself in any way and often goes unnoticed. Even moments of accomplishment are often overshadowed by others who attract the limelight. This is the lost child, the forgotten one in the family. Many lost children grow up to be lost adults. Sadly, they never find their place in life, living entirely in denial. You can imagine what happens when they marry. Look for low scores in the active social, expressive, and sympathetic traits on the Taylor-Johnson Temperament Analysis.

The Hero

Everyone seems to like having a hero around, someone whose success and achievement brings recognition and prestige to the family. The hero is addicted to pleasing others: parents, teachers, employers, God. When the family star successfully fulfills parents' dreams, he often accepts the dream as his own. And the acknowledgment he receives for his good deeds builds up the self-esteem of his family members.

But the personal cost for playing this role is astronomical. Heroes strive for achievement at the sacrifice of their own well-being. They don't develop a well-integrated personal value system because their focus is always on pleasing others. They tend to be very critical, so friendships are difficult to come by. Feelings are guarded closely because of the fears that if real feelings come rushing out weakness will be obvious.

Heroes are often the oldest children in families. As such, they often become enablers by denying themselves in order to care for younger siblings in order to please their parents. But the results in adult life can be hurtful.

Heroes eventually burn out because of their strenuous efforts to be good through overachieving. As the hero's external role gradually disintegrates, he begins to behave in ways that are totally foreign to him. Heroes often turn out to be the complete opposites of their assumed roles. What type of future spouse might this person tend to choose? Tend to attract?

The Mascot

The mascot is the family clown. He or she brings humor into the family through play, fun, and even silliness. Clowns are always joking and cutting up, especially when confronted by difficult situations. The fun-loving nature is a great cover for feelings of pain and isolation. The mascot's humor brings the attention that he is unable to gain in other areas. As you counsel a couple, it's easy to be so entertained by a mascot that you miss the pain he carries or the potential problems in a relationship.

The Manipulator

Manipulators are clever controllers in families. They learn early how to get others to do what they want them to do. They know how to seduce, to charm, to play sick, and to appear weak. They use every trick in the book to get their way. Sometimes it's difficult to identify this pattern in the limited time you have in premarital counseling.

The Critic

The critic is the fault-finder in the family. He sees the water glass as half empty instead of half full. Critics are characterized by sarcasm, hurtful teasing, and complaining. They would rather use energy to tear others down than build them up. Critics are not very pleasant to be around, but some families must endure them. Look at the Hostile scale on the T-JTA to help in identifying this tendency.

The Scapegoat

The scapegoat is the family victim. He or she ends up as the blame collector for everyone else. Everyone else in the family looks at his misbehavior and says, "If it weren't for him, our family would be all right." If the scapegoat tries to change his role, other family members won't let him off the hook. As long as he's around, they have someone to blame for their own irresponsibility.

Even though scapegoats don't seem to care what is going on, they usually are the most sensitive persons in the family. They're especially sensitive to the hurt they see in the family, so the stress they feel through their misbehavior is often acted out. Their actions may be a cry to the rest of the family to do something about the hurtful things that are happening in the home.

When the scapegoat is a child in the family, he feels responsible for keeping his parents' marriage together. If he senses problems between them, he may misbehave to unify them in attacking him. Victims may tend to marry someone who will help them continue this role since they are so accustomed to it. Or they may be looking to be rescued.

Daddy's Little Princess/Mommy's Little Man

Some parents refer to their children using the above terms, and often they do so in fun. But in some families these terms are not harmless nicknames. They're subtle and intense forms of emotional abuse. For example, a dysfunctional father may thrust his daughter into the role of little princess as a substitute for his wife in some ways. This father is afraid of getting his emotional needs met by his wife, so he elevates his daughter to princess status and uses her to gain emotional fulfillment. A mother could do the same with her son.

Being a parent's little princess or prince may make the child feel special. But, unfortunately, the youngster is denied his childhood because the parent demands adult responses from him. The boundaries of the child are not respected; they're violated. When the child grows up, in many cases he becomes the victim of physical or emotional abuse by other adults. It's a potentially dangerous situation.

The Saint

As the saint, this child is expected, in an implied rather than an explicit way, to be the one to express the family's spirituality. For example, parents may expect their daughter to go into full-time Christian work. But under the pressure of conforming to this role, she may end up denying her sexuality because her normal desires seem so unspiritual. Her worth as a person becomes dependent upon following the course of action laid out by her parents. A young man may learn to give the outward appearance of being spiritual, but it could be just a cover up. Anger could be repressed, and he may be hesitant to be totally honest with you or his fiancée for fear of tainting his image.

It's important to remember that the reason these roles are unhealthy is because they are just that—roles. In a healthy family, no one is pigeonholed into one slot and expected to remain there the rest of his or her life. In a healthy family one is allowed to be oneself and one's own personality is allowed to come to the forefront. Other family members encourage one another to develop and express individuality. Mother and father are united in their beliefs and values. Their children tend to be more secure since they don't feel the need to take on roles in order to keep the family in balance.

You may be wondering, "Why would anyone want to continue playing a role, especially those that are so unhealthy for the individual or the family?" It's not usually a matter of choice. A person adopts a role in a dysfunctional family as a means of defense, a way to deal with family difficulties and pressures. That role becomes part of that individual's personality. As he grows into adulthood, he continues to utilize that role to deal with problems in the world outside the family. He may realize to some extent the pain of the role, but it's usually easier to accept that pain than to face the world without the defensive armor of the role.

REACTING INSTEAD OF RESPONDING

One other major symptom seen in individuals from dysfunctional families is codependency. Most counselors have heard this term, but not all are aware of how widespread codependency is. Melody Beattie, author of *Codependent No More,* has defined the codependent person as "one who has let another person's behavior affect him or her, and who is obsessed with controlling that person's behavior."[2] The word commonly refers to a wife who doggedly stays beside her alcoholic husband thinking that she can help him. But now it describes more broadly anyone who subjects himself or herself to a problem person. A parent could be codependent to a problem child.

This definition takes on greater meaning through the experiences of codependents. One woman said, "For me codependency means staying married to an alcoholic." Another person said, "I'm always looking for someone to rescue." A thrice-married forty-year-old woman said, "For me it means looking for men with problems and marrying them. They are either alcoholic, workaholic or have some other serious problem." Still another person said, "Codependency is knowing that all your relationships will either go on and on the same way (painfully), or end the same way (disastrously), or both."

Sometimes codependency is confused with responding out of love, kindness, concern, or even righteous indignation. A man or woman may be a very giving, caring, compassionate individual and want to help others in difficulty. This is a normal and natural response. But there is a difference between helping and codependency. A codependent reacts to another person's problem instead of responding to his need. In fact, the codependent often overreacts or underreacts. Instead of measuring and controlling his responses, he allows the problems, pains, and dysfunctional behaviors of others to dictate his actions. If they're not careful, even professional care-givers, such as doctors, nurses, counselors, and pastors, can become codependents to the persons they are trying to help. Do you see any codependent tendencies in the couples you work with in your premarital counseling?

Codependency is also progressive. As the problems of those around him intensify, the codependent's reactions intensify. But, unfortunately, his reactions don't cure the problem.

When a codependent reacts he tends to express the first emotions he feels—anger, guilt, self-hate, worry, hurt, frustration, fear, or anxiety. Similarly, he latches onto the first idea that pops into his head. He speaks the first words that come to his mind, often later wishing he could retract them. There is little or no thinking until after his reactionary response. Melody Beattie writes:

> Reacting usually does not work. We react too quickly, with too much intensity and urgency. There is little in our lives we need to do that we cannot do better if we are peaceful. Few situations—no matter how greatly they appear to demand it—can be bettered by us going berserk.
>
> Why do we do it then?
>
> We react because we're anxious and afraid of what has happened, what might happen, and what is happening. Many of us react as though everything is a crisis because we have lived with so many

crises for so long that crisis reaction has become a habit. We react because we think things shouldn't be happening the way they are. We react because we don't feel good about ourselves. We react because most people react. We react because we think we have to react. We don't have to.[3]

Your task, then, as you minister to couples in premarital counseling will be to identify these roles and assist the person in becoming a transition person—one who breaks free from the legacy of the past and becomes whole and free in the present. This may entail individual counseling for the person and a selective reading program. Listed are some of the resources that have proven to be helpful.

Buhler, Rich. *New Choices, New Boundaries*. Nashville: Thomas Nelson, 1991.

Carder, Dave, *et al. Secrets of Your Family Tree*. Chicago: Moody, 1991.

Friel, John, and Linda Friel. *Adult Children: The Secrets of Dysfunctional Families*. Deerfield Beach, Fla.: Health Communications, 1988.

Townsend, John. *Hiding from Love*. Colorado Springs: NavPress, 1991.

NOTES

1. Sara Hines Martin, *Healing for Adult Children of Alcoholics* (Nashville: Broadman, 1988), p. 34, adapted.
2. Melodie Beattie, *Codependent No More* (San Fransico: Harper & Row, 1988), p. 28.
3. Ibid., p. 65.

CHAPTER
5

Goals of Premarital Preparation and Enrichment

Most people, layman and professional alike, believe that premarital counseling is a worthy concept. (The term premarital preparation and enrichment is a truer description of this process.) Traditionally, three main groups have provided most of the premarital counseling: ministers, physicians, and professional mental health workers.

The first mention of premarital counseling as a valued service occurred in a 1928 article in *The American Journal of Obstetrics and Gynecology.* Then and until the mid-1950s, most of the writing concerned physicians and the premarital physical exam. In the fifties, religious literature as well as mental health literature began to focus upon premarital counseling. Today many churches and public health agencies offer their services to young couples seeking permission to marry.

GOALS OF PREMARITAL COUNSELING

What does the pastor or other counselor hope to accomplish by spending several hours with a couple? There are numerous goals for Christian premarital counseling. In the following discussion, these goals are not listed in order of importance.

Planning the Ceremony

One of the goals of the counseling is to make arrangements for the procedural details of the wedding ceremony itself. The couple can express their desires, and the pastor can make suggestions and provide guidelines. Wedding invitations and ceremonies vary greatly today, and a pastor should be flexible in his approach to the ceremony. Christian couples are becoming more vocal and personal in expressing their faith in Jesus Christ through their invitations and ceremonies, thus allowing both to serve as vehicles for testimony as well as commitment and celebration.

Relationship with the Couple

Premarital counseling is a choice opportunity for the pastor or other counselor to build an in-depth relationship with the couple that could lead to a continuing ministry in the future. The rapport established now will make it easier to be involved in the excitement of the couple's marriage in years ahead.

Correction and Information

Correction of faulty information concerning marriage relationships, the communication process, finances, in-laws, sex, and so on, will be a regular part of the counseling for most couples. In fact, the pastor may be one of the few individuals involved in the life of the couple who can provide this corrective. Unfortunately, some pastors believe that, at this point, couples are not open to assistance and their minds are made up or romantically blinded.

To the contrary, if counseling is presented in the proper manner and the pastor is well prepared, couples will look forward to each session as a unique learning experience and value it highly. Many couples I have counseled think the premarital counseling material should be given to college students prior to mate selection and then again at premarital counseling.

Providing information is congruous with the process of correction. Probably more teaching occurs in this type of counseling than in any other. Part of this teaching involves helping the couple to understand themselves and what each one brings to the marriage, discover their strengths and weaknesses, and be realistic about the adjustments they must make to have a successful relationship.

Better Understanding of Self and Partner

Each person needs to come to a better understanding of who he or she is. Hopefully, through the various assignments, including books, tapes, and testing, each one will become more aware of his or her own thoughts, strengths, weaknesses, beliefs, values, feelings, and fantasies. This can contribute to a stronger identity.

The counselor wants to help each person develop a clearer and more realistic perception of who he or she is marrying. The partner is unique and has his or her own set of feelings, beliefs, fantasies, thinking processes, strengths, and weaknesses. If each one can grasp the fact that he or she is marrying a foreigner and will need to understand the other person's culture and learn to speak his/her language, much will have been achieved.

Relationship with Parents

This is a time to help couples determine if they have adequately separated from their parents and their past in a positive manner.

Relationship with One Another

The counselor also helps the couple to assess their beliefs, values, behaviors, and patterns of relating to one another. You will be guiding the couple to make the assessment and at the same time drawing some conclusions yourself.

Growth and Change

In order to accomplish these goals another foundational but strange goal is part of the process and it is this: to create a sense of unrest and questioning within each person. In other types of counseling, including marital and crisis, we often endeavor to have the person or couple leave the session with a sense of hope and resolution. Premarital is different. We don't want them to be that comfortable. Why? So that learning, growth, and change can occur.

One of the ways to accomplish this is to create a series of miniature crises. When the couple experiences a crisis, they are thrown off balance. They essentially feel out of control. Things are not proceeding the way they anticipated, and they are looking for a resolution. Their typical way of solving problems may not be working, and their defenses may not be as strong. Thus they are open to considering something new in order to bring some harmony back into their lives. This needs to occur within the premarital counseling to help the couple confront the realities of married life. But how?

There are several ways to do this. One approach I strongly recommend is the use of gentle, but firm and persistent, questioning.

I would rather see a couple leave my office questioning and pondering unanswered questions than leaving always feeling settled. I have had couples return for their next session and state, "You know, we talked for five hours after our last session. We really had some serious questions about our relationship. We struggled." And I usually respond with, "Good. That's important and healthy. You're probably a bit different this week than last because of that time."

I keep asking the question, "But, what if . . ." and push and push. Sometimes they admit, "I guess I don't know . . ." and I respond with "I guess you need to find out. How will you do that?" And they often leave the session with that question.

Sometimes I ask, "What is the worst type of behavior that your spouse could engage in that you wouldn't want?" And when they reply I ask, "Let's say that actually happened. How would you handle that? What effect would it have on your love for him?" We endeavor to take questions as far as we can in order to create somewhat of an unsettled state.

One of the other questions I pose is: "I don't know of any couples who marry with the purpose of getting a divorce, abusing their spouse, having an affair, or having a marriage that is unhappy. But it sometimes happens. What will you do to make sure this does not occur in your marriage?"

"Well, we're both Christians and with Christ in our lives, that will make the difference," many couples respond. My reply is, "I see fifteen to twenty couples a week in here with the very problems I just mentioned, and they are all born-again Christians from the evangelical churches in our area. When they married they had the same response as you just gave. But these problems still happened. Why? Why will yours be different?" With each answer I keep pushing until they seem to have no other answers. This is often a good place to end the session by saying,

"I guess that's something for you to talk through this week and bring your conclusions for the next time. I'll see you the same time next week."

Here is a series of "what if . . . " questions you can give to the couple to complete and discuss during the week. Ask them to share the results of their discussion:

How would you react to the following circumstances? What if this happens to you after you are married?:

1. Your spouse has to work night shift instead of day shift.
2. You discover your spouse's attraction to someone else.
3. You discover your spouse no longer has time for daily devotions.
4. A friend begins to indicate nonverbally he/she is interested/attracted to you or your spouse.
5. You cannot get along with your sister-in-law.
6. You have a definite communication problem with your mother-in-law.
7. You cannot become pregnant.
8. Your apartment is far too small, and you cannot afford a larger one.
9. Your spouse spends more money on himself/herself than on you.
10. You find yourself in major debt.
11. Your spouse loses his job.
12. Your sex life is less than exciting.
13. Communication is becoming increasingly difficult.
14. Discovering that your spouse cannot let go of (leave) his or her mother.
15. You find yourself living in the city rather than the country.
16. You find yourself attracted to another person.[1]

We also use questions to cause the couple to think and anticipate marital conflict and crisis. One question/scenario I use at the conclusion of the initial session helps them understand commitment. First I ask them their ages. Since many couples are young, I often hear one say, "I'm twenty-three, and Phyllis is twenty-two." I ask them at this time to face each other and look at one another. I then say, "You're both in your early twenties. If you live to the normal life span of individuals in our society, you'll both live until sometime into your seventies. This means that you are about to commit yourself to that person across from you for the next fifty years. The next half-century. I'd just like you to think about that. I'll see you next week." And the session is over. Sometimes I will rise and walk toward the door or gather up my materials.

Many of the couples are strongly affected. I've often heard the comment, "I'd never thought about it in that way. A half a century sure puts it in a different perspective."

Here is where the Taylor-Johnson Temperament Analysis can be very helpful. The test is taken twice by each person: once as they see themselves, and once as they see each other. Repeatedly I run into situations in which one person views himself a certain way and yet his partner sees him quite differently.

In one case a thirty-five-year-old man saw himself as being very expressive, a bit indifferent, and tolerant. But his fiance saw him as being nonexpressive, quite indifferent, and very hostile rather than tolerant. We took the individual questions in each of the categories and went through them one by one. She responded with her answer to each question and gave an explanation as to why she responded in that manner. With each response I could see him becoming more and more thoughtful and pensive until he finally asked, "If you actually see me this way, why would you want to marry me?" They both had unsettled feelings about getting married.

Each week we continued to pursue their differences and asked, "Can these be worked through enough so that you are comfortable enough to marry?" In a later session with the couple I began by asking each one, "On a scale of 0-10, how do you feel about getting married?" '0' meant not at all and '10' meant deeply and firmly committed. Her response was a 7 to 7 1/2, as was his. But she added that before they started their premarital counseling it was higher. We explored her feelings some more and then discovered that her feelings vacillated from a 2 to an 8. This led to the question, "And what does that tell you about whether you're ready to marry or not?" This proved to be one of the deciding questions for this couple. My feeling is that it would take at least a constant and steady 8 for the commitment level to be high enough to make this important commitment.

Communication Style

A new but critical goal in premarital counseling involves the communication style. The counselor needs to be able to communicate with the people he/she is seeing and help them to learn to communicate with one another. One of my own personal goals in counseling during the initial session is to discover the person's style of communication and communicate back to the person or couple in the same way. The principle is very simple. If I speak their language, we will understand one another and real listening will occur. And by doing this, I will have a platform for teaching a couple the importance of speaking one another's language.

I try to discover whether the person is more visually, auditorially, or kinesthetically (feeling) oriented. I listen to the tone of voice, volume, and the phrases the person uses. I study the nonverbal communication. Some people are loud, expressive, and gesture a lot. Others are somewhat quiet, reserved, very proper, and choose their words carefully. Some are amplifiers and some condensers. I join their type of communication, which builds rapport, trust, and eventually a willingness on their part to listen to me and follow my guidance. (For additional information on this, see *How to Speak Your Spouse's Language* by this author [Revell]).

As I work with couples, invariably I end up spending time teaching them the importance of speaking one another's language and how to do it. They read how to do this as part of their homework, and in the session I assist them in applying the principles. As you work with premarital couples it is important that you read and become proficient in your own communication ability so that you are capable of teaching others.

Prediction and Recommendation

This is also a time of prediction and recommendation. In the prediction process each couple must identify their weaknesses and potential problem areas in their marriage, evaluate what each has to offer to handle these trouble spots, and begin developing greater skills in these areas. The recommendation part of premarital counseling may be difficult for some. But couples do want our assessment and recommendation of their relationship and prognosis for their marriage. At times you will have a sense that a particular couple should not marry. This will be both an objective and a subjective value judgment on your part. How is it objective? Here are some guidelines:

1. A couple may not be motivated enough to complete the assignments.
2. There is indication of possible pathology in one or both of their Taylor-Johnson Temperament Analysis results.

3. One or both is unwilling to work on weaknesses indicated from the testing.
4. One or both has unresolved issues stemming from the past which are apparent and will damage their marriage.
5. One or both is unwilling to fully separate from their parents. The Family History Analysis will assist you in this area.
6. One of them is still involved in substance abuse and is unwilling to seek help. Their partner may be a "Rescuer" at this time, but it will probably not last.
7. The results of the PREPARE Test indicate an excessive number of conflicts which they are unable to resolve at this time.

The subjective element enters in also, as you will need to assimilate all of what you see and hear from the couple and then make your own value judgment. Sometimes you may be troubled because your intuition is saying something and yet you can't come up with any specific facts. And if you are very analytical and tend to base decisions on facts, you may tend to discount that other voice you are hearing. *Listen to it!* Bring it out in the open. I have done this on occasion by saying, "I guess at this time I need to share something with you. For some reason which I can't figure out, I am troubled in a way about your relationship. I don't know why or what it is. I wonder if you could help me? Why might I be feeling uneasy?'

I many cases the couple felt the same way and needed permission to raise their own uncomfortable feelings. On a few occasions I have just said, "Based on our sessions together and what we have talked over, I am wondering how you are feeling about proceeding with your wedding?"

Some were surprised at my question while others have known what I was driving at. On three other occasions I have said, "I would like to recommend you not marry one another, and I would like to give you my reasons." I proceeded to do just that and then asked, "How do you feel about what I have said?" Sometimes you will find resistance and upset and other times you will find that all three of you are feeling and thinking the same.

On one occasion after the third session I said to a couple who had been dating for five years, "I would like to suggest that we terminate the premarital counseling and that you not even consider marriage at this time. I think it would be much better for you to become involved in individual counseling to deal with other issues rather than consider marriage." The couple looked at one another, and I heard sighs of relief. The man said, "Finally someone has given us permission not to marry. All of our friends and relatives have been pushing us to marry since we have gone together for so long."

Of those I've worked with so far, most of the couples who made the decision to postpone or terminate the relationship did so on their own. It is vital that you be blatantly and lovingly honest in your appraisal and assessment of any couple. Your responses can serve as small loving shocks that carry the impact of a brief crisis shock.

One couple in their early thirties came to their last session. We had worked through some difficult issues, and at one point it appeared that the woman might call off the wedding. They were able to somewhat work through the issues, but I still felt unsettled. They would be carrying more potential adjustments into marriage than most.

In the last session I asked, "On a scale of 1-10, with 10 totally comfortable and satisfied and 1 being just the opposite, where are you in terms of your feelings about getting married next month?" He looked at her and then me and said, "Well, before our session today it was a high 9 but now it's about an 8." She responded, "It's about a 7 or 8. I looked at them and said, "I guess my response would be a 5." They both looked a bit startled and taken back. But it had its effect to encourage them to do some further work.

Realistic Expectations

One of the main purposes is to help the couple eliminate as many surprises as possible from the impending marriage. By helping them become more realistic about the future, the counselor can lessen marital conflict. I tell the couple this is my goal in disclosing their fears and hopes—to reduce conflict in marriage. I also let them know that by doing this they will have a greater opportunity to build and enrich their marriage. Too many couples today are committing marital suicide because of lack of preparation.

The counselor must have expertise in many areas, because the couple is looking to him or her as the conveyor of helpful information. This is an opportunity to provide an atmosphere in which the couple can relieve themselves of fears and anxieties concerning marriage and settle questions or doubts that they have. This may also be a time in which strained and severed relationships with parents and in-laws will be restored.

Marriage Enrichment

Another goal is to help a couple plan for the continuing enhancement and enrichment of their marriage. This is accomplished by helping them develop a plan for enrichment and by anticipating the various stages of their marriage.

Spiritual Growth

A very high ranking goal of premarital counseling is spiritual growth. This is a time for each person to evaluate his or her commitment to Jesus Christ individually and as a couple. One of the important questions to consider during this time is, "In what way will the presence of Jesus Christ make a difference in your marriage and how will this occur? In what way is He a part of your courtship relationship?"

And from there you will have the opportunity to assist them in establishing and developing the application of the Scriptures in their lives as well as a prayer life together.

The Decision to Marry

The final purpose for counseling may seem foreign to some and yet could be one of the most important goals. This is a time to assist the couple in making their final decision, "Should we marry?" They may not come with that in mind, but engagement is not finality. Research indicates that between 35 and 45 percent of all engagements in this country are terminated. Many people do change their minds. Perhaps during the process of premarital counseling, some couples will decide to postpone their wedding or completely terminate their relationship. Furthermore, in some cases the pastor may decide that he cannot, in good conscience, perform the wedding because of the apparent mismatch or immaturity of the couple. Some couples will listen to his advice; others will simply go elsewhere and find someone who does not require so much and will perform the ceremony.

Couples will change their minds. One couple I counseled decided to cancel two weeks before the ceremony. Two couples had such poor relationships that I planned to tell them their marriages would be too much of a risk; before I did, they told me they had decided to break off their relationships.

The Marriage Question

If we accept these goals as the foundations for our premarital counseling, we must then deal with several important yet difficult issues. The first and possibly the most difficult is deciding whether we should marry a couple whom we believe is not ready for marriage. It is my deeply held conviction that a minister has the responsibility to withhold the decision to marry a couple until he is assured in his own mind that the marriage has a chance of making it. It is also essential that you make this clear to the couple when you begin counseling them.

If it should become necessary to delay a couple from marriage, the minister must be willing to continue working with the couple either directly or through referral until the couple is ready to be married or decides to postpone or cancel the marriage plans.

After discussing this issue with ministers across the United States and Canada, at the premarital seminars I conduct, I have found most to be in agreement. Being ordained to marry someone is not only a privilege, but a great responsibility. Most of us would not question the criteria our churches have for accepting an individual into membership. In addition, we would not fail to deny a person membership if he failed to meet them. Yet, we question our authority and responsibility not to marry someone we believe is not ready for marriage.

If our practice becomes one of marrying anyone who comes to us to be married, then we really become no different from a justice of the peace or a marry-for-profit wedding chapel. It has not been uncommon to hear the argument some give that if they marry couples that are not ready, then they have a better chance of working with them and getting them involved in the church. The experience we have heard from most is that few couples stick around over the long run. This may be due to the instability and problems that were inherent in the relationship (impulsiveness, idealism, hostility, subjectivity, etc.).

Most experts in the field agree that premarital couples do not receive input or concern from family and friends when the relationship is questioned. Too often premarital couples are in an isolated environment and thus they do not receive sufficient information from people regarding themselves and their relationship. Friends or family members are often hesitant to speak to the couple for fear of meddling. And too often the couple is somewhat blinded or infatuated and cannot see reality. Because of this deficit, it is even more essential that we counselors be willing to not only say what we see, but stand behind what we see with our behavior.

Wedding Plans

Fortunately, in most cases when there are major problems, couples see them early in the counseling process and choose to postpone the marriage or cut it off entirely. The exception to this brings up our second issue: the effects of beginning preparations for marriage before finishing the counseling. When a couple has been allowed to put their date on the church calendar, and plans begin to be made, finances deposited and invitations sent out, the wedding seemingly must happen. The potential embarrassment and loss of finances seem to be so overwhelming that it blinds the judgment and perceptions of couples who would otherwise choose to postpone or cancel their wedding. When this occurs we have abandoned our first goal, which is deciding whether or not they should marry at this time.

This blinding also occurs in well-adjusted couples, who, while looking at potential troublesome issues, seem to ignore relevant facts that might help them in their future adjustment. When this happens, we are abandoning the second goal of helping couples gain skills that will enable them to nurture the relationship toward intimacy and maturity.

One way we have found to deal with this problem is to make it mandatory for couples to complete their premarital counseling before being allowed to place their wedding date on the calendar.

We also encourage couples to begin the premarital counseling before becoming engaged, thus leaving them plenty of time to deal with the issues before them without the pressure of having to meet deadlines. Although this policy raises some questions when first instituted, once explained it is often supported and desired by all involved. Most ministers say it takes about a year to educate the congregation.

These procedures have worked well in most of the situations of which I am aware, when they have been instituted over time with plenty of promotion. The only situations that have been problematic are when one or more members of a multiple pastoral staff has gone contrary to the policy. Unfortunately, the mindset that develops with couples is that if you want to be assured of getting married "go to X Church or Y minister. He doesn't make you work hard." This process only reinforces a tragic pattern that possibly already has begun and will continue into marriage. Simply stated, it is "do it the easy way." Its implications spell disaster when applied to communication and conflict resolution. In addition, confusion and feelings of unfairness are often experienced by couples who do not understand why the requirements are so different among ministers at the same church.

These recommendations are not harsh but loving and concerned. We care about the couple's marriage and future enough to be involved. And the goals and process described here can best be attained by the personal investment of time to conduct premarital counseling on an individual basis rather than the group premarital process.

THE IMPACT OF COUNSELING

What are the results of this program of counseling, and are they significant? Very little has been done in terms of extensive research and long-term statistical studies. Two research reports will be cited, as well as individual responses.

Lt. Col. John Williams, a faculty member of the United States Air Force Academy in Colorado Springs, reported in his doctoral thesis that divorce among U.S. military officers is significantly lower than among the population as a whole. Among military officers, Air Force officers were found to have the lowest divorce rate, with the lowest of all found among officers graduating from the Air Force Academy. Between 1959, when the first class graduated, and 1970, only 21 of the 4,500 Air Force Academy graduates (.004 percent) were divorced.

Those statistics may be explained in part by the high value placed on stable marriage. A premarital counseling program conducted by the chaplaincy is an indication of the importance of successful marriage to the Air Force. Cadets and their fiancées are given intensive preparation for marriage, which takes place after graduation from the academy. Protestant, Catholic, and Jewish chaplains conduct their own programs.

Catholic chaplains spend eight to fourteen hours counseling each couple, covering basic areas of communication, finances, love, responsible child planning, and in-laws. The final preparation takes place at a weekend retreat where marriage counselors, gynecologists, and lawyers share their views and experiences with the couples.

The Protestant program includes seminars on Sunday afternoons in January, February, and March. The subjects discussed include the success rate of Air Force marriages, methods of communication, and the physical and spiritual aspects of marriage. A marriage retreat is conducted in April.[2]

I conducted a research study in 1976 surveying more than 1,000 churches; 407 returned usable surveys representing twenty-five different denominations, with churches ranging in size from 30 people to more than 6,000. Church staffs indicated the types, extent, and results of their premarital counseling programs.[3]

The survey contained several important findings. Premarital counseling was required by 369 ministers, whereas thirty-eight did not require counseling. The average number of required sessions was three. Forty-five pastors required only one session, and forty-five required at least six sessions. More than half, 274 ministers, said they performed weddings for nonbelievers; sixty-nine reported they did not. Two of the most significant questions asked the participants were:

1. If counseling is mandatory, how do couples react? How does the church respond to this? More than 90 percent of the responses to this question were positive. People were in favor of the policy, felt that it helped, and encouraged their friends to come for counseling. Some couples were hesitant or went elsewhere.

2. What are the results of premarital counseling in your experience, and how do you know? A representative sampling of responses follows:

- It has opened up couples to marital counseling that they otherwise would not have had.
- Many have expressed gatitude. Only two have been divorced (about 70 marriages in 22 years).
- Several have postponed or canceled weddings.
- About 20 percent do not marry. They cancel their arrangements.
- Some couples decide that they are not ready for marriage; some have come to know Christ as Savior.
- Most couples have appreciated the sessions.
- In one church 25 percent of the couples decided not to get married. Almost another 25 percent have postponed their wedding dates. Many couples have been very outspoken in their appreciation and in encouraging friends to take the course.

One pastor counseled fifty-seven couples and conducted weddings for twenty-three. Out of the first eleven he married before he learned how to conduct premarital counseling, one couple had divorced and five couples were having serious struggles. After training he counseled forty-five couples. They now have proper ground rules for their marriages and even for disagreeing and are developing successful marriages.

In 1978-79 Christian Marriage Enrichment conducted an extensive marriage and family survey throughout the United States upon a Christian population. More than 8,000 couples responded, representing more than twenty-five denominations.[4] Of the 109 questions, several were focused upon premarital preparation.

One survey item asked: "Prior to your own marriage did you receive premarital counseling from the church or pastor where you were married?" Although 3,045 said yes, almost 5,000 said no. An additional 571 said they received premarital counseling from a professional counselor. Thus 45 percent of those participating in the survey received some preparation.

A very significant question was: "If you did receive premarital counseling, do you feel that it helped you in your marriage?" Positive responses greatly outnumber the negative, as shown below.

Definitely Yes — 29.3 percent
Possibly Yes — 45.5 percent
Possibly No   — 13.2 percent
Definitely No — 11.2 percent

Only 15 percent of those who participated in one session stated that it definitely helped their marriage, and 31 percent of those who received two sessions of counseling said it definitely helped. Significantly, of those who attended five sessions, 53 percent said that counseling definitely helped their marriage, and 75 percent of those attending seven or more sessions said that premarital counseling definitely helped their marriage.

A statistical study and analysis was done upon the effect of premarital counseling as seen by responses to other questions. Some of the findings derived from this research include the following:

• More of those who received premarital counseling say they entered marriage with an adequate understanding of what it would be like than those who did not receive counseling.
• More respondents who received premarital counseling described their marriage as fulfilled and continuing than did the respondents who did not receive counseling.
• More of those who received premarital counseling strongly believe that knowing and having a personal relationship with Jesus Christ has had a positive effect on their marriage than those who did not receive premarital counseling.

- More of those who received premarital counseling believe that the teachings and application of Scripture have helped their marriage relationship in a positive manner than those who did not receive premarital counseling.
- Among those who received premarital counseling the major responsibility for disciplining the children is equally shared more often than among those who did not receive premarital counseling.
- Fewer respondents who received premarital counseling listed how to resolve conflicts in the top four areas in which they would like the most additional help than those who had not received premarital counseling.

NOTES

1. Couple's Premarital Notebook, Dove Fellowship Church, Ephrata, Pennsylvania.
2. Article, *Religious News Service*, May 15, 1974, p. 2.
3. H. Norman Wright, research survey, Talbot Theological Seminary, 1976.
4. A research report by Christian Marriage Enrichment and Christian Counseling and Enrichment, Tustin, Calif., 1979.

CHAPTER
6

*Strategies
for an Extended
Counseling Program*

ORGANIZING THE SESSIONS

Earlier I suggested that a couple be required to have at least six sessions of premarital counseling. Here is how those sessions are organized: During the sessions the pastor or counselor meets with both partners. On some occasions you may want to see them individually, but usually they are together. Sometimes individual sessions may be necessary because of emotional difficulties discovered through testing.

The counseling setting is very important. Your office or a study at home could be used if there is sufficient privacy and a homey, informal atmosphere. Freedom from interruptions is crucial; make arrangements to prevent people from walking into the room, knocking on the door, and calling on the phone. When you and the couple sit near each other in easy chairs, an informal setting is created that helps alleviate the couple's anxieties.

Premarital counseling is highly structured, but great flexibility can occur within the structure. The number of sessions, content, assignments, and evaluative tests are set (see next chapter), but changes and additions will occur with almost each couple because of their unique issues.

The basic structure for premarital counseling follows this pattern:

1. Couples should contact the church several months in advance of the time they are planning to wed. At that time arrangements will be made to begin the process of premarital preparation. No date is placed on the church calendar at this time.
2. There will be a minimum of six one-hour sessions with the individual couple prior to the wedding and one session nine months to a year following the wedding.
3. In larger churches there might also be a number of group premarital classes conducted at the same time as the individual. An alternative to this is using the video series "Before You Say I Do."
4. There will be one meeting between the premarital couple and a selected married couple for the purpose of interviewing this couple about their own marriage.

TIME REQUIREMENTS

The basic structure of the premarital counseling suggested in this book is six one-hour sessions before the wedding plus one session three to six months after the wedding. Some counselors may ask, "How do we fill all of that time?" The problem is actually just the opposite—sometimes the time allotted is not sufficient to cover all the material. (I find now that I often need at least seven sessions.)

Other readers might react by saying, "I marry twenty to thirty couples a year. What you're suggesting could amount to two hundred hours. Where do I get that time, with everything else I have to do?"

It is true that counseling takes time. However, it might be well for each minister to regularly analyze his use of time. Sometimes our gifts and abilities are not being used to their best advantage. It is very easy in the ministry to become overwhelmed with tasks that have little to do with a real ministry to people. Often it comes down to a matter of priority; we do what we feel is important. Premarital counseling is one of the most important opportunities for ministry.

There are several ways to approach the problem of time. One is to restructure one's use of time so that counseling takes a higher priority and other activities are delegated. When we keep adding ministries to our already busy schedule and fail to relinquish or delegate some, a number of difficulties arise. (See Ex. 18 and Num. 11; note the difficulty Moses experienced because he had not delegated responsibilities to others.)

Use Lay Counselors

The answer is to develop a support team of qualified, committed, and trained lay individuals or couples to conduct the very same type of premarital counseling that you present to couples.

In many churches mature individuals and couples have the capabilities to become helpers in the ministry of premarital preparation. Some could serve as teachers in the class sessions and others can be trained to conduct the actual premarital sessions, including using the various tests and evaluation forms. Numerous churches are currently involved in this ministry. The entire field of lay counseling has been expanding over the past decade. Involving lay people is very effective.

In general, lay or paraprofessional helpers have shown a level of effectiveness comparable to professionals, according to many outcome studies reported in the literature. A recent issue of the *Journal of Psychology* highlights the effectiveness of using lay counselors and concludes that current research findings show that lay or paraprofessional counselors are, in general, as effective as professionals in helping people with their problems.[1]

Train Lay Counselors

The main question is: How do you train lay people to conduct premarital counseling? I recommend a six-step format for each person participating in the training.

First, announce to your congregation that you are looking for individuals or couples who are interested in considering this ministry. You may want to approach personally some people of known ability and empathy. Be sure to let everyone know that not all who are interested or take the training will be selected, as everyone will be going through a screening and supervision process. Some of those interested will drop out as they become aware of the requirements, and you will find some who are not really capable of counseling others. Any person or couple involved in this ministry must reflect a healthy, growing marriage themselves. The fifth step in the training (see below) will give you information about each person that will aid you in the selection process.

93

Second, have each person read this resource. Meet with the group to discuss what was read and answer questions.

The third step requires the potential counselors read each of the books recommended for premarital couples and listen to each of the tape series.

The fourth step involves each person completing the same tests the premarital couple will complete: The Taylor-Johnson Temperament Analysis, the Family History Analysis, and PREPARE II. It would be best to use the Enrich form of PREPARE for your group as it will assist them in evaluating their own marriage. In addition to these I would encourage you to have each person complete the "Marital Assessment Inventory," another assessment tool that will assist a couple in looking at the strengths and weaknesses of their marriage.[2] Make time to go over the results of these tests with the individual or couple.

Fifth, if you plan to have your lay counselors use any of the tests in their counseling, set aside the time to train them in the use of PREPARE II and the Family History Analysis. Each of these comes with an instructional manual. Some of your people may have the necessary educational background to participate in training lay people to use the T-JTA. The training couple can take the survey measurements themselves. If they participate in a seminar or if you have used this extensively for several years yourself, you could provide some of their instruction and they could use them under your supervision. Furthermore, if you have the audio tapes of a seminar you attended, you may also use these.

The final step is for the lay counselors to observe live counseling sessions. This is the most important part of the training. For years in my graduate classes at Talbot Theological Seminary and Biola University I have conducted premarital counseling with a couple in front of my students. The class size has varied from thirty to eighty students, yet none of the couples was inhibited or bothered by being observed. After each session the couple left and for the next hour we would analyze the session and deal with questions. Over the years students have continued to comment about the impact and effectiveness of that approach.

There are three ways to conduct such counseling-observation sessions:

1. Have an individual or couple observe you in your office as you lead the premarital session for a couple. Naturally you need to have the couple's permission. To ease any discomfort the couple might have, I have given them the freedom to ask the class members any

questions they would like, and the class must respond. You may want to do this in your session as well.

2. Conduct your premarital counseling in front of all those being trained. Be sure to leave time for analysis of the session with your group. It may be helpful to tape-record the sessions so that you can refer to specific situations or issues if needed.

3. Use the series of video training tapes titled "Helping Couples Resolve Marital Conflicts." This is a series of actual marital sessions with couples, and the counseling is conducted by this author. There are two videos for each session. One contains selected scenes from the session, which are left open ended so that those watching can respond to questions in their participant's manual. Once they have viewed all of these scenes, you can present the second video, which contains the complete session together with the counselor's responses. Though this series is on marital counseling, it will also help the participants learn about the counseling process.[3]

As noted in chapter 2, the premarital program at Grace Community Church in California uses lay couples for much of its premarital counseling. The church's approach in training the couples is similar to the program just described. The couples are instructed in a class setting and have the opportunity to observe six sessions of actual premarital counseling. Class members are trained to counsel both on an individual and group basis. This is encouraging to see and hopefully multitudes of churches, large and small, will begin to employ more lay people in their counseling ministry.

Once the reading, listening, and observing has been completed, you can make your selection of those you would like to have minister to engaged couples. I would encourage you to give them one couple at a time until they become more proficient. It is important to schedule some sessions where all the lay helpers can meet together with you to discuss their cases and concerns. Supervision is a necessity until those conducting the counseling are comfortable and have refined their skills.

MANDATORY COUNSELING

The pastor-counselor must educate the congregation concerning the pastor's policy of premarital counseling task; this education process could take a full year. Through the pulpit, classes, the church newsletter, and the bulletin, the pastoral staff has the opportunity to educate the congregation concerning the importance of marriage and the family and to describe in detail what is covered in premarital counseling. People in many congregations have expressed the wish that premarital counseling had been available to them years before.

Maintain Requirements

On the other hand, some will resent a mandatory program and will threaten to go elsewhere for their wedding and perhaps even find another church home. That is their choice. If they so decide, the pastor should not allow himself to be manipulated and pressured into lowering his standards. Too often it has been too easy to be married within the local church. A couple must be willing to take time to adequately prepare for marriage. Through a consistent program such as this, the community and the people in the congregation will come to a deeper level of respect for the ministry of the church.

It is also true that a pastor may have fewer weddings under his new policy. But those he does have will be significant. Robert Dulin, Jr., expressed this standard in his excellent address at the Congress on the Family in 1975 when he said, "Pastors should refuse to sell the birthright of their ministry to nurture marriages for the pottage of conducting a wedding. The church's ministry is not to conduct weddings. Its ministry is to nurture marriages, before marriage and during marriage. If couples cannot make a commitment to nurture their marriage prior to the event, then the church should say we cannot have your marriage solemnized here."

Some board members or relatives of members of the church may ask for a special dispensation in the case of their own young person. A son who is home on leave from the army for a week wants to get married; a couple where there is a pregnancy wants a quick and quiet wedding. Many other unique circumstances will arise. Couples involved in these situations are usually in even greater need of counseling and preparation than the ordinary couple, and they too should complete the total program of premarital counseling.

Part of the process of educating the congregation will be to give periodic reminders about the steps involved in scheduling a wedding at the church. Couples should consider starting their counseling at the time of engagement or, in some cases, prior to engagement. It is best to conduct the counseling no later than four to six months before the wedding.

There are two reasons for this. One is that the counseling lasts six to eight weeks, since the sessions are a week or ten days apart. The second reason for starting counseling early is that the wedding date is not put on the church calendar when the couple first calls the church. The pastor waits until he feels that he favors the marriage and that he can conduct the wedding: at that point the couple can go ahead and set the date on the church calendar. That may occur after two sessions or, for some, after five. A couple may ask to have a date on the calendar held for them, with the clear understanding that this does not constitute setting the date officially.

Evaluate the Couple

Undertaking the counseling does not automatically ensure the couple that the wedding will be performed. The pastor will have several criteria to use in making this determination. (They will be discussed later.) With that approach, couples will soon learn to make their plans well in advance. That has advantages for the entire church.

If several churches in a community would adopt this approach, couples would soon begin to see how deeply the church values the marriage relationship and how important the preparation is.

MARRIAGE INVOLVING A NON-CHRISTIAN

Most pastors ask two common questions concerning standards in marrying couples who have come for counseling: Do we marry just Christians, or do we become involved with non-Christians? What about those who have been divorced?

A pastor will have two Christians coming to be married, two non-Christians, and one Christian and one non-Christian. One cannot assume that just because two believers are involved the marriage should occur automatically. A Christian profession alone is not sufficient. And that is what the premarital counseling is all about—making that determination.

A counselor should strongly advise a couple to postpone the marriage if they are immature, have unrealistic expectations about marriage, have low motivation to complete the assignments during counseling, and cannot adapt or change. Some couples might be urged not to marry at all.

A counselor also should consider several questions during the evaluation. Here are several to help a counselor establish criteria for marrying or not marrying.

Are any legal requirements being violated, such as license, consent of parents for minors, health test, or waiting period? Are any of your own church requirements being ignored?

Do these persons give frivolous reasons for wanting to get married? Is one (or both) entering marriage under duress?

Are they so immature mentally and emotionally that they do not understand the meaning of the vows or give reasonable promise of fulfilling them?

Are there indications that they do not intend to fulfill their marriage vows?

Are there any serious mental, emotional, physical, or other handicaps that might endanger their marriage? Have those been adequately understood, accepted, and dealt with insofar as possible?

Is there such marked personality incompatibility that the need for psychological testing is indicated?

Some pastors favor a brief preliminary session with the couple to discuss their spiritual life. Whether this is done prior to the onset of the actual premarital counseling or during the first session is up to the individual counselor.

The Scriptures clearly forbid the uniting of a believer and an unbeliever in marriage (see 2 Cor. 6:14); this would be the standard for refusing to perform the ceremony. As a couple comes for the interview where this information is shared, the pastor's response in love and concern and his high regard for the scriptural teaching could make an impression upon the unbeliever so that the door for discussion remains open. This is an opportunity for evangelism. Yet if one does make a response at this time it is important to spend time with the person to eliminate the possibility that it was a pseudoprofession designed to get the pastor to conduct the wedding.

It is very difficult to judge motives. The pastor dealing with a premarital conversion should engage the person in a thorough discussion of the meaning of a commitment to Christ. He should watch for external evidence that indicates a change of life.

If a person does respond to the claim of the gospel, he or she should be guided into a group that will assist him or her in the Christian life. In many such cases the wedding date, if it is relatively close at hand, might be postponed in order to let the new convert grow in the faith. That growth is especially important for men because of the biblical concept of the leadership role of the Christian husband. If both partners are at a similar level in their Christian walk it is easier for them to grow together and study together.

The pastor should be satisfied that both the man and the woman are believers in Jesus Christ. The biblical standard must remain the guide for the church. Wayne Oates vividly summarizes the church's position:

> Marriage under the auspices of the church is an institution ordained of God, blessed by Christ's presence, and subject to the instruction of the Holy Spirit. This is what is meant when a church says it will not "join any person together other than as God's Word doth allow." If there is any other standard, the church is consciously yoking two people together unequally. The Christian experience of regeneration is a necessary prerequisite for a congregation's participating in a Christian wedding through the ministry of its pastor. God has not promised that even a Christian marriage will be free of tribulation. However, when a church joins couples together apart from the Christian faith, it shares the responsibility for any future failure of the marriage for the very reason it did not communicate the redemptive transforming love of Christ at the time of the wedding.
>
> One very real objection can legitimately be raised here. Some people say that a pastor and a congregation can marry a couple, even if one or both may not be Christians, with the hope that by being kind at this point, by doing things they may want it to do, it will have an opportunity later to win them to Christ. However, being kind to people does not necessarily consist of doing what they want done. It may even be the deepest sod of unkindness. Furthermore, there is always suspicion of the wisdom of the man or woman who marries with an eye to "reforming" the mate. If this is true of the couple's individual relationship to each other, it certainly is true of the relationship of the pastor and the church to them. When a church offers the services of its pastor with a view to the couple's being changed at some later date, it forthwith misrepresents reality to the couple.[4]

Pastors are divided over the question of what to do for couples when *both* claim to be unbelievers. Such a couple seeks a church wedding not to reflect their commitment to Christ but because of sentiment, status, or because the church represents the place to be married. Some pastors agree to perform this service for a couple, acting more as an agent of the state than as a minister of the gospel. The ceremony is usually held in the pastor's study and does not involve a regular church wedding. The content of this ceremony includes only what is necessary to fulfill the law. Yet it seems that this function could be performed by a justice of the peace. The pastor's time should be committed to bringing people to

Christ and building strong, enriched marriages; time available for weddings should be reserved for believers.

A Christian wedding involves vows taken before God, scriptural teaching and references that pertain to Christians, a blessing and benediction from God upon the husband and wife, a time of testimony to their faith in Christ, a commitment to build their marriage upon biblical teachings, and a time of celebration and praise. It should also be a time when those who attend the celebration are asked to uphold the couple in prayer and encouragement. Is it possible that nonbelievers could honestly go through this type of ceremony? Could a pastor honestly lead them through it?

When unbelieving couples ask for a wedding, those reasons can be clearly and lovingly explained. The pastor could also suggest that they continue meeting to explore together the meaning of the Christian faith. Some will respond, but some will never return; they will seek a place where their request will be honored. If a couple remains and professes faith in Christ, then the process of Christian growth begins, and a wedding is a possibility in the future.

In an article entitled "Church Weddings Are Not for Everyone," Pastor Grant Swank, Jr., expressed his philosophy:

> I will not perform the wedding ceremony for persons who are not, both by profession and by practice, Christians. Because of this, I have been regarded by some as a strange sort of clerical animal, unkind at best, cruel at worst. Yet no matter what the reaction, my convictions are firm.
>
> How did I reach this position? Partly through the realization that a very large percentage of the marriages I had performed had ended in divorce! At the outset of my ministry, I married any couple who asked me to do so. I counseled them before the wedding. Courtesies were exchanged among all concerned. The manners were well polished both in the study and in the sanctuary. However, often something disastrous happened after all the hoopla died down. As time passed—in some cases only a brief time—the vows and prayers of the ceremony were forgotten, and the marriage crumbled.
>
> This happened time and time again among those who had little or no real spiritual commitment to begin with. I was pressed to the conclusion that I was wrong in officiating at a wedding of two unbelievers.
>
> The more I thought about it, the more it seemed a charade. Was I called of God to perform marriages for people in the house of the Lord when those persons had not committed their lives to the Lord?

Was I to say prayers for two people who did not pray? Was I to read passages from the Bible to a bride and groom knowing full well that they did not intend to build their home upon that Bible? Was I to ask these two people to utter their promises in the presence of Jesus when they did not regard Jesus as the Lord of their lives? Was I to conclude the ceremony by earnestly beseeching God's blessing upon their new life together when they were not founding that life on the rock of salvation? They gave the Almighty only a nod of attention day in and day out: but on their special day, I, the man of God, was to call forth heavenly beatitudes upon their future.

Enough of this, I decided. I was being used. God was being used. The church and the truths the church stood for were being used. What the couples wanted out of it all was the beauty of the sanctuary, the noble sound of the organ, the dignified image of the clergyman, the luxury and respectability of a "church wedding."

What if I allowed a person to be baptized, knowing full well that he did not profess Jesus as Saviour? What if I told the congregation that anyone could receive communion, whether or not he was committed to Christ? What if I accepted into church membership anyone, no matter what he thought about the doctrines of the body of Christ? I would be asked to leave my pulpit. The governing session of the congregation would not stand for a minister with such a loose regard for those things held sacred. Yet I could go on year after year performing weddings that apparently were little more than hollow recitations of time-honored words.

My conclusion jelled when I reread in a new light the plain words of Second Corinthians 6:14: "Do not be mismated with unbelievers. For what partnership have righteousness and iniquity? Or what fellowship has light with darkness?" (RSV).* I realized that I had been partner to "mismating." I had joined light with darkness. And I had more times than not joined darkness with darkness.

Now when I perform a wedding, it is a time for genuine rejoicing in the Spirit of God. All persons gathered in the sanctuary know that the two being brought together are dedicated to the Lord. What a glad time it is, and what a peaceful time for me, the officiating clergyman! My prayers are sent to God with a new sense of earnestness. The Scriptures are read to the worshipers with the knowledge that the bride and groom have grounded their lives upon the Book. The vows are taken with the understanding that God is entering as a third party into those promises. And my conscience is clear before all concerned. . . .

*Revised Standard Version.

Some fellow ministers ask if I am missing witnessing opportunities because of my policy. But I do have an opportunity to witness. When asked to marry a couple, I invite them to come for a talk. When we meet I confront them with the forgiveness and new life that Jesus offers, asking them if they will become disciples of the Lord. At that moment the encounter with God is established. If they respond negatively, then I kindly state that I can go no further, for my first obligation is to see that they are saved. If they refuse that salvation, then I cannot in good conscience proceed.

If they respond positively, then I congratulate them, pray for them, give them a Bible and Christian literature, tell them of the times of our church services, and invite them to attend. And I tell them that six months hence I will be glad to perform their wedding if they are still living daily for Christ, are active in the church, are spending time in prayer and Scripture reading.

The divorce rate keeps on increasing. One out of three marriages in the country ends in divorce (two out of three in California). But according to a study cited by Billy Graham, one out of forty marriages ends in divorce when parents attend church regularly, and only one out of four hundred ends in divorce when both parents with their children attend church regularly and maintain family devotions.

I have a feeling that I am on the right biblical track—for the good of the people, the good of sound doctrine, and the good of my own conscience. And the marriages performed since I adopted this policy will bear me out.[5]

MARRIAGE AFTER DIVORCE

We cannot leave this chapter without facing what some have called a dilemma. What are the guidelines to follow when faced with a couple of whom one or both have been married and divorced? One concern should be with the person's relationship to Christ and his or her Christian walk. Another concern should be with the previous relationship. The discussion should determine whether all past matters have been settled biblically.

There are many views today concerning divorce and remarriage. Some take the position that there is no biblical basis for divorce or for remarriage. However, it does appear from certain passages that divorce is permissible in some cases, and if so, remarriage would also seem to be accepted. It is difficult to obtain all the facts concerning the previous marriage situation, but the pastor ought to try to determine whether the divorce occurred according to biblical grounds, if there were attempts at reconciliation, if the divorced person is bitter or forgiving, and so on.

If a person states that the spouse was the one at fault, the one who did the cheating, it is still important to ask, "Can you think of any way in which you might have had some responsibility in the demise of the first marriage?" or, "In what way do you feel that you contributed to the problems?" It is rare that only one person is at fault.

Other questions to ask are: What would you like to be different in this second marriage, and how will you make this difference? What did you learn from the first experience that will benefit you in this new relationship?

If one or both have children, spend time exploring their understanding of the process of child rearing from a biblical perspective. Philosophies of discipline usually conflict; the counselor can provide suggestions for handling the situation. (See chapter 14 for specific ideas.)

As a pastor interviews a person or a couple considering marriage after divorce, the following questions should be considered:

What is the level of spiritual maturity of each individual? What is the evidence of the presence of Christ in their relationship?

Were those people Christians at the time of the divorce (one or both), or have they become Christians since the divorce? What effect has divorce had upon them in terms of their relationship to Christ?

Has the person undergone some type of counseling or therapy during the first marriage or since that time? I strongly recommend that the divorced person completes a divorce recovery program before entering a new marriage. (Other issues and strategies for counseling a couple when either partner is divorced are discussed in detail in chapter 14.)

Is the couple capable of making a marriage work financially? The man's financial commitments to the first marriage may jeopardize the second. Finances undermine many marriages.

What do they see as the church's response to their marriage, and what are they seeking in terms of their future life in the local church?

Again Wayne Oates summarizes the church's position:

> If a couple have become faithful Christians and have demonstrated their change of heart and life since they have been divorced, a church will be hard put to refuse to marry them without placing its teaching concerning divorce above its doctrine of regeneration. Especially is this true if these people are deprived of a Christian wedding and at the same time awarded the privileges of church mem-

bership and of holding positions of leadership in the church. The wisdom of an earlier Episcopal ruling is still valid: a couple is required to wait at least one whole year after the date of the legal decree of divorce before remarriage. This ruling prevents a couple from "by-passing" the grief process of the previous marital break-up and from hastening into a premature relationship that may have been one precipitating cause of the previous marital collapse.[6]

NOTES

1. See Siang-Yang Tan, "Lay Christian Counseling: The Next Decade," *Journal of Psychology and Christianity,* vol. 9, no. 3 (1990), pp. 59-65. Published by the Christian Association for Psychological Studies, this issue is vital for articles on preparing and training lay people to conduct premarital counseling, and it contains helpful bibliographic references.

2. The Marital Assessment Inventory is available from Christian Marriage Enrichment, 17821 17th St., Suite 290, Tustin, CA 92680.

3. The videotape series "Helping Couples Resolve Marital Conflict" is available from Christian Marriage Enrichment in Tustin, CA.

4. Wayne Oates and Wade Rowatt, *Before You Marry Them* (Nashville: Broadman, 1975), p.34.

5. J. Grant Swank, Jr., "Church Weddings Are Not for Everyone," *Christianity Today,* August 27, 1976, pp.26-27. Copyright by *Christianity Today* 1976 and used by permission.

6. Oates and Rowatt, *Before You Marry Them,* pp. 38-39.

CHAPTER
7

Resources for Premarital Counseling

I n this recommended counseling program, the couple must agree to complete the assignments given during the time of training. Several books, tapes, and tests are used in the assignments. Many books could be used; each counselor will probably have certain volumes that appeal to him. In this handbook I outline a curriculum that specifies four books for the couple, one additional for the man and the woman, and two audio tape series.

Significantly, the counselor will benefit greatly by being widely read in the area of marriage and family, as some books are more applicable for one couple than for another.

When the couple comes for the first session it is vital that they be told that they will probably spend fifty to sixty hours of work outside the sessions. They should look over their schedules and arrange time for study and discussion. That is another reason the actual counseling should take place well ahead of the wedding, for wedding preparations could end up taking precedence over the counseling and its homework.

CONTENTS OF THE SESSIONS

Prior to the initial session, the counselor should give three individual tests to the couple, who also should write out ten indications as to "Why this is the time of my life to marry" and "Twelve specific reasons why I want to marry this person." These must be completed and sent back to the church or person conducting the premarital counseling. None of the tests or the written work is to be discussed by the couple. The three tests that we use are the Family History Analysis, the Taylor-Johnson Temperament Analysis,® and the PREPARE II Inventory.

In addition to the testing, which is an essential part of the premarital process (sessions 2 to 5 are spent discussing the results of the testing), each couple will study books and tapes as part of the requirement.

Each person will read and complete the workbook *Before You Say I Do* and *So You're Getting Married*. If this is a remarriage, the book *Before You Remarry* would replace *Before You Say I Do*. Each person will need a copy of each book. In addition, each will read the book *How To Speak Your Spouse's Language* by this author. One copy is sufficient per couple. This book lays the groundwork for learning to speak a partner's language. The man will also read *If Only He Knew*, by Gary Smalley, and the woman will read my *Understanding the Man in Your Life*. I also ask the couples to read two chapters from *The Mystery of Marriage*—"Love" and "Wedding Vows"—and to share a summary of what the chapters said to them.

These are the basic books needed. In many cases the counselor may choose additional resources based upon the results of the Taylor-Johnson Temperament Analysis test.

The couple should listen to the tape series on sexuality by Dr. Ed Wheat, "Before the Wedding Night." They also listen to Larry Burkett's series on finances, "Your Finances in Changing Times." This last series is very extensive and contains six tapes. I usually have the couple use this series after the sixth session of premarital counseling and give them two months in which to work through the tapes. This actually extends the process of premarital counseling.

All couples purchase their own books, but we do loan them the tape series. The counseling pastor also should have the books and tapes accessible at the church, including several sets of the tapes. And it is essential that you, the counselor, read the books and listen to the tapes prior to seeing any couples in order to properly discuss the material with them and answer their questions. In addition to the couple's purchasing the books, you may want to include an amount in the wedding service fee to cover tape breakage and loss as well as the cost of the various tests. (PREPARE II costs $21.00 per couple. Approximately $1.00 for the Family History Analysis and $2.00 for the T-JTA would cover your own costs for those tests.)

One series of video tapes suitable for classes or to send home with the couple is called "Before You Say I Do." Produced by Evangelical Films, the series features four speakers: Tim and Beverly LaHaye on sexuality, Larry Burkett on finances, and this author on the specific issues of marriage. All of the books, tapes, and videos are available from Christian Marriage Enrichment, 17821 17th St. Ste.# 290, Tustin, CA 92680.

The chart "Premarital Assignments" shows the recommended content and preparation for six premarital sessions. The seventh and final session occurs nine months to a year after the wedding. During this marital evaluation and enrichment session I ask two questions of each partner, which I believe is all that is needed to use the time effectively. The questions are: What are the most positive experiences you have had during the first six months of marriage? Where have you had the greatest difficulty during the past six months?

EVALUATION INSTRUMENTS

The Family History Analysis

The Family History Analysis (FHA) is the newest tool to be used in premarital preparation.[1] This eight-page fill-in form is designed to help couples become aware of how the families from which they have come will influence their own style of marriage. Each person brings to his or her own marriage a model of marriage; marital dreams, expectations, attitudes, and behaviors are not innate. Some will tend to repeat the pattern of their parents' marriage. Others will exercise energy and effort in trying to prevent their parents' marital dynamics from infiltrating their own. Thus they tend to behave and react in the opposite manner.

The counselor should give the FHA to the couple prior to the first session; they return it to the minister or counselor at session one so that he will have an opportunity to read through the form and indicate significant items. At the conclusion of the first session he returns the forms to the couple so they can discuss those items before the second session. Often much of the content of the second session will involve information

PREMARITAL ASSIGNMENTS	
Topic	Assignment

Session 1

Questions 1-8 found in the next chapter

Prior to the first session the couple completes ten indications and twelve reasons they are marrying the other person. They complete the tests. They could begin reading *So You're Getting Married.*

After the first session read *Before You Say I Do*, chaps. 1-2, and *The Mystery of Marriage*, chaps. 4, 6. Complete *So You're Getting Married* before session 4. The in-law forms are sent home at the end of session 1. (These are discussed in the next chapter.)

Session 2

Family History Analysis and the questions 9-16 in the next chapter

After the session read *Before You Say I Do*, chaps. 4-5, and *So You're Getting Married,* chaps. 2, 4-6.

Session 3

Taylor-Johnson Temperament Analysis

After the session read *Before You Say I Do,* chaps. 6-7, 12, and complete *So You're Getting Married*, chap. 7.

Interview a married couple. Listen to "Before the Wedding Night," by Dr. Ed Wheat.

Session 4	
T-JTA and PREPARE II	*After* the session read *Before You Say*, chaps. 8-9; *How to Speak Your Spouse's Language*; and *So You're Getting Married*, chaps. 8-11, 13.
Session 5	
PREPARE II	*After* the session complete *Before You Say* and *If Only He Knew* (for the man) or *Understanding the Man in Your Life* (for the woman).
Session 6	
Discuss finances and budget. Discuss their spiritual life. Counselor shares letters from their parents.	*After* the last session listen to "Your Finances in Changing Times" tape series.

Chapter 3 of *Before You Say I Do* can be used for devotions on the couple's honeymoon.

RESOURCES: Burkett, Larry. "Your Finances in Changing Times," tape series, Moody.

Mason, Mike. *The Mystery of Marriage*. Portland, Oreg.: Multnomah, 1985.

Smalley, Gary, and Steve Scott. *If Only He Knew*. Grand Rapids, Zondervan, 1982.

Wright, Norman. *How to Speak Your Spouse's Language*. Old Tappan, N.J.: Revell, 1988.

_____.*So You're Getting Married*. Ventura, Calif.: Regal, 1985.

Wright, Norman, and Wes Roberts. *Before You Say I Do*. Eugene, Oreg.: Harvest House, 1978.

Wheat, Ed. "Before the Wedding Night," tape series, Springdale, Ark.: Scriptural Counsel derived from the FHA. The value of this form is that it will help couples become aware of their past and how it might affect their future. It will assist them in gaining the freedom to develop their own style of marriage.

Family History Section. Here is a portion of the instructions for using the FHA Family History Section.

1. Upon receiving the FHAs, prior to the initial session with the couple, read over each one from beginning to end carefully and note any outstanding features. Then compare the two to note similarities and differences.

Note that you are looking for their perception of positive and negative responses of their parents—How might these feelings affect their response to their new spouse and his/her parents? What type of expectations do they have because of their relationship with their own parents? A man or woman might desire parental similarities within their spouse. This expectation, however, could lead to conflict. Some may purposely choose a partner who has characteristics opposite those of their parents because of a negative relationship. Or they could choose someone with similar negative characteristics as a parent with the hope of reforming this person.

2. Patterns of emotional expression and communication in the past can affect this new relationship—expectations both negative and positive will need to be explored.

3. Parents' expectations for a son's or daughter's life goal may have an influence upon whom one chooses, such as their continuing education, where they live, etc. Do parents have goals for them? Have the goals been fulfilled? How strong are the parents' expectations that these goals be attained? What are the individual reactions to the goals? These are a few of the questions or issues which may need to be discussed.[2]

Birth Order Considerations. It is important to note the number of brothers and sisters and the individual's own position in the family order. Was he the oldest, youngest, or middle child? Was he the oldest of brothers or sisters? If they were the youngest, were the others brothers or sisters? For example, if the man is the oldest child and had three younger sisters and the woman was the oldest child and had younger brothers, how might that affect the marital relationship? Or suppose the woman was the oldest sister with younger brothers and the man was the youngest child in his family, and had older sisters. How will that affect the marriage?

One theory holds that sibling position can be looked upon as a role that a person has learned in the family and has the tendency to assume in situations outside of the family. These roles may be quite similar or modified. That theory is discussed in detail in *Family Constellation*, by Walter Toman (Springer Publishers) and in a newer book, *Birth Order Roles and Sibling Patterns in Individual and Family Therapy*, by Margaret M. Hoopes and James M. Harper (Aspen Publishers). Though the concept remains only theory, it does warrant consideration, especially in establishing a marital relationship. For an example of how birth order characteristics can affect adjustment in marriage, see Hoopes and Harper, *Birth Order Roles and Sibling Patterns*, pages 35-43.

Knowing the birth order of a person is helpful in understanding his or her tendencies, or "his peculiar bent." The birth position can affect the relationship to his/her partner. For instance, consider what happens when (as it often does) a firstborn marries a secondborn.

A secondborn, whether male or female, is often difficult to describe or generalize about. So often, her lifestyle is determined by her perception since she plays off the firstborn. The tendency is to be the opposite of the firstborn. She could be a pleasant pleaser or an antagonistic person, a controller or manipulator, a victim or a martyr.

Secondborns have good emotional antennae. They are able to identify the emotional needs and feelings of others. As they interact with others they tend to be tender, sensitive, and caring. Quite often they act on feelings and intuition rather than facts. They pick up subtle messages that others fail to notice.

Since they are usually not as structured as firstborns, secondborns are freer in their interpersonal relationships. They might even ask inappropriate questions, or give too much information. They are often more concerned about getting the job done correctly than a firstborn and focus on the details. In a task setting they will also pick up the emotional undercurrent and respond to that. Often they tend to add stability to a relationship by their tendency to adapt easily to another's style of responding. In the communication process a secondborn individual will tend to zero in on implicit messages, feelings, and process more than actual content. This can be frustrating if one is married to a person who focuses on the apparent and obvious bottom-line content. But don't be surprised if this same person responds totally to feelings at one time and then deals with facts to the exclusion of feelings at yet another time.

Secondborns tend to draw close to others quickly in contrast to the firstborn. Because they are adept at picking up subtle emotional cues, they are alert to the intimacy needs of other people. Their intuition level helps them know what others are experiencing, often before the other person is even aware. They are good at sensing but have difficulty translating it clearly into factual statements. They need more assistance from others with intellectual intimacy. It helps if their partner engages them in factual intellectual conversations. They can develop into even better communicators by becoming more explicit verbally and by not assuming that others understand what they know and are thinking.

What happens if a firstborn and a secondborn marry? Both have the ability to talk about facts, so this level of communication will function well. They can both communicate on thoughts, interpretations, and ideas. Sometimes, though, when a secondborn is responding emotionally, and the firstborn factually, they will talk past one another. Firstborns can help their partners when they are too engrossed in emotions. Secondborns can encourage their partners to become aware of the emotional side of life, which they tend to overlook. Sometimes firstborns become so involved and independent in what they are doing that their spouses may feel rejected and left out.

Firstborns do well in a marriage when their partner confirms that they do their tasks well. They also appreciate knowing that they do well in social situations. It is important for secondborns to make sure their messages, expressions of encouragement and approval, are crystal clear and obvious. Firstborns don't do well with subtleties.

A secondborn spouse needs to know his partner values him and that he is important in the marital relationship. Both obvious and subtle messages get through to the secondborn.

Both firstborns and secondborns tend to feel responsible for their original families. This could cause difficulties within the marriage. Secondborns tend to bring more unresolved emotional issues with them into their marriages. If these issues continue unresolved they may begin to resurface in the marriage.[3]

This is just one way in which to consider differences and assist the couple in their future relationship. If you are interested in exploring birth order differences further, for the most detailed analysis available see *Birthorder Roles and Sibling Patterns*, by Hoopes and Harper. Another highly informative book is *Were You Born for Each Other? by* Kevin Leman.

The parents' history. The parents' history section on the Family History Analysis is very helpful in understanding influences and attitudes of each person. The section will explore seven areas:

1. The economic history and future expectations. Some individuals desire a different economic lifestyle and others a similar pattern. How
   will this affect the marriage?
2. The happiness ranking of the parents' marriage and the personal relationship with either parent. As you note the results, focus on the factors that made these relationships this way. What influence will these
   have upon the new marriage?
3. Birth position in the family. The position among brothers and sisters
   can be significant, as stated earlier.
4. Decision making, influence, and style of negotiation. What are their
   feelings about the familiar style? How will this affect their own marriage?
   What changes do they desire? How will they bring about a change?
5. Similarities and differences. Are the similarities or differences desirable? What if their partner changes in the future? What are their feelings about the changes?
6. Descriptive adjectives. The adjectives can indicate a positive or negative self-concept. Note if they stand out as unique or different in relationship to others that they compare these adjectives to. What types of
   people do they feel most comfortable with? How do they respond to
   others with these characteristics?
7. Dependency on parents. Is there an indication of dependency? If so,
   in what area, and how will this affect the marriage?

Listed on the following page are a few of the actual questions from
this form so that you may see how it can be used. "Family History—
Father and Mother" is an excerpt of some of the actual questions from
this form and shows how the counselor can promote discussion of the
family history.

Here are some sample responses I have received on the FHA. Some
people will give the counselor detailed and elaborate responses. This
gives insight into their thinking and expression style as well as their
personality.

1. *List what you feel are the positive qualities of your father.*

> My father believes in people. He trusts God's hand in all things.
> His family has always been his priority in life, and his faith has been
> strong in the Lord. He is not influenced by outward circumstances, and
> does not give in to materialism and negativity easily. He has stood fast
> in God and the church. He is emotional, loving, gentle, caring, and
> supportive in other peoples' cares, desires, needs, and problems.

FAMILY HISTORY—FATHER AND MOTHER

I would like to know about your father. (If you have a stepfather, please describe the one you feel closest to or the one you regard as your father.)

1. List what you feel are the positive qualities of your father.
2. List what you feel are the negative qualities of your father.
3. Describe how you feel about your father.
4. What emotions does he express openly and how?
5. Describe how you and your father communicate.
6. Describe the most pleasant and unpleasant experiences with your father.
7. What was/is your father's goal for your life?

In making decisions or solving interpersonal conflicts, people use different styles of negotiation for handling conflict. Please indicate the style of each family member by placing a check mark in the appropriate column.

	WIN	LOSE	YIELD	WITHDRAW	RESOLVE
Yourself					
Father					
Mother					
Brother					
Brother					
Sister					
Sister					

Where on the following line would you place yourself currently in relationship to your parents?

COMPLETELY   COMPLETELY
DEPENDENT   INDEPENDENT

Who managed the finances in your family?

Describe how your mother and father demonstrated affection to one another and to you.

---

2. List what you feel are the negative qualities of your father.

A bit too trusting at times. Maybe a little too emotional about some practical issues. At times materialism plays a practical part in the human life. My father disregards the practical applications which may become a disadvantage for himself as well as the family. Nevertheless, his commitment to his faith prevents him from capitalizing on earthly/human opportunities.

3. Describe how you feel about your father.

I am not in agreement as to his human and practical decisions. Not happy with his commitments at times. Feel sorry for missed opportunities, benefits, and advantages. However, I am fully satisfied with his commitment to God, his commitment to his family, his decisions of compassion, goodwill, support, and care. I am proud of my father for his efforts and achievements in adverse conditions. I am very satisfied as to how he taught us to love the Lord and make God, church and family our priority.

4. What emotions does he express openly and how?

He displays love, care, concerns, ambitions, desires, and also some negative feelings of anger, subordination, stubbornness, fears, insecurities, misunderstandings.

5. Describe how you and your father communicate.

We argue points and issues. We talk freely. We assist each other by supplying needs and wants. We compliment each other for a job well done, for accomplishments, for our attitudes to others. We work to reach common goals and objectives. We argue our disagreements.

Don't be surprised if you receive some brief and simple responses, such as the following:

1. *List what you feel are the positive qualities of your father.*
Strong-willed, determination.
2. *List what you feel are the negative qualities of your father.*
Closed mind, set in ways.

3. *Describe how you feel about your father.*
Have no relationship now.
4. *What emotions does he express openly and how?*
Shows love by buying or doing.
5. *Describe how you and your father communicate.*
Talking to arguing.

Below are the responses from a woman in her twenties. Needless to say, the substance of her responses changed the direction of the premarital counseling. It's not uncommon for a person to be drawn to someone similar to a parent with whom they have an unfulfilled relationship. Her fiance, unfortunately, was much more controlling, angry, and dogmatic. After three sessions and a three-month wait between the third and fourth session, the woman began to recognize what was not so obvious to her before and broke off the relationship. What do her responses tell you about herself, her relationships, and future problems?

1. *List what you feel are the positive qualities of your father.*
—Is dependable
—Willing to provide for family
—He's organized and intelligent

2. *List what you feel are the negative qualities of your father.*
He's impatient, insensitive, critical, easily angered, has a harsh tongue, and is overly hard-working at the expense of neglecting his family.

3. *Describe how you feel about your father.*
I appreciate all he has provided for me, but I resent the way he treats my mother. He yells at her in public, even in front of my friends, and is always ridiculing her.

4. *What emotions does he express openly and how?*
He expresses frustration and anger by criticizing my mother all the time. At the dinner table he always finds something to complain about.

5. *Describe how you and your father communicate.*
We only communicate about trivial things and rarely get down to gut feelings or emotions. I no longer share very many things with him

at all about my fiance since I know he does not share my joy. He usually likes to talk about business, and I usually don't even understand what he's talking about.

6. *Describe the most pleasant and unpleasant experiences with your father.*

I've never enjoyed being with my father. I can only think of one pleasant memory.

7. *In what way is your fiance similar and dissimilar to your parents?*

My fiance is like my father in that he is very stubborn and authoritative. He is unlike him in that he has a completely different pattern of thinking, has more patience. He does not take his frustrations out on me. He also has a temper, but it usually comes out when he sees others violating what he considers to be Christian principles, not out of selfishness.

The Taylor-Johnson Temperament Analysis

The major test used in premarital counseling is the Taylor-Johnson Temperament Analysis® (T-JTA).* The American Institute of Family Relations has given this test to more than 70,000 couples over the years, and thousands of other counselors and ministers have used it extensively. It is used for individual, premarital, marital, and family counseling, business and industry placement, placement of Sunday school teachers, evaluation of counselors for Christian camps, and assessment of college and seminary students.

The test requires between thirty and forty-five minutes to complete. The profile derived from the test is very readable; lay people can understand it readily. Norms for the test are available for high school, college, and adult ages. It is important to remember that a minister must take a training course in order to qualify to administer and work with the test. Many seminaries give that training. Numerous one-day seminars are conducted throughout the United States that qualify ministers and counselors to use this test. For information regarding a seminar in your area write to Christian Marriage Enrichment, or to the test publisher, Psychological Publications (5300 Hollywood Blvd., Los Angeles, CA 90027).

---

* Taylor-Johnson Temperament Analysis and T-JTA are registered trademarks of Psychological Publications, Inc.

The T-JTA can be used with individuals, couples, or families. The test manual states that the T-JTA "is designed primarily to provide an evaluation in visual form showing a person's feelings about himself at the time when he answered the questions." But it also reflects who the person is over a longer period of time as well. Although the T-JTA is not designed to measure mental abnormalities in psychiatric terms, it does provide measures of temperament and personality patterns with sufficient validity and reliability for emotionally normal couples in a developmental-educational premarital counseling context. It can also assist in identifying persons who might benefit from more individual or marital counseling.

The T-JTA manual is thorough and complete. The T-JTA itself is available in two levels of difficulty, the regular edition, at the eighth-grade reading level, and the secondary edition, at the fifth-grade reading level. It is available in Braille and is published in a number of foreign languages (Spanish, German, French, Taiwanese) with appropriate norms. Before the couple comes for their first counseling session, they are asked to take the test. They may pick up the forms at the church office, or the forms may be mailed to them. The counselor goes over the instructions with them before they take the test. Each one takes it twice. The woman takes it as she sees herself, and then as she sees her fiance. He takes the test as he sees himself and then as he sees her. This criss-cross testing provides invaluable information on each person's perception of himself or herself and of the partner and saves several hours of counseling.

After the use of the T-JTA criss-cross in premarital counseling, the typical response of couples is that they have gained great insight regarding themselves and their partner. The scales are comprehensive, yet easily understood and quite descriptive in their presentation of information. One of the distinct advantages of this tool is the readability of the profile. The shaded areas on the profile are designed to provide immediate information to the couple about traits that relate to successful and unsuccessful relationships.

Since many emotional problems, such as uncontrolled anger, depression, worry, lack of empathy, or a low self-image, are at the heart of numerous marital problems, it is crucial to take an intense look at the emotional areas. On the following pages are four profiles of a married couple, Richard and Helen Brown (not their real names). The first two profiles show the scores for themselves; the final two display the criss-cross. Look at the profiles, noting the nine traits and their definitions and the four shaded areas (from "excellent" to "improvement urgent"). Study the areas of difference in which Richard and Helen both have strengths and weaknesses. These areas could be problem areas between them as well.

By having the test returned to you before the couple's first session, you will have time to score the forms before you meet with them. Even though you do not go over the results until the individual sessions, you may want to probe into certain areas of their lives or relationships in this first session because of what the tests have revealed.

It is essential that anyone using the T-JTA be properly trained and follow the specific guidelines in interpreting and presenting back the results.

The Premarital Personal and Relationship Evaluation

Another helpful tool is the Premarital Personal and Relationship Evaluation, known as PREPARE II. This scientifically developed instrument is designed to assess the personal and relationship strengths and problematic issues for couples. It has been designed as a diagnostic tool for professionals working with premarital couples in either educational or counseling programs.

PREPARE II is a 125-item procedure that assesses attitudes and personal issues in twelve areas:

Communication	Realistic Expectations	Children and Marriage
Conflict Resolution	Religious Orientation	Personality Issues
Sexual Relationship	Equalitarian Roles	Leisure Activities
Financial Management	Family and Friends	Idealistic Distortion

The computer results can be readily obtained and include a seven- to ten-page analysis, which is easily interpreted. Results are returned within one week from the time they are received.[4]

PREPARE II results provide individual (male and female) scores and couple scores for each of the twelve categories. Individual percentile scores and revised percentile scores that correct for an individual's "faking good" are provided. Couple agreement and disagreement scores are provided to indicate potential strengths and problematic areas for couples. Both individual and couple scores are compared with continually updated norms based on all couples who have taken PREPARE II.

HUSBAND

SAMPLE PROFILE 1

TAYLOR-JOHNSON TEMPERAMENT ANALYSIS PROFILE
Profile Revision of 1984

These Answers Describe **BROWN, RICHARD** _____ Age **46** Sex **M** Date **10-1-84**

School **U. OF CALIF.** Grade ____ Degree **PHD.** Major **CHEM. ENG.** Occupation **CHEM. ENGINEER** Counselor **W.E.**

Single ____ Years Married **20** Years Divorced ____ Years Widowed ____ Children: M **1** Ages **18** F **1** Ages **16**

Answers made by: SELF and/or husband, wife, father, mother, son, daughter, brother, sister, or _____ of the person described.

Norm(s): **67-68** GEN. POP.	A	B	C	D	E	F	G	H	I	Attitude (Sten) Score:
Mids		1	2	1		1			1	Total Mids: **6**
Raw score	4	7	20	17	34	1	20	8	37	Raw score
Percentile	20	50	19	11	65	5	26	39	96	Percentile
TRAIT	Nervous	Depressive	Active-Social	Expressive-Responsive	Sympathetic	Subjective	Dominant	Hostile	Self-disciplined	TRAIT

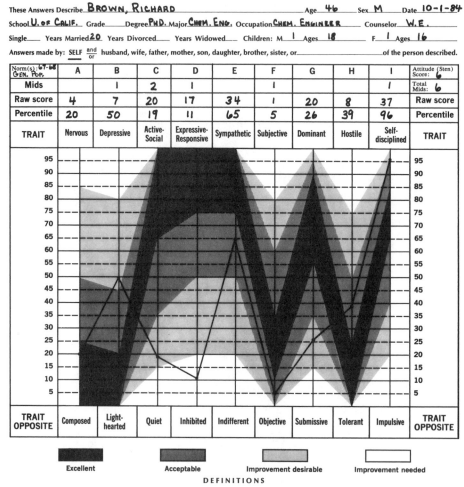

TRAIT OPPOSITE	Composed	Light-hearted	Quiet	Inhibited	Indifferent	Objective	Submissive	Tolerant	Impulsive	TRAIT OPPOSITE

■ Excellent   ■ Acceptable   ▨ Improvement desirable   □ Improvement needed

DEFINITIONS

TRAITS

Nervous — Tense, high-strung, apprehensive.
Depressive — Pessimistic, discouraged, dejected.
Active-Social — Energetic, enthusiastic, socially involved.
Expressive-Responsive — Spontaneous, affectionate, demonstrative.
Sympathetic — Kind, understanding, compassionate.
Subjective — Emotional, illogical, self-absorbed.
Dominant — Confident, assertive, competitive.
Hostile — Critical, argumentative, punitive.
Self-disciplined — Controlled, methodical, persevering.

OPPOSITES

Composed — Calm, relaxed, tranquil.
Light-hearted — Happy, cheerful, optimistic.
Quiet — Socially inactive, lethargic, withdrawn.
Inhibited — Restrained, unresponsive, repressed.
Indifferent — Unsympathetic, insensitive, unfeeling.
Objective — Fair-minded, reasonable, logical.
Submissive — Passive, compliant, dependent.
Tolerant — Accepting, patient, humane.
Impulsive — Uncontrolled, disorganized, changeable.

Note: Important decisions should not be made on the basis of this profile without confirmation of these results by other means.

WIFE

SAMPLE PROFILE 2

TAYLOR-JOHNSON TEMPERAMENT ANALYSIS PROFILE
Profile Revision of 1984

These Answers Describe **BROWN, HELEN** _____ Age **40** Sex **F** Date **10-1-84**

School **COMPLETED** Grade **11** Degree _____ Major _____ Occupation **HOUSEWIFE** _____ Counselor **W.E.** _____

Single ___ Years Married **20** Years Divorced ___ Years Widowed ___ Children: M **1** Ages **18** F **1** Ages **16**

Answers made by: SELF $\frac{and}{or}$ husband, wife, father, mother, son, daughter, brother, sister, or _____ of the person described.

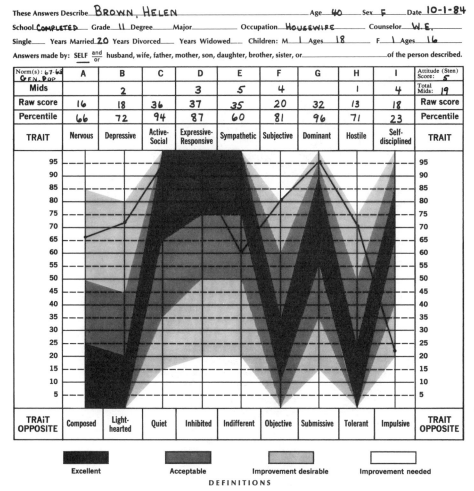

Norm(s): 67-68 GEN. POP	A	B	C	D	E	F	G	H	I	Attitude (Sten) Score: 5
Mids		2		3	5	4		1	4	Total Mids: 19
Raw score	16	18	36	37	35	20	32	13	18	Raw score
Percentile	66	72	94	87	60	81	96	71	23	Percentile
TRAIT	Nervous	Depressive	Active-Social	Expressive-Responsive	Sympathetic	Subjective	Dominant	Hostile	Self-disciplined	TRAIT
TRAIT OPPOSITE	Composed	Light-hearted	Quiet	Inhibited	Indifferent	Objective	Submissive	Tolerant	Impulsive	TRAIT OPPOSITE

Excellent   Acceptable   Improvement desirable   Improvement needed

DEFINITIONS

TRAITS

Nervous — Tense, high-strung, apprehensive.
Depressive — Pessimistic, discouraged, dejected.
Active-Social — Energetic, enthusiastic, socially involved.
Expressive-Responsive — Spontaneous, affectionate, demonstrative.
Sympathetic — Kind, understanding, compassionate.
Subjective — Emotional, illogical, self-absorbed.
Dominant — Confident, assertive, competitive.
Hostile — Critical, argumentative, punitive.
Self-disciplined — Controlled, methodical, persevering.

OPPOSITES

Composed — Calm, relaxed, tranquil.
Light-hearted — Happy, cheerful, optimistic.
Quiet — Socially inactive, lethargic, withdrawn.
Inhibited — Restrained, unresponsive, repressed.
Indifferent — Unsympathetic, insensitive, unfeeling.
Objective — Fair-minded, reasonable, logical.
Submissive — Passive, compliant, dependent.
Tolerant — Accepting, patient, humane.
Impulsive — Uncontrolled, disorganized, changeable.

Note: Important decisions should not be made on the basis of this profile without confirmation of these results by other means.

Published by Psychological Publications, Inc.
5300 Hollywood Blvd., Los Angeles, California 90027

THE PREMARITAL COUNSELING HANDBOOK

HUSBAND ~~BY WIFE~~
CRISS - CROSS

SAMPLE PROFILE 3

TAYLOR-JOHNSON TEMPERAMENT ANALYSIS PROFILE
Profile Revision of 1984

These Answers Describe **BROWN, RICHARD** _____ Age **46** Sex **M** Date **10-1-84**

School **U. OF CALIF.** Grade _____ Degree **Ph.D.** Major **CHEM. ENG.** Occupation **CHEM · ENGINEER** Counselor **W.E.**

Single _____ Years Married **20** Years Divorced _____ Years Widowed _____ Children: M **1** Ages **18** F **1** Ages **16**

Answers made by: **SELF** (circled) husband, wife, father, mother, son, daughter, brother, sister, or _____ of the person described.

Norm(s):67-68 G.P. c.c.	A	B	C	D	E	F	G	H	I	Attitude (Sten) Score: 6 6
Mids	4 1	2	2 2	1		1 1	1	2	1 1	Total Mids: 6 13
Raw score	4 10	7 8	20 12	17 6	34 19	1 9	20 10	8 2	37 37	Raw score
Percentile	20 36	50 39	19 13	11 2	65 23	5 36	26 9	39 9	96 95	Percentile
TRAIT	Nervous	Depressive	Active-Social	Expressive-Responsive	Sympathetic	Subjective	Dominant	Hostile	Self-disciplined	TRAIT

| TRAIT OPPOSITE | Composed | Light-hearted | Quiet | Inhibited | Indifferent | Objective | Submissive | Tolerant | Impulsive | TRAIT OPPOSITE |

Excellent   Acceptable   Improvement desirable   Improvement needed

DEFINITIONS

TRAITS

Nervous — Tense, high-strung, apprehensive.
Depressive — Pessimistic, discouraged, dejected.
Active-Social — Energetic, enthusiastic, socially involved.
Expressive-Responsive — Spontaneous, affectionate, demonstrative.
Sympathetic — Kind, understanding, compassionate.
Subjective — Emotional, illogical, self-absorbed.
Dominant — Confident, assertive, competitive.
Hostile — Critical, argumentative, punitive.
Self-disciplined — Controlled, methodical, persevering.

OPPOSITES

Composed — Calm, relaxed, tranquil.
Light-hearted — Happy, cheerful, optimistic.
Quiet — Socially inactive, lethargic, withdrawn.
Inhibited — Restrained, unresponsive, repressed.
Indifferent — Unsympathetic, insensitive, unfeeling.
Objective — Fair-minded, reasonable, logical.
Submissive — Passive, compliant, dependent.
Tolerant — Accepting, patient, humane.
Impulsive — Uncontrolled, disorganized, changeable.

Note: Important decisions should not be made on the basis of this profile without confirmation of these results by other means.

Published by Psychological Publications, Inc.
5300 Hollywood Blvd., Los Angeles, California 90027

RESOURCES FOR PREMARITAL COUNSELING

<u>WIFE BY HUSBAND</u>   SAMPLE PROFILE 4
<u>CRISS - CROSS</u>
TAYLOR-JOHNSON TEMPERAMENT ANALYSIS PROFILE
Profile Revision of 1984

These Answers Describe **BROWN, HELEN** _____ Age **40** Sex **F** Date **10-1-84**

School **COMPLETED** Grade **11** Degree ____ Major ____ Occupation **HOUSEWIFE** ____ Counselor **W.E.**

Single ____ Years Married **20** Years Divorced ____ Years Widowed ____ Children: M **1** Ages **18** F **1** Ages **16**

Answers made by: SELF **and/or** husband, wife, father, mother, son, daughter, brother, sister, or ____ of the person described.

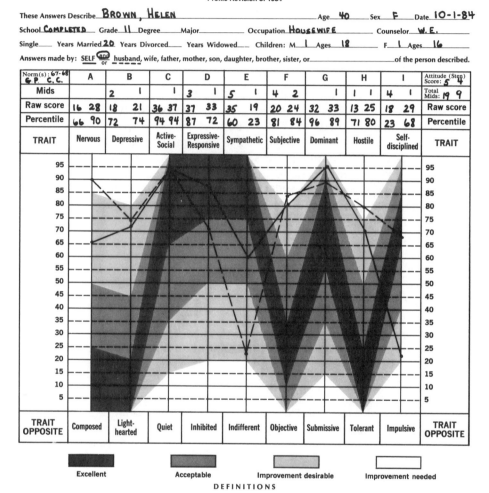

Norm(s): 67-68 G.P. C.C.	A		B		C		D		E		F		G		H		I		Attitude (Sten) Score: 5 4
Mids	2		1		1		3		5		4	2		1		1		4	1	Total Mids 19 9
Raw score	16	28	18	21	36	37	37	33	35	19	20	24	32	33	13	25	18	29	Raw score
Percentile	66	90	72	74	94	94	87	72	60	23	81	84	96	89	71	80	23	68	Percentile
TRAIT	Nervous		Depressive		Active-Social		Expressive-Responsive		Sympathetic		Subjective		Dominant		Hostile		Self-disciplined		TRAIT
TRAIT OPPOSITE	Composed		Light-hearted		Quiet		Inhibited		Indifferent		Objective		Submissive		Tolerant		Impulsive		TRAIT OPPOSITE

■ Excellent   ▨ Acceptable   ▧ Improvement desirable   ☐ Improvement needed

DEFINITIONS

TRAITS

Nervous — Tense, high-strung, apprehensive.
Depressive — Pessimistic, discouraged, dejected.
Active-Social — Energetic, enthusiastic, socially involved.
Expressive-Responsive — Spontaneous, affectionate, demonstrative.
Sympathetic — Kind, understanding, compassionate.
Subjective — Emotional, illogical, self-absorbed.
Dominant — Confident, assertive, competitive.
Hostile — Critical, argumentative, punitive.
Self-disciplined — Controlled, methodical, persevering.

OPPOSITES

Composed — Calm, relaxed, tranquil.
Light-hearted — Happy, cheerful, optimistic.
Quiet — Socially inactive, lethargic, withdrawn.
Inhibited — Restrained, unresponsive, repressed.
Indifferent — Unsympathetic, insensitive, unfeeling.
Objective — Fair-minded, reasonable, logical.
Submissive — Passive, compliant, dependent.
Tolerant — Accepting, patient, humane.
Impulsive — Uncontrolled, disorganized, changeable.

Note: Important decisions should not be made on the basis of this profile without confirmation of these results by other means.

123

Also listed are all the disagreement, special focus, and indecision items. The entire sentence and couple scores are fully printed for each of these items. A counselor's manual describes how to interpret and use the computerized results with couples.

Fowers reported positive findings in his study "Predicting Marital Success and Divorce Using Prepare." Here is his summary of PREPARE's validity:

> To test the predictive validity of PREPARE, this study was conducted to assess how well PREPARE scores could predict couples who are happily married from those who were unhappily married, separated or divorced. These couples had been married an average of 2 years and took PREPARE about 3 or 4 months before marriage.
>
> PREPARE proved to be very accurate at predicting marital success in these couples. Using PREPARE scores (individual, positive couple agreement and background), it was possible to predict with 86% accuracy those couples that eventually got divorced and with 78% accuracy those couples who were happily married. The average prediction rate for both groups was 81%.
>
> The PREPARE categories that were most predictive of marital success were: realistic expectations, personality issues, communication, conflict resolution and religious orientation. Couples who had relationship strength (scored high) on these categories had a higher probability of being happily married and those who had these as work areas (scored low) had a higher probability of being unhappily married.
>
> Another significant finding was regarding pre-marital couples who took PREPARE and later decided not to marry. About 10% of the couples who took PREPARE eventually decided to delay or cancel their marriage. In comparing these couples with the unsuccessful and successful groups, it appears that couples who delayed were very similar to those who later got divorced and very different from those that were happily married.[5]

The following are descriptions of the areas PREPARE will evaluate.

Idealistic Distortion. This category is a modified version of Edmonds (1967) Marital Conventionalization Scale. This scale has been well validated and correlates highly with other scales that measure the tendency of individuals to answer personal questions in a socially desirable direction. Since premarital couples tend to be highly idealistic, this scale is intended to assess the degree to which individuals attempt to present themselves in a highly favorable and often exaggerated way. Moderately high scores identify individuals who are responding in a way that presents a favorable impression of their relationship. Questions are extreme and therefore reflect a tendency that in all likelihood permeates the entire inventory and must be carefully attended.

Realistic Expectations. This category assesses the rational quality of an individual's expectations about marriage, love, commitment, and relationship conflicts. The intent of these items is to ascertain the degree to which expectations about marriage relationships are realistic and grounded in objective reflection. Low scores would suggest that individuals are too romantic or idealistic in their perception of marriage. In general, moderately high scores in this category reflect realistic expectations about relationship issues.

Personality Issues. This category assesses an individual's perception of the personality characteristics of his partner and the level of satisfaction or dissatisfaction with that perception. Items focus on traits such as sense of humor, temper, moodiness, stubbornness, jealousy, and possessiveness. Respondents also disclose personal behaviors and attitudes related to demonstration of affection, smoking, and drinking. Moderately high scores in this category are intended to reflect personal adjustment to partner and approval of partner's behavior.

Equalitarian Roles. This category assesses an individual's beliefs and feelings about various marital and family roles. Items include occupational roles, household roles, sex roles, and parental roles. Individuals respond to these questions and reveal information about their satisfaction with assuming particular role behaviors. There is an implied bias in the scale toward equalitarian versus traditional role behaviors. For that reason, moderately high scores would reflect flexibility and satisfaction with equalitarian role positions. Moderately low scores would reflect a more traditional role position and may or may not be problematic for the couple.

Communication. This category is concerned with an individual's feelings, beliefs, and attitudes toward the role of communication in the maintenance of marital relationships. Items focus on the ability of respondents to express important emotions and beliefs, the ability to listen to one's partner, the ability to respond appropriately in certain situations, and on the style or pattern of communication that exists between partners. Moderately high scores reflect an awareness of the communication skills necessary to maintain a relationship and an ability to use them.

Conflict Resolution. This category assesses an individual's attitudes, feelings, and beliefs toward the existence and resolution of conflict in relationships. Items pertain to strategies used to end arguments, satisfaction with the way problems are resolved, and the openness of relationship partners to recognize and resolve issues. Moderately high scores reflect realistic attitudes about the probability of relationship conflicts and satisfaction with the way most problems are handled.

Financial Management. This category focuses on attitudes and concerns about the way economics are to be managed in the family. Items assess the tendencies of individuals to be spenders or savers, the care in which financial decisions on major purchases are made, and decisions regarding the person or persons who will be in charge of specific financial matters. Satisfaction with economic status and responsibility for money management is indirectly assessed. Moderately high scores reflect satisfaction with financial management and realistic attitudes toward financial matters.

Leisure Activities. This category assesses each individual's preferences for spending free time. Items reflect social versus personal activities, active versus passive interests, shared versus individual preferences, and expectations as to whether leisure time should be spent together or balanced between separate and joint activities. Moderately high scores reflect compatibility, flexibility, and/or consensus about the use of leisure time activities.

Sexual Relationship. This category assesses individual feelings and concerns about the affectionate and sexual relationship with the partner. Items reflect satisfaction with expressions of affection, level of comfort in discussion of sexual issues, attitudes toward sexual behavior and intercourse, birth control decisions, and feelings about sexual fidelity. Moderately high scores reflect satisfaction with affectionate expressions and a positive attitude about the role of sexuality in marriage.

Each partner indicates his level of agreement to each of the 125 statements using the following scale: (1) strongly agree, (2) moderately agree, (3) neither agree nor disagree, (4) moderately disagree, (5) strongly disagree. The computer printout clearly shows areas of disagreement as well as the couple's overall scores.

The following three charts depict a sample printout of the overall scores and their comparison with the norms, and point out special situations and personality issues between the counselees.[6]

SUMMARY ANALYSIS FOR P R E P A R E CATEGORIES

	Individual Scores				Couple Scores				
					Item Summary			Positive Agreement	
	Male		Female		Agree	Disagree	Indecn.		
Category Title	Pct.	Rev.	Pct.	Rev.	Items	Items	Items	Couple	Norm
Idealistic Distortion	78		20						
Realistic Expectations	22	18	84	80	1	6	3	10	34
Personality Issues	88	70	10	10	4	5	1	20	35
Equalitarian Roles	10	10	10	10	8	1	1	20	44
Communication	72	60	19	17	5	4	1	50	47
Conflict Resolution	82	75	15	14	3	2	5	30	45
Financial Management	26	23	35	34	4	4	2	40	34
Leisure Activities	94	91	75	74	7	1	2	70	52
Sexual Relationship	45	42	45	44	4	2	4	40	47
Children and Marriage	91	81	88	85	7	2	1	60	39
Family and Friends	66	58	59	57	7	0	3	60	47
Religious Orientation	12	10	10	10	8	1	1	30	34
Average Positive Agreement								39	42

Percentile Scores (Pct) range from 0 to 100 and have an average score of 50. Moderately high scores (60 or more) reflect positive relationship attitudes and adjustment. Revised scores are an adjustment of an individual's pct score based on each person's tendency to present an idealistic image of their relationship. Revised scores will be low when individuals are unrealistic about marriage. Positive agreement scores reflect partners' consensus on attitudes believed to be related to positive adjustment in marriage. Relationship strengths are identified when a couple's positive agreement score is higher than the norm score for that category.

SPECIAL SITUATIONS

| | Individual Scores | | | | Couple Scores | | | | |
| | Male | | Female | | Item Summary | | | Positive Agreement | |
Category Title	Pct.	Rev.	Pct.	Rev.	Agree Items	Disagree Items	Indecn. Items	Couple	Norm
Personality Issues	83	79	24	19	5	3	2	20	35

The male—high score—has positive perception of partner and general approval of partner's behavior.
The female—low score—perceives her partner as having negative personality traits.
The low positive agreement also indicates that this may be a problematic area.
  *See p. 6 for listing of Items for Discussion for Personality Issues

| Equalitarian Roles | 27 | 24 | 17 | 14 | 9 | 0 | 1 | 10 | 44 |

The low individual scores and low positive agreement indicate that this couple do not desire an equal role in their family relationship and would prefer a more traditional approach. Their high agreement would suggest that this may not create a problem for them.
  *See p. 12 of the Counselor's Manual for an explanation of the implied bias in this scale toward equalitarian versus traditional role behaviors.

| Religious Orientation | 19 | 16 | 17 | 13 | 8 | 1 | 1 | 20 | 34 |

The low individual scores may mean that both partners regard religion as a personal decision or question traditional beliefs. This may not be a problematic area, however, as indicated by their high total of Agree Items.
  *See p. 14 of the Counselor's Manual for an explanation of the implied bias in this category toward traditional view of religion as an important component of marriage versus an individualistic interpretation.

STUDY THE CATEGORY DESCRIPTIONS
ALWAYS WATCH FOR THEMES AND PATTERNS

DISAGREEMENT ITEMS

8. M = 4. F = 2.

There are times when I am bothered by my partner's jealousy.

115. M = 5. F = 2.

At times I think my partner depends on me too much.

125. M = 4. F = 1.

Sometimes my partner is too stubborn.

The full 13-15 page printout gives the disagreement, indecision, special focus, and agreement for each of the 11 categories (but not for idealistic distortion).

SPECIAL FOCUS ITEMS

24. M = 2. F = 2.

At times I am concerned that my partner appears to be unhappy and withdrawn.

30. M = 1. F = 1.

I wish my partner would smoke and/or drink less.

78. M = 1. F = 2.

It bothers me that my partner is often late.

Although "special focus" items are agreement, it should be noted that they are agreeing to things that may be problems in their relationship.

The Meyers-Briggs Type Indicator

Another instrument that is widely used is the Myers-Briggs Type Indicator. The MBTI is an easy-to-use instrument that classifies individuals in one of sixteen personality types. This reflects an individual's preference in how they perceive information and make decisions. It also shows their preferred orientation to life and preferred ways of dealing with people, ideas, schedules, and the world around them. The results are presented in positive terms that emphasize the strengths of each individual type and the ways in which each person can better understand and build and encourage others. It does not measure possible emotional differences as does the T-JTA.

The MBTI can be used to identify differences and assist others in personal growth, making decisions, enhancing relationships, and increasing organizational effectiveness. It can be used in individual, premarital, marital, and family counseling.

According to the theory behind this test, every person is born with a predisposition for certain personality preferences. There are four pairs of preference alternatives. In each category a person is either:

Extroverted	or	Introverted (EI)
Sensing	or	Intuitive (SN)
Thinking	or	Feeling (TF)
Judging	or	Perceiving (JP)

Furthermore, the theory proposes that each person develops a preference early in life and sticks with it. The more one practices those preferences—intentionally or unintentionally—the more they rely on them with confidence and strength. That does not mean we are incapable of using our nonpreferences from time to time. In fact, the more we mature, the more our nonpreferences add richness and dimension to our lives. However, they never take the place of our original preferences. So, an extrovert never becomes an introvert, and vice versa.

Here are some descriptions of the first three preference alternatives:

Extroversion/introversion (E/I). The extrovert derives stimulation from the environment, the outer world of people and things. The introvert's stimulation comes from within, the inner world of thoughts and reflections. Everyone uses both attitudes, but one is usually preferred and better developed.

Some characteristics are:

Extrovert	Introvert
Energized by other people and external experiences	Energized by inner resources, internal experiences; exhausted by too much contact with people
Acts, then (maybe) reflects	Reflects, then (maybe) acts
Is often friendly, talkative, easy to know, outgoing	Is often reserved, quiet, hard to know
Expresses emotions	Tends to bottle up emotions

Needs relationships	Likes privacy
Gives breadth to life	Gives depth to life

E's may seem shallow to I's; I's may seem withdrawn to E's. Extroverts use both E and I, but prefer E. Introverts use both E and I, but prefer I. In our society, there are approximately three extroverts for every introvert.

Sensing/Intuition (S/N). These are known as "perceiving functions," as they describe two ways of perceiving or taking in information: sensing and intuiting. With sensors, the sensing function takes in information by way of the five senses: sight, sound, feel, taste, and smell. Seventy percent of our society are sensors.

In contrast, 30 percent of our population are intuitives, processing information by way of a sixth sense or hunch.

Both ways of perceiving and taking in information are used by everyone. But one is usually preferred and better developed. Some people have one that is very highly developed whereas others are quite close with each one.

Some of the characteristics are:

Sensing	Intuition
Looks at the parts and pieces of something	Likes to look at patterns and relationships
Lives in the present, enjoys what's there	Focuses on the future, anticipating what might be
Likes to handle practical matters	Prefers to imagine possibilities, speculates
Prefers things that are definite, measurable, tangible	Likes opportunities for being inventive
Starts at the beginning, taking one step at a time	Tends to jump in anywhere; bypasses some steps
Reads instructions and notices details and thinks everyone should	Skips directions, follows hunches
Likes set procedures, established routine	Likes change and variety

Sensors may seem too materialistic and literal-minded to intuitives; intuitives may seem fickle, impractical dreamers to sensors.

Sensing types use both the sensing (S) and intuiting function (N), but prefer S. Intuitive types use both S and N, but prefer N.

Thinking/Feeling (T/F). These are known as "deciding functions," as they describe two different ways of deciding or evaluating. The thinking function (T) decides on the basis of logic and objective considerations. The feeling function (F) decides on the basis of personal subjective values.

Both ways of deciding and evaluating are used by everyone, but again one is usually preferred and better developed.

Some of the characteristics are:

Thinking	Feeling
Decides with the head	Decides with the heart
Uses logic	Goes by personal convictions
Has a concern for truth, justice	Concerned for relationships and harmony
Sees things as an onlooker, from outside the situation	Sees things as a participant, from within a situation
Takes an overall, long-range view	Takes an immediate and personal view
Spontaneously finds flaws and criticizes	Spontaneously appreciates; is more relationship oriented
Good at analyzing plans	Good at understanding people

In relationships with each other, T's may seem cold and condescending to F's; F's may seem fuzzy-minded and emotional to T's.

Thinking types use both T and F, but prefer T. Feeling types use both T and F, but prefer F. This is the only gender-related preference in which two-thirds of American males are T's and the same number of women are F's.[7]

Preferences can affect a relationship many ways. Let's consider dating. Sensors are usually very realistic about dates. They see the other person for what he or she is. Remember: they're not necessarily impressed with a lot of phoniness or potential. Intuitives are different. For them, most of the date takes place in the mind. Their imaginations are rich; often their perceptions or dreams of the date are more exciting than what actually transpires. A sensor fantasizes, but after the fact. After an initial encounter, for example, they'll imagine what the next encounter will be like —they can imagine all sorts of exciting things, but it is all grounded in reality. It's based upon what did in fact transpire on the preceding date. But for an intuitive, facts only ruin their fantasies.

For sensors, an exciting date is one that involves all those senses—the two people ideally look good, smell nice, taste good food, hear nice music, feel cozy, and so on. It's through the five senses that the dating experience happens. For intuitives, it is through their sense of potentiality rather than reality that they experience a date. In some ways, the date is far more fantasy than fact.

Sensors and intuitives approach dates very differently. For a sensor, the date doesn't begin until the two parties get together. For an intuitive, the "date" may begin as soon as the arrangements are made, even if that is many weeks in advance. The resulting fantasies of what could happen may reach the point of obsession.

First dates tend to be conversation-intensive, allowing tastes, personalities, and images to emerge. A sensor is more comfortable talking about concrete things: people they've known, events they've experienced, things they've seen, places they've been—and the specifics on all of the above. In contrast, an intuitive is excited by conversations that involve their dreams, visions, and beliefs.

Time is always a potential sensing-intuitive problem. If an event starts at 8:00 and it takes twenty minutes to get there, at 7:50 a sensor will become frustrated at the possibility of being at least ten minutes late. Time is much more flexible for the intuitive. "Events usually start late," they think.

Let's consider the thinking and feeling function in regard to dating. You will find that there will be more T men attracted to F females. As a relationship evolves into a more intimate experience, this preference will be the one that can create major problems. Thinking types want to understand intimacy; for them, it is a state of being analyzed, mastered, and fine-tuned. Feelings types simply want to be intimate. The result is that thinkers may seem rather cold and aloof at times. And they may dislike being pushed to experience the intimacy their feeling partners are enjoying. T's can feel the emotions existing inside them; they must intellectually face those emotions before they can share and express them.

A thinker's need for understanding begins with the first date and continues throughout a relationship. It is important for a thinker to define expectations clearly: "Are we going to be just friends, or do we have expectations beyond that?" For a thinker, even "I love you" is subject to further discussion.

For feelers, all this analysis merely defeats the whole purpose. Even if it is only a one-time date, they feel, just "being together" is sufficient. The more you're together, the more the relationship develops on its own. They live with the phrase "Your heart will tell you." Their responses tend to be mushy and vague, and that's comfortable for them but not to a T. For a feeler, "I love you" speaks for itself. It needs no further discussion.

Let's follow a married T and F couple to their first wedding anniversary. Picture it—the end of a fairly normal first year—whatever that means. The man thinks there are several possible ways to celebrate their first anniversary. He may suggest to his wife one of the following:

"Our marriage is quite good. Let's leave well enough alone. We'll go out to dinner and a movie afterward."

"The year has gone pretty well. So we can improve what's already good. Here are some questions to help guide our development. Let's spend the evening evaluating and celebrating."

"Our anniversary conflicts with my softball playoffs, so we'll have to celebrate it on another date."

To any of these suggestions, a feeler's response is the same, "How cold! Obviously he doesn't care enough." A feeler knows the first anniversary is the most important of all. (For feelers, the first of almost anything is important—the first kiss, the first date, the first vacation, etc.) The anniversary, for the feeler, must be significant, experiential, cozy, warm, expressive, romantic, and meaningful. If the thinker fails to appreciate these factors his wife will interpret it as "You don't love me."

Perhaps you can see how important it is for you to clarify these differences for a couple in your premarital sessions. Since marriage involves so much decision making, looking at this function illustrates how differences hold the potential for conflict.

Decisions are influenced by a person's values. But for a thinker and a feeler, those values are arrived at very differently:

> For a thinker, it's a very objective experience. It shouldn't be involved in emotion. The more important the decision, the more objective one must be. The head must rule.
>
> For a feeler, decision making is a very subjective experience. You have to pay special attention to the people and issues involved. The more important the decision, the more carefully you must consider extenuating circumstances. Your heart must be the decision maker.[8]

COST OF COUNSELING SESSIONS

One final area must be noted: the cost of counseling. Is there any charge when it is done at the church? What would it cost if the couple went to a professional marriage counselor? In answer to the second question, it would cost a couple between $300 and $400 for the preparation. Most churches do not charge for counseling. However, the wedding service fee usually pays for church use, utilities, janitorial service, and other expenses. A number of churches have begun to include an additional seventy-five or eighty dollar fee to cover the cost of counseling. That money pays for the books that the pastor gives to the couple as well as the PREPARE Test. It is important for the couple to own the books. Many have stated that after they were married they reread the books, which took on a new meaning for them.

The fee also pays for the testing materials used by the couple and several series of tapes used in the counseling ministry. This cost is minimal when compared to some of the items in the actual wedding, which do not have any lasting value.

One final word about resources. Before proceeding with the ministry of counseling, the pastor or lay person must be totally familiar with the tapes, books, tests, and other materials to be used. It may take several weeks of study, but that in turn enhances the ministry of marital preparation. In addition to reading the books already mentioned, a pastor or counselor will benefit greatly and add depth to his counseling ministry by reading the following books. Remember that these authors hold various views, and you will not agree with everything they say. That will be beneficial because it will cause you to think and to examine your beliefs.

BIBLIOGRAPHY

Beck, Aaron T. *Love Is Never Enough*. New York: Harper & Row, 1988.

Wright, H. Norman. *Seasons of a Marriage*. Ventura, Calif.: Regal, 1983.

Lederer, William, and Don Jackson. *The Mirage of Marriage*. New York: Norton, 1990.

Swindoll, Charles. *Strike the Original Match*. Portland, Oreg.: Multnomah, 1980.

NOTES

1. The Family History Analysis is copyrighted by H. Norman Wright and available through Family Counseling and Enrichment, 17821 17th St., Suite 290, Tustin, CA 92680.

2. H. Norman Wright, Instructions to Family History Analysis (Tustin, Calif.: Family Counseling and Enrichment, 1981), p. 1.

3. Margaret M. Hoopes and James M. Harper, *Birth Order Roles and Sibling Patterns in Individual and Family Therapy* (Rockville, Md: Aspen, 1987), pp. 100-102, adapted.

4. Scoring is completed at PREPARE/Enrich, P.O. Box 190, Minneapolis, MN 55440. For more information, call their head office at 1-800-331-1661.

5. Blaine Fowers, "Predicting Marital Success and Divorce Using Prepare," *Journal of Marital and Family Therapy*, 12:4 (1986): 403-13.

6. PREPARE charts are used by permission of PREPARE/Enrich, Minneapolis, Minn.

7. This discussion of the differences among types is adapted from Otto Kroeger and Janet M. Thuesen, *Type Talk* (New York: Doubleday, 1988), pp. 23-48.

8. Kroeger and Thuesen, *Type Talk*, pp.122-40, adapted.

CHAPTER
8

Sessions One and Two

T he first session is about to begin. The couple has arrived at the
church for their first premarital interview. Prior to this session
they have completed the Taylor-Johnson Temperament Analysis®
and PREPARE II. They have also answered individually several questions
that will be covered in this particular session. The questions were given
or mailed to them along with the PREPARE, the Family History Analysis,
and the Taylor-Johnson test.

After the couple arrives, it is important to spend time getting acquainted. Some of the couples will be people you have known for years, others
will be strangers. Share information about yourself such as your background, family, hobbies, schools, and some of your interesting experiences in marriage.

QUESTIONS FOR SESSIONS ONE AND TWO

Here is the overall outline for sessions one and two. It is difficult to say how much is covered in each session since it varies with each couple. Often it takes three sessions to cover this material, and usually I take a total of seven to eight sessions with each couple. Our task is not to mechanically cover material but to do a quality job of application with each couple.

Generally, the counselor can use the first eight questions to promote discussion in session one; the final eight may be presented in session two (and perhaps session three).

1. What are your expectations for premarital counseling?
2. What would you like to see accomplished during premarital counseling?
3. If I were to ask you to describe your fiance what would you say?
4. Describe your personal relationship with Jesus Christ.
5. If you had one passage from God's Word that you would like your fiance to incorporate into his/her life, what would it be? (This can be answered the following week if they need time to select these passages.)
6. Describe your courtship—length, type. In what way will your courtship contribute to your marriage? Is there anything from your courtship that you would like to change after you're married?
7. (To one) What convinced you that you loved this person? (To the other) Please describe the love that you have.
8. What is the extent of your sexual expression?
9. Give twelve reasons you want to marry the other person and twelve indications as to why this is the time of your life to marry.
10. Family background—family position. Who makes decisions in your family? Who owns what territory? How is your fiance similar to your father or mother? How do you see your fiance getting along with your father and mother? (Questions 9-12 are incorporated into the discussion of the Family History Analysis.)
11. Is there any way in which there is still a dependency or something unresolved between you and your parents?
12. What is there about your parents' marriage that you want or don't want?
13. Is there anything about yourself or your past that you think might seriously affect your marriage? Was there alcohol or substance

abuse in your family, lack of affirmation, or emotional, sexual, or physical abuse?

14. In light of what is happening to marriages today, why will yours be different?

15. Which of you handles disappointments the best? Describe what you have experienced and how you have handled these.

16. What are your fears and concerns about marriage? (This might be asked in the initial session. It's important to ask this question in each session until you receive a response.)

What Are Your Expectations?

I often begin my initial session of premarital counseling by asking each person, "What are your expectations for our time together? What would you like to see accomplished?" Some have clear-cut goals and needs, whereas others are vague in their response. I take this opportunity to tell them one of my goals: to assist them in having the quality marriage they are hoping for by helping them eliminate as many surprises as possible following the wedding. Over the years time and time again I have seen how the unexpected tends to discourage and disillusion people and eventually causes them to question whether they loved their partner to begin with. A primary purpose of premarital counseling is to help both individuals determine if marriage to each other is the best choice.

One of the basic ground rules of the premarital counseling is stated to the couple in the beginning: there is nothing that cannot be discussed in these sessions. The couple should not hesitate to ask the counselor any questions they have, and the counselor will take the same privilege of asking them anything he thinks is necessary.

In addition, the counselor must remind the couple of the agreement that they complete their outside assignments if the counseling is to continue.

Ask the couple what they think marriage is. Do they have a definition of marriage? At this point you can share several definitions of marriage with them, perhaps your own and others that have been formulated. Many definitions could be explained at this point; sometimes they are incorporated into the wedding itself. One was written by David Augsburger:

> Is marriage a private action of two persons in love, or a public act
> of two pledging a contract? Neither, it is something other. Very much
> other! Basically, the Christian view of marriage is not that it is pri-

marily or essentially a binding legal and social contract. The Christian understands marriage as a covenant made under God and in the presence of fellow members of the Christian Family. Such a pledge endures, not because of the force of law or the fear of its sanctions, but because an unconditional covenant has been made. A covenant more solemn, more binding, more permanent than any legal contract.[1]

David Hubbard, president of Fuller Theological Seminary, has presented another interesting definition of marriage:

> Marriage does not demand perfection. But it must be given priority. It is an institution for sinners. No one else need apply. But it finds its finest glory when sinners see it as God's way of leading us through His ultimate curriculum of love and righteousness.[2]

Years ago I found this thought provoking statement reflecting what a marriage needs:

> —No marriage is perfect.
>
> —Marriage is a daily creation,
> not a packaged product.
>
> —Marriage is like a child
> who needs to be picked up and hugged,
> and given personal attention. . . .

You may want to ask them how they will "hug" their marriage.

I have been formulating one definition for several years, and I concentrate on that definition with the couple. It is given here, followed by an amplification that I share in counseling and in classes with married couples. This definition suggests the personal dimension every counselor can bring to the session.

> A Christian marriage is a total commitment of two people to the person of Jesus Christ and to one another. It is a commitment in which there is no holding back of anything. Marriage is a pledge of mutual fidelity; it is a partnership of mutual subordination. A Christian marriage is similar to a solvent, a freeing up of the man and woman to be themselves and become all that God intends for them to become. Marriage is the refining process that God will use to have us develop into the man or woman He wants us to become.

Have you ever thought of your marriage as a refining process? That God is going to allow certain events to happen in your life that will cause you to grow and develop into the man or woman He wants you to become? What would happen if you were to have that attitude toward the events that occur within your marriage—that those events are something that God can use to cause you to grow deeper together and to cause each to grow more as an individual?

Each of you has had different experiences. In every marriage it will be different. We've had a unique situation in our relationship. We had two children, a daughter who is now thirty and a son who died at twenty-two years of age. He was a brain-damaged, mentally retarded child, and was about eighteen months old mentally. He probably would have never reached a mental age of more than two or three years old. When Matthew was first born we didn't know this. At about eight months of age, he began having seizures. We took him to the UCLA Medical Center where the diagnosis was made.

The name "Matthew" means "God's gift," or "gift from God." Matthew is God's gift to us. We have experienced times of pain, disappointment, and heartache, but we've experienced other times of joy and delight. I can remember when we prayed for Matthew to walk. All of us in our family prayed for about three and a half years. And one day when we were together, he stood up and took about five steps. I said something like, "Isn't it wonderful?" Joyce said something like, "Isn't that great?" Then our nine-year-old daughter said, "Let's stop right now and thank God for answering our prayer." It is interesting how our children will teach us and will cause us to give thanks to the proper person. We learned so much about life through Matthew, even in his death.

You consider some of the events that may occur in your life and you wonder, "How in the world am I going to handle them when I don't even know what's going to happen?" But God gives us the resources to handle whatever happens; He does this in His wonderful and marvelous way, even when we're not aware of it. God can be preparing us for some of those situations that are going to hit us.

Before Matthew was born and I was in seminary, I had to write a thesis. I didn't know what to write about. When I went in, the professor said to me, "Nobody's written a thesis on the Christian education of the mentally retarded child. You write it." So I did. I read books, studied, went to schools, and observed Sunday school classes for these children. I learned a lot about them. Then I wrote the thesis.

My wife typed the thesis the first time, a second time, and finally a third time, and she learned about retarded children as well. After it was finally turned in and accepted, I went to work at my church while I was working on a psychology degree. I had to do an internship in the public school district for the school psychologist credential. I was assigned to test and re-test mentally retarded children. At my church I was given the responsibility of training teachers to teach mentally retarded children within the church and so I had to develop a program.

One night two years before Matthew was born, Joyce and I were talking; we said, "Isn't it interesting all the experience we've had with retarded children? Could it be that God is preparing us for something that is going to occur later in our life?" That is all we said. Two years later Matthew came into our lives. We saw how God prepared us.

When an event occurs in your life that some would call a tragedy, can you look back and see how God has been preparing you for that, or how He's going to give you the extra strength, wisdom, and patience right at the right time for you to handle it?

Marriage is a refining process. An adequate concept of what marriage is about is the first foundation of marriage preparation.

There are occasions when I ask the couple for their definitions, but I do not share my own with them at this point.

Describe Your Fiance

The next question I ask is, "If you were to describe your fiance, what would you say?" I am interested in knowing if their perception of their fiance is accurate. Some couples have not yet identified the personality traits and character qualities or defects. Individuals should share their answer to this question facing their fiance, so the counselor can note the level of comfort the couple has attained in discussing issues face to face.

Describe Your Spiritual Life

An important area to discuss is the couple's Christian beliefs. (Some pastors choose to have an extra preliminary interview for this purpose.) I do not ask the question, "Are you a Christian?" It is too easy to respond affirmatively, which terminates the conversation. You will learn more by phrasing the question differently. For example, the pastor might ask one of them, "Just tell me a little bit about your own personal spiritual growth and what you believe about the Person of Jesus Christ and God." Then sit back and let the person talk.

The majority of the couples that you and I see are born-again believers. But there can be differences between born-again believers. One might be a very strong, growing, maturing Christian. The other may have been a Christian for ten years but has never really developed any depth in Bible study and prayer, nor become particularly involved in the church. If those differences are sensed now, you can begin to work with the couple and help them develop some spiritual growth. That is especially important if the young woman is the one who is very strong as a believer and the man, who is supposed to be the spiritual leader within the marriage relationship, is weak at this time.

On occasion you will deal with a couple where one is a Christian and the other flatly declares, "No, I'm not a Christian. I do not believe." What do you say at that particular time? If I am counseling such a couple and one partner has shared with me the fact that he or she is not a Christian, I thank him or her for his honesty. Then I take the opportunity to present the gospel and talk about how important spiritual harmony is to a marriage relationship. The unbeliever may then say, "Well, I am really not interested," and that will close the conversation, at least for that particular time. Later on you may have another opportunity to speak of spiritual things.

Do you continue with the premarital counseling when one person remains an unbeliever, or do you stop it? I think it is best to go ahead with the counseling and explain again that you reserve the right to decide whether or not you will perform the wedding ceremony until later in the sessions. You can also take the opportunity to explain the teaching of Scripture regarding the marriage of a believer to an unbeliever. The believer may be aware of it and could already have some conflicts over it. Or perhaps he or she is not aware of it. You can point out that the Scripture teaches that a couple is not to be unequally yoked together. You might experience some different reactions at that point: the Christian could be angry or hostile, or he or she might be very agreeable to continuing the premarital counseling.

Pastors who have followed this procedure say they have had varied experiences. A number of the couples have agreed to continue the premarital counseling, realizing that without it the pastor would not agree to perform the ceremony.

What happens when the non-Christian responds and receives Christ as savior? Would that solve the difficulty? Would you feel like going ahead with the ceremony on the date the couple had planned? It might be best to talk to the couple about postponing the wedding date so that the new Christian will have an opportunity to grow in his or her new Christian life. That is important, especially when the new Christian is the young man. A marriage relationship in which the woman is spiritually stronger and more knowledgeable of Scripture can have problems unless she is very sensitive about her role. You will have many different experiences here.

When a person has accepted the Lord, you could put him or her in contact with other Christians who are involved in Bible study and help them assist the new Christian person in his or her growth. If the new Christian is not concerned about developing his or her spiritual life, that should raise questions as to the genuineness of the decision.

Here are some questions developed by one pastor to facilitate discussion about spiritual matters. You may want to make this into a form with blank lines provided for the couple to complete or simply ask them some of these questions.

1a. How can you be sure that your mate will always live according to God's ways? What makes you so convinced that your future mate will not walk away from the Christian faith and become a burden to you instead of a help?

1b. How can you be sure that you will always live according to God's ways?

(Answer: You can't, but based on one's commitment patterns; i.e., maturity level, their character traits, and their disciplinary measures of personal devotion to God and His Word, one can perceive his or her own seriousness and that of others. Prayer sees that seriousness takes root into determination and ultimately culmination.)

2. Do you have regular private devotions now? How often and to what extent?
3. Do you know if your fiance has regular private devotions? How often and to what extent?
4. Do you both pray together much now? Aloud?
5. Do you both read/study God's Word together now?
6. What do you like most about your future mate's spiritual life?
7. Have you had any major spiritual conflicts in your relationship so far?

Give Scripture Passage to Your Fiance

Probably one of the strangest questions asked is: "If you could suggest one passage of Scripture that you would like to see your fiance incorporate into his or her life that would make him/her an even stronger and more mature person than he/she is now, which Scripture would it be?"

About 50 percent of the couples need a week to process this question and come up with their selections. The purpose of asking it is to encourage each of them to look to the Word of God as a guide for asking their partner to make changes in his/her life. Couples do desire their partner to change, and perhaps it helps if we consider that change in light of the Scripture. Perhaps the change would help them to be stronger and more mature, or perhaps our reason for asking them to change is simply because of our own bias or because we are threatened by some of their differences.

Another area to consider in the first session is the extent of their preparation for marriage. You may ask, "What preparation have you had for marriage? Have you been reading any books? If so, what books have you read? Have you taken any classes in church or in college, and did you take the classes separately or together?" It is necessary to find out what preparation they have had, because some might have been good and some might have been poor.

Describe Your Courtship

Another topic is the dating background of this couple: How long have they been going together, and what kind of dates have they had?

For example, consider two different couples: One couple has been dating for the past two-and-a-half years. They live in the same town. Their dates occur mostly on Friday and Saturday nights, and sometimes on Sunday evenings. During the week they have very little contact with one another. Quite often when they go out on Friday or Saturday nights they go to a movie or some type of entertainment. Now and then they go to a party, but they really do not have much time to communicate with one another.

On the other hand, the second couple may have been dating for eight months, but during that period they have spent quite a few hours together each day. They have been thinking seriously about marriage. During the summer they worked together washing dishes in the kitchen of a Christian camp, and they saw each other at times when they were happy, when they felt sad, and when they were in bad moods. All of that contributed to a good relationship.

As you look at the two couples, you might think, "Well, there's a couple who has gone together for over two years. They might have a better relationship." That is not necessarily true. The couple who spent more varied and realistic time together, even though the time was shorter, could have a better adjustment.

The couple to be counseled should be asked what they have done on their dates, where they have gone, whether they have included other friends, or if they have just gone places alone.

It is also important that each individual has become acquainted with the other's parents. In fact, young couples who are seriously dating should be encouraged to spend time in the evenings in their partner's parents' homes. On some occasions I have met couples whose families have gotten together on vacations and all spent a week together in the mountains. This has contributed to a healthy relationship.

Realistic dating is essential. An additional question to ask at this point is, "In what way will the type of courtship you have had contribute to your marriage?"

How Do You Know You Love Her/Him?

As stated earlier, the next question to ask one of the partners is, "What convinced you that you loved this person?" Ask the other person to describe the love that he/she has for the other person. I listen to what they say and then respond.

I always listen closely to the couple's definition of love. There are two definitions that I like to suggest to them. One is this: "A person is in love with another individual when meeting the emotional needs of that person becomes an emotional need of his or her own life." We discuss and explore that statement to discover what it means in practical daily life.

Another definition is: "Real love means an unconditional commitment to an imperfect person." That is the love that one needs to have for the person one marries. It is also an illustration of the kind of love that God has toward humanity. His is an unconditional commitment, and all of us are imperfect. If each person realizes that the future mate is imperfect and accepts him or her that way, there is hope!

One young couple I counseled had an interesting experience. The young woman was delighted about it. She was so happy and jubilant when I saw her that I had to ask, "What are you so happy about?" About three days before, she said, they had been out in the evening and her fiance was miserable. She said he was stubborn, obstinate, and out-of-sorts. He was really a rat, and yet, in spite of all that, she had the firm conviction that she really loved him. She said, "That was so affirming to me to realize that even at the times when he might be very disagreeable and I might not really like everything he was doing, I'd still have this conviction of love."

An important biblical passage to discuss is 1 Corinthians 13. I read it and talk about the ideas it contains, using the *Amplified New Testament*.

I also mention the need for self-esteem. I discuss with the couple that in order to really love another person you must love yourself first—you must have a good feeling about yourself. That concept may come up again in connection with the couple's T-JTA scores.

Several other definitions of love may be mentioned at that point. One is, "Love is a learned emotional reaction . . . One does not fall in or out of love; one grows in love."[3] Another is "Love is not a commodity that can be bartered for, or bought or sold; nor can it be forced upon or from someone. It can only voluntarily be given away."[4] Erich Fromm gave an extended definition:

> Love means to commit oneself without guarantee, to give oneself completely in the hope that our love will produce love in the loved person. Love is an act of faith, and whoever is of little faith is also of little love. The perfect love would be one that gives all and expects nothing. It would, of course, be willing and delighted to take anything it was offered, the better. But it would ask for nothing, it can never be deceived or disappointed. It is only when love demands that it brings on pain.[5]

That statement sounds very basic and simple, but it is difficult to practice.

Having the couple read the chapter on love in Mike Mason's book, *The Mystery of Marriage,* can be an enlightening experience.

The Question of Sex

The next area that is discussed can be delicate. The counselor should be concerned about the extent of the couple's sexual involvement and the attitude they have toward this important aspect of their relationship. This topic may be introduced by asking each of them about the sexual information that has been given to them over the years: "Who prepared you in terms of your understanding about sex? Who talked with you? What books have you read?"

One of the questions I ask that quite often brings silence is, "When a couple is looking forward to marriage they desire to express their affection in some physical manner. To what extent have you had the opportunity to express your affection to one another?"

I have experienced various responses to that question ranging from "Why do you want to know?" to long silences, guilty looks, or positive statements that "We kiss and hold each other a lot and really enjoy our time together." One couple confided that they allowed themselves ten minutes of kissing, holding, and hugging and then stopped, since during that time span they could control themselves. They said after that they seemed to run into difficulty. If I do not get any response from the couple at that particular time, then I might go a little more into detail by explaining that when a couple is in love they have certain feelings toward each other and they like to express those feelings sexually. Now I may get continued silence from a couple. Or I might get a response that says, "Well, I do not think I understand what you mean." Most of the time a couple does understand what is meant. No matter what they say, I respond with, "How do you feel about that level of involvement?"

These questions are not an attempt to pry and probe into a very personal area of their life. I am not trying to be voyeuristic in any way, but I am concerned about the extent of the physical relationship for a very sound reason. If the couple has built their relationship upon a physical basis only, they are asking for difficulties later in the marriage. And if they have gone too far, or further than their standards permit, they might have feelings of guilt, fear, resentment, or even hostility.

In counseling it is important to provide the atmosphere and the opportunity to explore the physical relationship. From time to time the couple sits there, and then one of them might volunteer: "Well, I think we've gone a little further than we really wanted." And then I can say, "Well, could you be more specific for me? Are you saying that you were involved in light petting or heavy petting, or have you been sleeping with each other?" The attitude depends upon the couple. Some couples feel bothered, upset, and guilty if they have been involved in petting. Other couples are bothered only when they have been going to bed together.

I explore further by asking, "Can you tell me some of the feelings that you've had about the extent of your physical relationship?" Are you satisfied with it? Have there been problems? What attitudes do you have?" If they have been engaging in sexual relations, I simply share with them part of my beliefs. I tell them that I believe it is very important at that particular time for them to stop having complete sexual relations for two basic reasons. One reason is to find out if their relationship is built on something other that just the physical; refraining from intercourse will really help them to make that decision.

The second major reason for asking them to stop having sexual relations is based on Scripture. The New Testament teaches that we are not to engage in premarital relations. The Scripture calls that fornication. Scriptural teaching should be discussed thoroughly with the couple. An excellent resource to use is *Intimate Deception*, by P. Roger Hillerstrom (Multnomah).

So far I have not encountered a couple who have refused to follow this guideline, though from time to time you might run into one. The pastor of a large church in Southern California follows this particular principle. On many occasions, directly from the pulpit, he has stated this principle that he holds for premarital counseling. He also states that if a couple is not willing to refrain from premarital intercourse, he will not agree to continue the counseling nor to perform the ceremony. That is basically my feeling, too. If a couple will not follow that guideline, then the counseling ought to stop.

It is very important for a couple to go into marriage with the proper attitudes and proper behavior. If they have been involved in premarital intercourse, there should be a discussion of their feelings. There should be confession of sin to one another and to God and a time of forgiveness and prayer.

In some cases the man and woman should agree on a covenant that will help them maintain a proper sexual standard. Here is a covenant one man made with his fiance:

> I vow to you, to endure to treat you as my friend in the Lord, because I know you desire that my affections for you be channeled toward your personality. I will put all conscious effort into assuring that my affections for you are directed toward you as a person, not simply toward your body.
>
> What I have written down here is an outline of definite actions to be taken, and definite situations for us to avoid in order to honor this vow.
>
> 1. Pray concerning this one specific area for 5 to 10 minutes a day during our prayer times.
> 2. Spending 15 minutes a day when we are together sharing with each other what the best part of our day was.
> 3. The next time we are together, we will both bow before the Lord and spread out this petition before Him.

4. Judging from the past, what we shall not do is to find ourselves in any room with the doors closed especially after your parents have gone to bed.

5. In those times when we will hug and kiss, then I will take the responsibility to notice when we need to separate ourselves, probably spatially. This will be interpreted not as rejection, but as necessity for the growth of the relationship.

6. You can anticipate that I will channel some of my strong urges into writing, because I know you like this.

7. While driving to Hemet there will be no touching above the knees, nor below the shoulders.

One area that must be considered as one talks about sex is whether the young woman is pregnant. If she is pregnant, then various alternatives must be considered. Marriage might not be the best one.

If pregnancy is the main motivation for marriage, it is not sufficient. If the couple is mature, deeply committed to one another, and willing to wait to complete the counseling, and if they realize the adjustments that will be necessary, then marriage could occur. Many couples, however, feel pressured to marry by parents, friends, their own guilt, and even the church.

Other alternatives would be not marrying and either giving the child up for adoption, or, in some cases, keeping the child. The number of abortions each year is increasing steadily; there are many different views regarding that procedure. Pastors differ greatly in their attitudes. My own personal stance is that abortion is not an alternative; if the subject arises, I advise against it.

ADDITIONAL QUESTIONS

Depending on the depth of the disclosure, the couple's interaction, and, of course, the nature of their answers, the counselor may present the following questions in session two.

Why Marry This Person—Now?

I ask the couple to share their lists of the indications for marriage and their reasons for marrying the other person. The couple is asked to sit face-to-face as one shares his list of indications with his fiance. The lists are to be read in the first person. After that, the partner responds with her list. Then each gives his or her reasons as to why this is the time in life to marry in the same first-person manner. Here is a list of one person's indications. (All names in this chapter have been changed to protect the individuals' privacy.)

"Eight Indications As To Why This Is The Time Of My Life To Marry"

1. I now have enough experience living alone to know that I prefer not to.
2. I now know that I am able to financially support a wife.
3. However, I expect to be much more secure financially in the relatively near future, and I want to get married before then because I think it can be beneficial to a good relationship to share some minor economic deprivations in the beginning.
4. I may be making my final career decision in the near future, and I would like my wife to be able to share in that decision.
5. I want to leave the Riverside area as soon as is practical, and I want to be able to take Mitzi with me.
6. If I am going to have children, I don't want to wait much longer to start having them.
7. I want to go to Europe with my wife while we are both still young enough to enjoy doing it on a very limited budget.
8. But mainly, having made the major decision that getting married will greatly improve my life, I am just naturally eager to start enjoying that improved life-style as soon as possible.

Here is a twenty-eight-year-old man's list:

"Twelve Reasons Why I Want To Marry Jean"

1. Jean loves the Lord, her God, with all her heart and soul.
2. She is far and away my best friend . . . who better to commit for life to than your best friend? Best friends have fun together.
3. She is a fun-loving person who enjoys the simple and sophisticated life styles . . . yet is not caught up in the "World Lifestyle Ordeal."
4. Jean is a wonderful person who treats all people with respect. She understands the meaning of "honor."
5. She will be an energetic mother who will love and nurture her kids.
6. Jean is very level-headed . . . which makes her extremely fun to be with.

THE PREMARITAL COUNSELING HANDBOOK

7. She is ready to go out and conquer life with energy and enthusiasm. She looks at and sees problems and tests in life as a God-ordained circumstance and as a time to show her faith in our Lord.
8. She is sensitive and secure . . . wise but not cocky, friendly, yet not overbearing.
9. I think Jean is very attractive . . . she has a well-kept figure and outside beauty.
10. She has a deep inner beauty in which she manifests the fruits of the Spirit.
11. Jean is secure in our relationship. She is committed to making our relationship not only work, but something special. We both have high expectations and plan to have high goals.
12. Jean is not afraid to learn and change.
13. She even loves me. I know it, I feel it, I like it, I want it, and I want to love her and protect her.

Look for a balance as the individuals read their reasons for wanting to marry each other. Occasionally somebody will give reasons like these: I want to marry him because he fulfills all my needs, he takes care of me, he does this for me, he does that for me. The reasons focus on "what the other person can do for me," without the balance of "what I can do for the other person." When a counselor encounters that kind of situation, he should confront the person with what he or she has said.

I remember an occasion when a young lady was listening to her fiance's reasons for marrying her. The more he read the angrier she became, and before he completed the reasons, she broke in and said, "The reason you want to marry me is for me to do everything for you! What are you going to do for me? Don't you really love me?" The rest of the session was spent talking about the reasons and motivations for their marriage. We were able to settle some of the differences right then and there.

We should be just as concerned, however, when we see an individual giving reasons that indicate that he is going to do everything for the other person. Can that individual accept love? Can he accept the other person's doing something for him? There has to be a balance.

When couples write their reasons for marriage and for marrying this partner, they often are able to clarify and even discover the specific reasons for marriage. In most instances it is a delightful experience to observe the nonverbal responses in those who are hearing the indications and reasons for the very first time. I have seen several respond with silence and/or tears of delight.

The "face-to-face" seating arrangement is important. I tell the couple that too often married couples fail to communicate face-to-face in that manner. They learn to communicate on the run or doing two or three things at the same time. It is vital for intimacy development that couples spend time in uninterrupted face-to-face communication.

Questions About Family Background

At this time you are probably into your second session and much of this will focus on the Family History Analysis. The Counselor's Guide will provide you with instructions for its use, but here are some practical illustrations and examples.

Often I use the question, "How would you like feelings of love, warmth, and tenderness shown to you in public and in your home?"

Part of the problem you are looking for is the fact that when people come out of their own homes they might carry with them some of the behavior that was detrimental in that home. They also might have certain expectations. For example, a person might come into marriage with the expectation that his or her mate will be like a parent whom he or she admired. Or, one partner may have the expectation that the mate will not be like a parent with whom this individual had a number of differences. One may believe that the lifestyle in the new home will be the same as in the parental home; another may wish it to be radically different.

For instance, consider Bob. His mother died in childbirth. He had no brothers or sisters. He was reared solely by his father and had no contact with women in his home as he was growing up. His father was lower middle class. They moved every year or two. Bob went to many different schools, lived in cities all over the nation, and had no settled roots.

Bob did not date very much. When he was in high school he dated a girl only once or twice. Later at college he spent a lot of time studying as well as working very hard at a job. When he was twenty-three, he met a young woman named Janet; they fell in love and decided to be married.

Janet came from an upper middle-class home. The family had lived in the same location for the past fifteen years. Janet had two brothers and three sisters and the family was very stable. They did many things together and were a very close-knit group. The grandparents lived nearby, and there were aunts and uncles in the same town. Janet never lacked much of anything. She had money when she needed it, and the parents took a great deal of interest in all their children.

Here was a couple with great differences in their backgrounds. Premarital counseling was vital for them. There were some major differences that needed to be explored, for the marriage could have suffered greatly because of those differences. The young man had very little contact with females. He did not know what it is like to live in a home with women around. Since he did not have a mother or any sisters and did not date much, after marriage he could have been in for a real cultural shock. He had not had much experience in sharing a home with other individuals.

What happens when he is married? In the morning he walks into the bathroom and discovers pantyhose drying on the towel rack. He realizes that he is living with a person who is very different from himself. If he is quite frugal and she is accustomed to spending money freely, what conflicts will come about? An unfortunate factor in this situation is that, at least from what we know, this young man did not have a good model of what a family should be like.

Those are just a *few* of the areas of adjustment. The couple must be made aware of differences and must be asked to develop a plan and approach to solve these potential problems.

You will find some couples who have come out of poor backgrounds with tremendous hostilities, fighting, and multiple divorces within a home. Either the man or the woman might have suffered sexual abuse as a young child, and as a result has some problems with his or her feelings and attitudes in the area of sex. You need to explore and talk with the couple about their backgrounds.

Another helpful question is, "What is there about your parents' marriage that you would like in your marriage, and what is there you would not want?" After they disclose any trait or characteristic that they do not find desirable, ask, "How will you prevent this from occurring within your marriage? Your parents were models for you, and you have probably incorporated both positive and negative tendencies whether you wanted to or not. What can you do to make sure those traits do not occur in your marriage?"

In a session with one couple, I noticed some information on the woman's Family History Analysis that needed further clarification. Here is how the dialogue proceeded:

NORM: You described how you felt about your father, and you said, "Good"—it seemed very, very strong. You are encouraged about his wisdom and how he loves the Lord. Question number five said, "Describe how you and your father communicate." You said, "Usually it is through Mother when we communicate." I am interested in knowing a bit more about that.

SUE: Um, Dad's usually gone—he's a doctor—gone a lot. He's usually communicated with patients all day long, so when he comes home he just wants to relax—not to talk much. So the things I want to know, I've usually asked on the run—when I come home, before I go out at night, or something I find out from Mom because she's told Dad about what I am doing. The only time I really communicate with my father is for pleasure—you know, getting to know him personally. But otherwise, financial things or information about friends or family I usually get from my mom.

NORM: What are your feelings about having to communicate through your mom to get to Dad?

SUE: Well, I wish it wasn't that way. I wish Dad and I could go out to dinner sometime alone, but that would have to come if I initiated it, and I know he would feel uncomfortable. If it was something Mom initiated for the two of us, he would feel a lot more comfortable.

NORM: What would happen if you would call your dad and say, "Dad, I would like to take you out to dinner on a date"?

Sue laughs and giggles.

NORM: I know he might feel uncomfortable, and you might, too. But I am wondering if that couldn't turn into a very special evening.

SUE: It could. I don't want to assume how he would react, but I think he would say: "When is there time?" or, "What's the special occasion?"

NORM: Maybe you could say the special occasion is that "I would just like to go out to dinner with my father."

SUE: Uh huh.

NORM: Why don't we make some time?

155

SUE: It's worth a try (*laughs*).

NORM: The reason I am pushing on this is because it sounds like there's a little bit of unfinished work, an unfinished relationship there. There's been a void, and I've become a bit concerned about that. When we have had some unfulfilled needs in our parental past, we usually transfer those onto the person we marry. Consciously or subconsciously, we think our mate will fill the need that was not filled in the past. So what we need to do is to bring that to a conclusion and build an even stronger relationship so that you can say, "I did communicate with my dad. It was possible to get him to quit seeing so many patients and give me the attention that I feel I needed and that I deserved."

SUE: I feel content, though. Is it something subconscious?

NORM: I hear the contentment, but I also hear sort of a wanting, a desire, a wistfulness that says, "Gee, I wish that could have happened." Now is the time to begin to resolve that before you move into a marriage relationship.

SUE: OK.

NORM: That's why I'm more concerned with your feelings rather than simply this is what Dad did. In a sense, I think you used Mom as a go-between or a buffer. As we look at your marriage coming up to Greg, you will not have your mother there to be the buffer. Greg is going to be talking to a number of people at work, and he is going to come home tired and he might not want to communicate. What will you do when that happens?

SUE: I don't know.

Another question that I have asked on occasion is: "What would you like your marriage to become and to reflect?" Some couples will need time to think about that, for it may be a totally new concept to them. In a way that question can lead them into thinking about goals for their marriage. The word *reflect* could refer back to their own personal, individual qualities or qualities within the relationship. That could be an opportunity to share with them about the spiritual qualities their marriage could reflect.

MARITAL SATISFACTION

Next, I usually ask the couple, "In light of all of the marriages today that are ending in divorce or are unhappy, why will yours be different?" After a brief discussion I show the couple the following chart depicting the level of marital satisfaction over the family life cycle. This chart is the result of a number of research studies over the past fifteen years.[6]

Husbands' and Wives' Marital Satisfaction over the Family Career

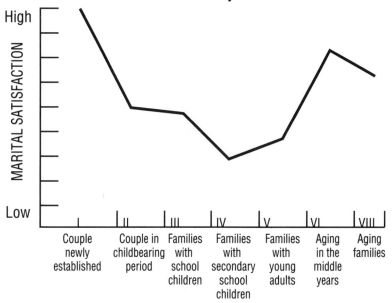

IDENTITY VERSUS INTIMACY

Many predictable changes occur as couples proceed through the various stages of the family life cycle. Some of those changes can cripple a marriage in the process. That happens because the couple neither anticipates nor plans for the events and changes that often occur at each stage.

Often a man builds his identity through his occupation or profession. Many men pursue goals of making a good living and finding a good life, which prove to them they are adequate and of worth. (That typically male process is undergoing some change, however, as many women are now pursuing careers and professions.) Because their identities are built in that manner, men devote their time and energy to their work. The marital relationship often takes a secondary position. When couples marry, the timing is such that most men are just at the point of establishing themselves in their line of work. Their main task at that time is establishing identity through their work. But at the onset of marriage a wife is seeking to build an intimate relationship with her husband. That is where frustration may occur. The struggle can be described as identity versus intimacy.

Underlying part of many wives' strong emphasis upon intimacy is their striving to build their own sense of identity. Often a wife builds an identity through her husband or family. (That typically female process is undergoing some change, too, as many women are now being employed outside of the home and some marital roles are changing.)

Many wives become discouraged after a few years of marriage because the intimate relationship with their husband does not develop as expected. In time a wife may turn her efforts for intimacy toward the children. Perhaps that accounts for many mothers finding it so difficult to let go of the children when they are old enough to leave the nest.

If that situation continues—the husband building identity through work and the wife building intimacy and identity through the children —a crisis will occur eventually. Many husbands in their forties realize they have reached the end of the line for upward progress in their work. There is nowhere else to go, so their goals begin to change. They may now turn back to their wives with a desire to build intimacy. They could be in for a shock, because many wives, after the children leave home, begin to consider how their own identities have developed. They may now decide either to complete their own education or to pursue a career. Their desire for an intimate relationship with their husbands is not very intense after so many years of no reciprocation on his part. The issue of the meaning of achievement and values in relationships needs attention during marital counseling because often they are the underlying cause of the symptomatic problems married couples bring to counseling.

I ask the couple to notice the drop in marital satisfaction on the chart during child-rearing years. Then I ask, "Why does the presence of children affect marital satisfaction so much? Why does the level continue to drop?" We then talk about the idea that the trend, or tendency, on the part of couples does not have to occur. What will they do so that does not happen to them in their marriage?

Flexibility and adaptability are important on the part of the pastor or counselor conducting the premarital sessions. Each couple will vary in their abilities, needs, or problem areas, and the amount of time given to each topic will vary. With a few couples all of this material may be covered during the first session. With most, however, it will carry over into an additional session with the couple together, or you may extend the first session to an hour-and-a-half. Often it takes more than six sessions to complete the series.

FEARS AND CONCERNS

An additional question to ask the couple is: "What fears do you have about marriage?" Reassure them that most people looking forward to marriage have certain fears, questions, and doubts; you want them to have the opportunity to talk about some of those. You might not get a response. The couple might say, "Well, we really have no fears. We've talked this over, and we really think we know all about it." You may want to drop the question at that point. But later on, you probably will discover that they do have some fears. Do not pressure them when they are not ready to discuss their fears. Ask the question each session, and you will discover some.

Here is a list that a woman, twenty-two years old, shared in the third session of counseling. Needless to say, the entire direction of our counseling changed after these concerns were shared.

"My Fears and Anxieties Entering Marriage"

1. That we will be too busy to have quality time for each other.
2. I will not be able to keep him and my mother happy—she will have her feelings hurt.
3. His priority for working out and exercising will still be greater than mine.
4. We will not have devotions or prayer together every day.
5. There will be times when I will want to go into debt for a particular item and he will not.
6. After a few years of marriage I will not want to give in and will want to "have it out."
7. I will want to concentrate on my career when he would rather begin having a family.
8. I'll want to buy a new car—he'll want to buy a used one.
9. That I will get pregnant before we plan!

At the end of the first session I explain about the required books and tapes and help them develop a time schedule for the books. They purchase the books so that they will have them to keep, and the tapes are loaned to them.

BUILDING TIES TO FUTURE IN-LAWS

At this time the prospective in-law forms are introduced. If both sets of parents are in favor of the marriage, I give one final assignment, not to the couple but to their parents. I have each person ask his or her parents to write a letter to me telling why they want this young man or woman to become their son- or daughter-in-law. They are not to show this to their son or daughter but to mail it to me. During the last counseling session I read these letters to the couple. This is an affirming time and greatly enhances total family relationships.

In addition, each parent (both mother and father) receives a copy of the "Becoming an In-law" evaluation form (shown below), and they are asked to complete it and return it to the pastor. This will be given to the couple, and they will probably want to respond to their parents' response. As you can see from the questions, the purpose of this questionnaire is twofold: to build positive concern and communication between the parents and future in-laws and to help eliminate potential problems.

BECOMING AN IN-LAW—BUILDING POSITIVE RELATIONSHIPS

1. How would you describe your relationship with your parents and in-laws during the early years of your marriage?
   Parents: _____
   In-laws: _____
2. Would you like your married children to approach you in the same way you approached your parents and in-laws? Why or why not? ____
   _____
3. What would you list as some major needs of your soon-to-be married son or daughter? Could those needs be best met (1) with your help, (2) by himself or herself, or (3) with the new marriage partner? _____
   _____
4. Are there some unique needs of your mate related to the leaving of your child? How might you help him or her in these areas? _____
   _____
5. What will be the greatest adjustment that you will have to make as your son or daughter leaves home? _____

6. If you could ask your son or daughter to pray for you as you make this transition, how would you ask him/her to pray? _____

7. Will you expect the new couple to visit you often? How do you define "often"? How will you go about suggesting they visit you? _____

_____

8. When the newlyweds choose something that is not your choice, what do you think your response will be? (Can you think of an example?) _____

9. Do you expect the newly married couple to call before visiting you and vice versa? Can there be spontaneous "drop-ins"? _____

10. What plans, secrets, and problems do you expect the new couple to share with you? If that does not happen, what do you think your reaction will be? _____

11. In what way do you think and speak of your son- or daughter-in-law as a positive addition to your family? _____

12. In what way are you taking into consideration the feelings of the other family (parents-in-law) in making wedding plans? _____
Scheduling holiday visits? _____
Giving gifts? _____
Seeing the grandchildren? _____

13. Please describe six expectations that you have for the couple after they are married. _____

14. Please take another piece of paper and together compose a letter describing in detail why you are looking forward to your son's or daughter's fiance becoming your son- or daughter-in-law. This should be addressed to that person. Please write at least three paragraphs. _____

Here are three additional questions that I have been asking couples that elicit some thoughtful responses:

1. As you proceed through your marriage relationship, what would be some of the worst problems that could occur that you definitely would not want to happen in your marriage?

2. I don't know of any people who marry with the intent to divorce or abuse their partner, but this does happen in Christian marriages. How will you make sure that your marriage never ends in divorce? What will you do to ensure the fact that neither of you will ever have an affair, that neither of you will physically abuse one another, or that incest would never occur in your family?

3. "What type of wake and sleep pattern do you have?" Asking such a simple question can lead to an enjoyable discussion. After you receive a puzzled look, proceed to explain the issue of contradictory wake/sleep patterns.

MORNING AND EVENING PEOPLE

Research studies have found that couples whose wake and sleep patterns are mismatched (an evening person married to a morning person) reported significantly less marital adjustment, more marital conflict, less time spent in significant conversation, less time spent in shared activities, and less sexual activity than couples who were matched in their wake and sleep patterns. This does not mean that only couples whose patterns match should marry. It just means that couples with this pattern will have to learn to be more flexible in the use of their time. The potential for more conflict is evident for several reasons.

The two people may experience efficiency and energy peaks at different times during the day. This can lead to frustration and disagreements over when to go to bed, how much sleep each needs, laziness, and resentment because their partner is never around when they are at an energy peak. The amount of sleep each needs may vary because of basic psychological and metabolic differences.[7]

The alert morning person may feel that his/her partner is lazy, whereas some merely need more sleep; they are slower in coming alive and may be fully awake within two hours after arising. My wife, Joyce, and I are like this. We have learned to accept these differences and not pressure the other to change. For one thing, it will never happen. But the early morning person will have to make a greater concession in that he or she will have to back off and not overwhelm the partner with too much input when the mate first arises. They just cannot handle it. This is one of those areas where it is best to back off in terms of activity, noise, and intensity until their partner comes alive. It is showing sensitivity to the needs of the other person.

As you share information like this with your couples you may also want to remind them of the pertinent Proverb: "If you shout a pleasant greeting to a friend too early in the morning, he will count it as a curse" (27:14 TLB*). In addition, you may ask these three questions to detect and remedy a potential conflict: (1) What is your individual sleep/wake pattern? (2) How will this affect your marital relationship, especially

*The Living Bible.

162

if they are different? (3) What accommodations will you have to make in order for this not to be a marital problem?

At the conclusion of the first session it is important to give the assignments for the remainder of the sessions from the *Before You Say I Do* workbook. (The pastor may choose to photocopy the assignments and other questions.) Some of the assignments from *Before You Say I Do* and *So You're Getting Married* will be discussed during the sessions, and some will not. The counselor can base the decision upon the maturity of the couple and what he believes each couple needs to cover. Remember that each person is to have his/her own copy of the workbook.

A FAMILY LOG

One of the newest assignments that I now give is to have each person keep a daily log and a family year overview, noting daily activities and amount of time spent in each activity for a week and then compare. This is very detailed and includes a step-by-step view of a person's day; the time they arise, whether they shower or eat first, work out, read the paper, have devotions, whether they like to talk early in the morning or prefer quiet, and so on. Do they go to bed early, read in bed, shower at night? Do they like to eat the minute they get home, eat in quiet or in front of the TV, have quiet evenings or be on the go? You will find that most couples have never considered the significance of understanding and blending the daily activities of their individual habits.

The first year of marriage is important, yet also a time of major adjustment. By helping the couple to identify their distinct characteristics prior to the marriage, some conflicts are eliminated. I've seen conflicts in married couples because one wants it absolutely quiet and totally dark when they go to bed and the spouse wants a light on and the radio on low. And each behavior came as a surprise to the other.

The counselor should ask each person to complete a family year overview, a listing of each family event and celebration such as birthdays observed and in what way, holidays and how they are celebrated—large family gatherings or quiet observances, whether the Christmas tree is flocked or left green, whether gifts are opened Christmas Eve or in the morning, where the family has gone on vacation, and the like. This overview includes which of these traditions will be brought into their own marriage and what new traditions they would like to establish for themselves. Again clarifying these in advance will lead to a smoother adjustment and help the couple to begin considering the blending process.[8]

MARRIED COUPLES AS COUNSELORS

Churches are beginning to take advantage of the mature married couples in their church who have the capability to minister to those about to be married. As noted in chapter 2, lay counseling by couples can be very effective as an adjunct to professional counseling. Programs vary; one such program, called "Wedding Song," gives the engaged couple and their married-couple counselors copies of the questions. The engaged couple will ask the married couple these questions during a ninety-minute interview, usually held at the married couple's home. The open sharing and guidance from this selected couple has proved to be beneficial. The side benefit of this program is the growth that occurs in the couple selected to minister. For if they want to respond well to these questions, they find that it is necessary to respond to them ahead of time and begin growing together in areas that are lacking in their own relationship.

The interview covers six areas: biblical foundations for marriage; communication; the engagement, wedding and honeymoon; finances; sex; and a wrap-up. Here are the questions:

The Biblical Foundation for Marriage

1. How has your relationship with Christ affected your relationship with each other?
2. As a married couple, how do you encourage each other's spiritual life?
3. In Galatians 5, the fruit of the Spirit is mentioned. Which of these qualities have been most important to you in your marriage relationship?
4. What has been the practical outworking of authority and submission in your relationship (Ephesians 5:1ff)?
5. Do you believe divorce is an option for Christians? How has your position on this issue strengthened the quality of your commitment to one another?

Questions on Communication

1. Was there a change in the quality of your communication from your engagement period to your first year of marriage?
2. Were you as good communicators as you thought you were?
3. What are the most serious challenges to ongoing communication?

4. What does your spouse do or say to encourage (or discourage) your desires to actively communicate?
5. How do you handle arguments and disagreements?

Questions on Engagement, Wedding, and Honeymoon

1. What advice would you give us for the best use of our engagement time?
2. What did you two do that was most memorable at your wedding ceremony?
3. How did you resolve in-law differences of opinion?
4. Do you have any advice for us on planning a honeymoon?

Questions on Finances

1. Have you consistently used a budget to control your finances? If not, what system do you use?
2. What are your convictions about the wife's being employed outside the home?
3. Who determines what you will buy and what you won't buy?
4. How have your differences (i.e., background, sales-resistance, temperament, etc.) affected these decisions?
5. Do you have a shared conviction about giving to the Lord's work? How was that decision arrived at?
6. What is the easiest way for a couple to get in debt over their heads?

Questions on Sex

1. How did your individual backgrounds mesh to form your own sexual adjustment as a married couple?
2. Can you describe the differences between your perception of marital sex before you were married and the realities of marital sex after you married?
3. How does sex fit into the whole concept of married life?
4. How do you keep romance alive in your relationship?

Wrap-up Questions

1. Is there anything that we have not covered that you feel would be valuable for us to know as we anticipate a Christian marriage?
   NOTE: Why not spend a few moments together in prayer as you conclude your meeting?

The questions act as a springboard for the discussion. Naturally, other questions arise during the interview that are prompted by the ones listed here. A number of churches have used forms such as these.[9]

In conducting your premarital sessions you need to have a direction and a plan but also flexibility. Each couple will be different, and your own sensibility as well as the leading of the Holy Spirit will guide you to the areas of emphasis with each couple.

NOTES

1. David Augsburger, *Cherishable: Love and Marriage* (Scottsdale, Pa.: Herald, 1971), p.16.

2. Chapel address by David Hubbard at Fuller Theological Seminary, n.d.

3. Leo Buscaglia, *Love* (Thorofare, N.J.: Slack, 1972), pp. 61-62.

4. Ibid., p. 63.

5. As quoted in Buscaglia, *Love,* p. 66.

6. The chart first appeared in *So You're Getting Married*, by H. Norman Wright, copyright 1985, Regal Books, Ventura, CA 93003. Used by permission.

7. Jeffrey H. Larson and D. Russsell Crane, "Morning and Night Couples: The Effect of Wake and Sleep Patterns on Marital Adjustment," *Journal of Marital and Family Therapy*, 17 (1991): 53-64.

8. A helpful book to explain differences in a positive manner is *Type Talk*, by Otto Kroeger and Janet Thuesen. The focus of the book is the differences as indicated on the Myers-Briggs Type Indicator.

9. For further information, contact the Wedding Song Premarital Program, First Evangelical Free Church of Fullerton, California.

CHAPTER 9

Sessions Three and Four: Using the Taylor-Johnson Temperament Analysis

The content of the third and fourth sessions in premarital counseling is listed together because it is difficult to know how much will be covered in the third session. Often we don't begin this material until the fourth session since the other material demands more time. Most of the time will be spent talking about the Taylor-Johnson Temperament Analysis.® As you work with different couples you will find that with some you will need three sessions to cover all this material; with others you will be able to cover it very comfortably in two sessions.

USEFULNESS OF THE INSTRUMENT

When the couple arrives for the third session they are usually very interested in looking at the Taylor-Johnson test. It's important to remember that the T-JTA® measures a person's inner responses about himself/herself at the time when the person answered the questions. But it also gives you a reflection of the person's inner thoughts and feelings for the past few weeks. It tends to measure the inner life of the person rather than behavior. How much a person has changed over the previous months has to be identified in your counseling session.

Note that this tool is not designed to measure mental abnormalities in psychiatric terms. It does provide measures of temperament and personality patterns or indications of problems. These may necessitate additional evaluation to identify the full extent of the issues. It is also important that we not attempt to make the T-JTA say more than it was intended to say or use it in a way for which it was not designed.

The T-JTA is available in two levels of difficulty. The regular edition is at the eighth grade reading level, the secondary edition is at the fifth grade reading level. You may need to use this edition with young couples. It is also available in a braille edition for the blind and is published in Spanish, German, and French with appropriate norms for these groups. This could be very helpful if you do much cross-cultural work.

GUIDELINES FOR USING T-JTA

As you work with your premarital couple, be sure to view the T-JTA score in each trait as a tendency. Use the wording "according to the way in which you have answered the questions, there appears to be a tendency toward . . . " Being tentative is safer and much more acceptable than stating "You are definitely a . . . "

Here are four other cautions in presenting the results. First, *always* have the individual or couple predict their score for a specific trait prior to your giving them their scores. The mindset and expectation level is far different when this is done. Premarital couples are usually very eager to see the results.

Second, use pertinent questions. This will greatly facilitate couple communication and the resolving of conflicts. During the past five years I have been using the individual questions of each trait more and more in counseling and discovered a previously untapped source of useful information and couple interaction. It may take additional time, but it assists you in moving from the surface to root issues.

Third, remember that the shaded areas are there to assist you and the counselee in understanding the significance of the score. Generally speaking, the more closely a person's scores follow the darker shaded areas on the profile, the better the indications for both individual and marital adjustment. But the shaded areas were developed based upon a consensus of opinion by a number of professional counselors who had used the T-JTA extensively. These are not absolute indications but must be interpreted with some latitude. Not using the shaded profiles greatly reduces the effectiveness of this instrument.

Fourth, be aware of how your own personality tendencies (and scores on the T-JTA) will tend to influence your interpretation of the test results of others and your own counseling approach.

Strong positive scores in various trait areas can suggest ministry opportunities. Several years ago a pastor told me how he explained certain results to the couples. If a couple both had strong positive scores in a specific trait, he encouraged them to develop a ministry to other people who had difficulty in that trait area. If one of them had a strength in that trait area and his/her partner needed work in that same area, the one with a strength was called upon to minister to the partner who needed assistance. If both of them needed work in the same trait area, he encouraged them to seek the assistance of a third party. This is helpful for couples just starting out in marriage.

The counselor should focus on the personality differences, the areas of possible adjustment. I like to focus on how the two people are alike and how they are different. You are not looking for a couple to have identical profiles. Very few couples are identical in their T-JTA profiles. In fact, some who are too much alike may have difficulties. Perhaps the man and the woman both score 95 on the dominant scale. Look at one of the Taylor-Johnson profiles now, and you will see what the potential problem might be for that couple. Two individuals who are very dominant may be headed for trouble if they do not learn to ease off, to give, and to adjust to the other person.

Some individuals will have profiles that clearly indicate that additional testing is needed to discover the depth of the emotional difficulty. Other profiles will indicate that individual counseling is needed before the person marries. Carrying a pattern of anxiety, depression, emotional blockage, negative thinking, overcompliance, anger, or impulsiveness into a marriage adds additional and sometimes disastrous struggles. On numerous occasions I have recommended individual counseling before proceeding with the premarital preparation.

The T-JTA is a launching pad for identifying and releasing areas that otherwise might slip by.

A typical situation in using this test may be that of a young man who scores himself very high on the Sympathetic/Indifferent trait; when he sees that his fiancée scored him very low, he wants to know, "Why do you see me like that? I am a very loving and caring individual." Perhaps he is, but he might not be sharing this with her or verbalizing it so that she perceives it.

When you work with a couple on the results of their Taylor-Johnson Temperament Analysis, you have unlimited opportunities to focus on their individual differences. Learning to blend, to become complementary and compatible are major tasks for any couple during the initial five years of marriage—personality differences, behavioral differences, and communication differences will emerge during this session. That's why I often tell couples they will be marrying foreigners.

A CASE STUDY

To illustrate this adjustment process, here is a conversation taken verbatim from the third session with Bill and Jan, who were planning to be married within six months. (All names in this chapter have been changed to protect the individuals' privacy.) We were reviewing the Active-Social/Quiet category and the Expressive-Responsive/Inhibited traits on the T-JTA when I mentioned to them that each was actually marrying a foreigner. Jan was surprised to hear that; so was Bill.

BILL: What do you mean, marry a foreigner? We're both from this country. In fact, we couldn't be better matched or more alike. We were both born and raised in California; we're both white; our parents were born and raised in this country, and so were their parents. How are we foreigners?

NORM: Well, this comes as a shock to most couples, and I share this with almost everyone I work with now. You and Jan are similar. But you were both raised in different homes with different parents, siblings, experiences, and in effect a different culture. You may eat the same types of foods, but they were prepared differently. You have different customs, different rituals in your families, different beliefs and values, and thus you each learned a different "language." If you want to have the kind of marriage you have described to me, your biggest task is going to be to learn about the other person's culture, to develop the flexibility to be comfortable with either set of customs, and above all, to learn your partner's language so that you can speak it.

JAN: You mean, Bill and I, even though we've gone together for three years, still need to learn more about communication and how we talk with each other? (*Pause.*) You know, I have felt that way at times. On occasion I've sensed that Bill and I were sort of out of touch with each other, even though we had done a lot of talking and sharing. We would talk and talk, and at the time we each seemed to grasp what the other person was sharing, but later it felt as if we hadn't talked at all. He didn't catch what I had said. Other times he has a difficult time understanding me. And I don't understand why.

NORM: Jan, right now you're sensing and sharing something many individuals feel perplexed about for many years of their marriage. Bill, what do you think about this?

BILL: Yes, I see what you're getting at now. Jan and I do talk quite a bit, but sometimes I wonder why she doesn't understand my perspective. I state my point of view, but from the questions she asks, it's as though she'd never heard me. So I try to explain again. In fact, at times I think we *over* talk about some things. I like to make everything clear and simple and to the point, but we tend to go on and . . .

JAN: Bill, the reason we go on and on at times is because you don't seem to understand what *I'm* feeling. I need to make sure that I'm understood by you, so we don't have misunderstandings.

NORM: Jan, it's important to you that Bill understands your feelings, right? Bill, you want Jan to understand your perspective and view it your way, right? (*They both nodded.*) Could it be that some of the words you use aren't in the other person's vocabulary? Could it be that in some way you're not speaking the other person's language?

JAN: Perhaps that's what's happening. (*She thought for a minute and then continued softly.*) Now that we are talking about this, I've become aware of something else. I feel we've made more progress, but at first we had to work on how we shared with each other. I didn't understand what was going on until I went to Bill's home for dinner the first time. What a shock!

BILL: Yes, it was a shock for her (*laughing*).

NORM: What happened?

JAN: We went to his home and had dinner with his parents and two brothers and sister. Naturally, I felt a bit apprehensive, since I wanted to make a good impression. I felt a little on edge, and when I do, I tend to quiet down somewhat. Not that I don't talk as much as I usually do, but I get more hesitant and soft-spoken. Once we got into dinner, I'm afraid I sat there with my mouth open in shock—at least I felt as if I did. Bill's family is totally different from mine. My family is polite and quiet, and they rarely raise their voices. If they do, watch out! It means that someone is angry, but that doesn't happen often.

But Bill and his family raise their voices, interrupt, carry on two or three conversations at once, even shout at times! I was numb by the time dinner was over and felt very uncomfortable. When we left, the first thing I said to Bill was, "Bill, your family is such an angry group of people—and they didn't seem very polite toward one another, either. They interrupted and didn't let people finish."

BILL: That came as a big surprise to me. So I said, "What do you mean? My family loves each other. They're very close-knit and loyal. In fact, they were just themselves tonight, which is good. That means they liked you and looked at you as someone they could be themselves with. Nobody was angry. That's just the way we talk! We've always been that way, and so are my grandparents and aunts and uncles and their families. We're just loud and have our own style of communicating. I'm that way, too."

JAN: It was a shock for a while. The more I went with Bill, the more I discovered that he communicated that way. When he first raised his voice, I froze, because I thought he was angry, but I have since learned that he does that when he is excited and wants to emphasize something.

NORM: So when you first went to Bill's home, it was like entering another country, since they did things differently and in a sense spoke a different language. At first you felt a bit awkward, until you began to translate what they were saying into your own language. Am I right?

BILL: (*Laughing*) You're right. Nobody ever put it that way before, but I can sure see how the idea of speaking another person's language makes sense.

NORM: This picture of marrying a foreigner is clearing up a bit for you then, isn't it?

BILL: Oh, yes. In fact, I can see how both of us have already started to learn each other's family language and to adapt to each family.

NORM: How?

BILL: Well, after some time I noticed that Jan started to open up when we were with my family. She actually raised her voice and even interrupted at times. She really has learned to become one of us. I don't even think she was aware of the changes.

JAN: Bill's right. I didn't think about how I was gradually changing, until one Christmas we had a tape recorder on during the family meal—or celebration as they call it. We sat and listened to it after dinner, and I was amazed when I heard myself. I sounded like them!

NORM: How did that feel to you, changing your way of communicating?

JAN: It was very comfortable. I enjoyed myself, and I was getting closer to Bill's family as well. I felt good about this new relationship with his family.

As the interview proceeded, I chose different communication styles for Bill and Jan; my choice of words varied in subtle yet distinct ways. Bill reported that he had adapted to Jan's family, becoming more soft spoken, though he understood his own family better. Then I asked Jan how well she understood her family.

NORM: Jan, do you and your family understand each other when you share together? Are you in touch with each other?

JAN: Oh, yes. We always are. I get along especially well with Mom. Dad, I must admit, doesn't always say too much. I wish he would. He's short and to the point with very little detail. At times I feel we have to drag any information out of him. When he does talk, he sounds like a newspaper reporter giving a condensed version of the daily news. He just gives the facts. And feelings? I don't know when I've heard Dad share his feelings. That's frustrated Mom over the years, too. But Mom and I really click.

NORM: So your father responds more like a condenser, and your mother is more of an amplifier.

JAN: Yes, that's exactly it.

NORM: Bill, you and your family seem to focus in well together as you talk, and Jan, you feel good about your communication with your mom. Now, what about the two of you together? What will it take for you two to communicate so that you understand each other (*Pause*)?

NORM: By the way, Bill, are you and I communicating? Do you think we see eye-to-eye? Do we understand each other?

BILL: Oh, yes. You seem to see what I'm talking about, and I am getting the picture of this whole discussion of marrying a foreigner. I wonder, though, if I don't need a passport to marry Jan (*laughter*)!

NORM: Jan (*in a soft voice*), how do you feel about our communication? Does it make sense?

JAN: Very much so. You seem to have a handle on what I'm feeling, and what you say registers. We seem to speak the same language.

NORM: It's important that we learn not only to speak the same language but also to make sure we mean the same thing with our words. I have run into so many couples who get irritated and upset in their marriages because of such a simple matter as having different definitions for their words. You each come to your marriage with a different dictionary. You know, two people can speak Spanish and not mean the same thing. Two people can speak German and not mean the same thing. We're sitting here speaking English and using some of the same words, but we might have different meanings for them. Your experiences in life, your mindset, what you intend can give meaning to your words. My wife might ask, "Could we stop at the store for a minute on our way home? I'll just be a minute." I might take the word *minute* literally, but I had better not, because years of experience have taught me we're talking about fifteen to twenty minutes.

At this point, I decided to personalize the issue to Bill and Jan by asking Bill a question. His answer prompted a lively discussion.

NORM: Bill, has Jan ever said to you, "Bill, could I talk to you for a minute about something?" and you said yes, assuming she meant a minute, but you're still discussing the issue thirty minutes later?

BILL: Tuesday night. That very thing happened Tuesday night. Jan wondered why I was getting uptight.

JAN: Well, it was important. Did it matter how long it went on? You agreed we needed to talk about it, and I had felt that way for some time.

BILL: Oh, no, it was all right. I just figured it'd be short, since you said *a minute.*

JAN: (*With more feeling*) But many times I feel *you* have set a time limit on our conversations. I almost sense that you're impatient and want to get to the bottom line. You don't want to hear all my reasons or feelings. In fact, I wish *you* would share more details with me. I wear a new outfit and ask you how it looks, and all you say is, "It looks fine." Can't you tell me any more about how you feel about it?

BILL: (*Rolling his eyes upward and then turning to Jan*) But I said it looked fine. What else do you want to hear?

NORM: On a scale of zero to ten, with zero meaning it looks terrible —like it's out of the rag pile—and a ten meaning it's outstanding, where does the word *fine* fall?

BILL: Oh, it's somewhere between an eight and a ten.

JAN: How would I know that? That's the first I've heard that *fine* had any meaning at all!

NORM: This is what I mean when I say you need to define your words. Bill, if you couldn't use the word *fine* and had to give a three-line description of the dress Jan is wearing, what would you say?

BILL: (*Pause*) Well, I like it. The color looks good. The dress looks like you, and I like some of the detail around the waist. It fits well, and I like the curves. It just seems to look like you. And the style is flashy.

NORM: How do you feel about Bill's response?

JAN: That really feels good. He really seemed to notice, and I enjoyed hearing his description.

BILL: Well, I could do that, but when I'm with some of my other friends and we say *fine,* we know what we mean.

NORM: I can understand that, Bill. When you're with them you speak the same language, but when you're with Jan, you need to speak her language. She wants more detail, more description, more adjectives. That's what registers with her. This is a good example of what I mean by speaking the other person's language. Now that we're talking about it, which one of you tends to give more detail when you talk?

JAN: I'm the detail person. Quite often Bill asks me to get to the point and give him the bottom line so he understands what I'm taking about. I just want to make sure that he's going to grasp what I'm sharing. I've always given a lot of detail and feelings, but sometimes it's as if he doesn't hear my feelings. He ignores them.

BILL: I don't ignore what you are saying. I do see what you are getting at, but I don't always know what to do with those feelings. It's not that I always mind the detail, but I wish you would focus on the bottom line first, instead of going around the barn several times and then telling me what you're talking about. I like it straightforward and to the point. In fact I really like it when you're precise. The other day I asked you the time and you replied with 'A little before six.' It was actually 5:50. I guess I need information concise, simple, and exact. I like clean instructions, too.

NORM: Bill, you want Jan to communicate with you like a newspaper article.

BILL: A newspaper article?

NORM: Most newspaper articles are structured like a pyramid. The first sentence is a complete summary statement of what is in the article. Next comes a brief paragraph with some of the most significant summary items expanded. The final larger portion of the article will contain the minute details.

BILL: That's it. An approach like that makes sense to me. I can follow what's going on a lot better, and (*looking at Jan*) I would be willing to hear some more of the detail. But I don't think I need to hear as much detail as you enjoy hearing. I don't want a two-line news summary of what you say, but a *Reader's Digest* condensation would be helpful.

NORM: Bill, you're asking Jan to condense some of the details a bit and identify the bottom line right at the start. That helps you focus on her conversation better. Is that accurate?

BILL: Yes.

NORM: That also means, Bill, since Jan enjoys detail, that when you share with her, you will give her more detail than you do now.

Now, does my statement about marrying a foreigner make more sense to you?

JAN AND BILL: Yes, definitely!

COUNSELOR: Once again let me go back to the question I asked a few minutes ago. Jan and Bill, what is it going to take, in addition to what we have already pointed out, for the two of you to understand each other and no longer be foreigners? What do you think, Bill? What do you feel, Jan?

Before reading on, reflect back on what you just read. Were my words different when I spoke to Jan compared to Bill? If so, in what way? Why? What were the principles being taught to them in this session?

Before continuing, let me emphasize your role as a counselor. The best way a counselor can teach any couple how to speak one another's language is by you, the counselor, modeling this process as you interact with them. This necessitates becoming familiar with various types of personality styles. The most accurate of these and the easiest to learn is the Myers-Briggs Type Indicator, and the most helpful resource is *Type Talk*, by Kroeger and Thuesen.

CREATING RAPPORT

Styles of Communication

In addition to this, learning the characteristics of a person who speaks like a condenser and one who speaks like an amplifier is necessary. It means using the same style of speaking and the same terminology that your counselees use. Some are more cognitive and factual, whereas others are much more feeling-oriented and expressive. It means being able to speak right to the point as well as going off on tangents before returning to the main point.

One important principle for you to remember is: The person who has the greatest flexibility in his communication style will have the greatest influence and impact on other people. He also will establish rapport with them very quickly. This has ramifications for a minister's preaching as well. Too often we allow our own thinking and speaking style to permeate the sermon. If we tend to be more precise, structured, and factual we communicate well with those in the worship service who are the same. But what about the others who are more feeling-oriented or who like word pictures or illustrations that contain emotions? Sometimes we leave some people out of the sermon. I have heard a number of ministers who have developed the ability to speak to all the different learning, thinking, and speaking styles in their congregation. And it shows by the response of the people. Listen to your sermons. Listen to your conversations with others in and out of the counseling office. What is your style of communicating?

Establishing rapport was mentioned earlier. It is vital for the counselor to establish rapport with each premarital couple but also for them to do the same in their relationship with one another.

A Definition

We use the word *rapport* when we talk about establishing relationships with other people, and in the field of counseling, psychologists are encouraged to establish rapport with the clients as soon as possible. Rapport has been defined as "a relationship marked by harmony, conformity, accord, or affinity." It reflects a relationship that has agreement or even likeness or similarity.

How far does establishing rapport actually go? Do we have to become so much like others that we become clones? That we begin to lose our own identities? Not at all. You will still be who you are and reflect your own unique mannerisms and patterns of speech. However, by emphasizing similarities, you will be able to respond to a much greater variety of people in your counseling and other church ministries. In order to establish rapport, you have to take the opportunity to learn to be quite flexible. In fact, no doubt you already subconsciously do a lot of what I will suggest. Here I want only to identify it, refine it, and explain it so that you can become an even better communicator.

Mirroring

Some of the outstanding therapists of our time are adept at establishing rapport quickly. In watching them you discover that part of their process of developing rapport relies on mirroring. *Mirroring* simply means giving back to the person portions of his or her own *nonverbal* behavior as though the person were looking in a mirror.

We all do this to some degree. You go to a dinner party, and you find yourself matching your table manners and body postures to the expected level of informality or formality you feel is needed for that group.

Mirroring does not mean mimicking. From early childhood we have been taught that copying is not acceptable. We believe that to mimic is the same as making fun of a person, but mimicry is usually characterized by some exaggeration of a behavior or speech trait.

In contrast, mirroring occurs when you become sensitive to portions of your own behavior and response and to the other individual. What do you begin to become aware of? Portions of the other person's body posture, specific gestures, facial expressions, voice tone, tempo, and intonation patterns. In some cases I have even seen the therapist match the person's breathing rhythms. But remember that these are very slight and subtle responses. If the person you talk with begins hitting himself on the side of the face every so often, don't do likewise!

I'd suggest a subtle matching of slight behaviors, mannerisms, and voice. For this to be effective you don't have to be a therapist. Friends talking together, a teacher with a student, two business associates—anyone can do it. Unconsciously (and now more consciously) I have done it in conversations with people in social situations as well as in the counseling office. A slight shifting of the body in order to sit in a fashion similar to the other person, using a slight hand gesture that reflects one of his, pausing in much the same way she does are all examples of mirroring. Matching the level of their volume and types of wording is easy to learn. Be aware of what you do when you are with other people. Watch their interactions as they communicate. Notice the quality of the interaction when mirroring is there and when it isn't. It goes on all around us every day.

Let's continue with Jan and Bill:

NORM: Once again let me go back to my question of a few minutes ago. Jan and Bill, what is it going to take, in addition to what we have already pointed out, for the two of you to understand each other and no longer be foreigners? What do you think, Bill? What do you feel, Jan?

BILL: Well, we need to speak the other person's language.

NORM: Yes, but how do you do that, Bill? What does that mean in actual day-to-day communication?

JAN: (*Interrupting*) I might be off on this, but I'm beginning to catch a sense of what you've been doing with us.

NORM: What have I been doing?

JAN: I've noticed, now that I think about it, that you really have been doing this. You talk differently to Bill and me. Now I know what you mean by speaking the other person's language. Bill, have you grasped it yet? No, let me take that back. Bill, do you see what has been happening?

NORM: You did it very well just then, Jan. You switched from your vocabulary, which made sense to you, and used a word that's part of Bill's vocabulary. Bill, did you notice that?

BILL: Well, I noticed something different, but I'm not sure yet.

NORM: Go on, Jan.

JAN: Bill, you use words like *see, look, focus* all the time with me and everyone else, so they must have some significance to you. Those aren't my words, but I can learn to use them. When I use feeling words, I don't usually get much response from you, so perhaps I need to listen to your words more, and you need to listen to mine, and we can both learn to use each other's way of speaking.

BILL: "OK, I think I'm beginning to see. . . " He caught himself and then said, "You're right. I do use that word a lot."

JAN: If we had a tape recording of this session—no, if we had a tape recording and a video recording, like the ones we used in our teacher-education courses—I imagine we would discover that you have been doing more than using our language. Is that right?

NORM: Yes, it is. You're perceptive to sense that so soon.

JAN: Now, if you had made that same statement to Bill, how would you have said it?

BILL: (*Interrupting*) Wait, I do see it now. You might say the same thing to each of us, but with different words, based on how we talk. I just noticed something else. When you talk to me, you give a bit more volume to what you say. You raise your voice just a bit, because I talk louder than Jan does. I noticed something else, too. You don't waste any words with me on long explanations. You seem to make it short and to the point, and I like that. Maybe that's because that's the way I talk. This is really something. We haven't been here long, but it seems as if we've been together or known each other for a long time.

JAN: Yes, I agree. I feel—and that's one of my comfortable words— the same way. I've noticed you do more than just speak our language with your choice of words. When you talk to Bill, you seem to shift in your chair and sit almost the way Bill does. It's nothing major, but you have done this several times. You sit up a bit more, which is the way you sit, Bill. When you talk to me, I've noticed you tend to sit back and put your hands on the arm of the chair, which is exactly what I do. You even slow down your rate of speaking and speak more softly to me than to Bill.

NORM: You're right, Jan. Since the two of you are just now becoming aware of this process, it will take some work on your part to refine your communication with each other. I feel you've discovered the fact that you have probably responded this way already with other people, and you just were not aware of it. Now you will become more aware and will work consciously on how you communicate, not only with each other, but in a wider range of contacts as well. What will each of you be doing differently in your communication with each other at this point? Bill, what do you think?

BILL: Well, since this is in my lap, let me think a minute. Boy, this is something. I feel as if—how do you like that, one of Jan's favorite words!—I've just come back from an archeological expedition and made a gigantic discovery, and I'm still trying to put together all the pieces I've unearthed.

NORM: Bill, is that the way you usually describe things? Jan, was that a typical description for Bill?

JAN: I haven't heard descriptions like that too often, but it was great. It said so much more than, "I'm thinking about it," or something to that effect.

BILL: Well, it's just the way I was feeling, and that's the best way to describe it.

NORM: Bill, that was great. That was a beautiful example of how to expand your description and give your conversation more life, meaning, and richness. As you begin to communicate more and more like that, you will be amazed at your own ability and other people's response to you.

BILL: Sometimes I even amaze myself! Well, here is what I'm going to be doing differently as I communicate with you, Jan. I guess the first step is to really learn your language, and that means I need to listen to you, to what you say, and how you say it. I'll have to listen to you with my eyes as well as my ears. I know that there are times when I don't have eye contact with you when you talk; then when I do turn and look at you, your message somehow seems different.

I don't think I will totally change my way of communicating, since I want to be me. But when I talk with you, I can use some of your words and phrases. . . .

SPOTTING PREFERENCES

It is important to explore a couple's preferences and find specific activities that could lead to a conflict or already have become a source of contention. In another premarital session, I was discussing Active-Social/Quiet trait scores with a couple. A score higher than 50 indicates either a desire to be actively doing things and involvement with people or it could refer more to extrovert tendencies. A score less than 50 suggests a quieter life style such as not being on the go so much, doing things by oneself, or it could reflect introvert tendencies. Tim's score was 79 and Jean's was 34. In the ensuing discussion, she expressed concern that her score was not very reflective of who she really is. But we explored this, and her fiance spoke up and said, "I think it is. The only thing she enjoys going out and doing is shopping." She agreed with that. Since the word *shopping* had arisen before, we talked further about this.

NORM: After you are married, how frequently do you want Tim to shop with you?

JEAN: Twice a week. *(Tim grimaced a bit at this, and I was mildly surprised at her expectation.)*

TIM: And when she shops, she means from 10:00 in the morning until 5:00 at night!

NORM: Tim, could you describe to me your style of shopping?

TIM: I know what I want when I go to a store, and I know the store to go to. I walk in, find it, and walk out.

NORM: Do you see shopping as something to enjoy or a necessity?

TIM: A necessity. It should be done fast and efficiently.

NORM: Jean, tell me about your style of shopping.

JEAN: I like to look around and try everything on and go from store to store.

NORM: Is shopping an enjoyable pastime for you?

JEAN: Definitely!

NORM: Could I make a suggestion? After you are married, why not plan to shop together perhaps once every two months and limit the time to two hours. How does that sound?

JEAN: Once every two months? That's all? Why, my mother and I go every Saturday for the entire day!

TIM: It sounds good to me. After all, what's the longest I've ever lasted shopping with you? It's never been two hours yet.

JEAN: Well, that's right, it hasn't. And usually you're in a hurry and you don't like to look like I do. Maybe that would work.

NORM: I just feel it would eliminate a great deal of conflict. There are other activities that you could plan or learn to do together that would bring you a greater sense of satisfaction.

The discussion proceeded as we explored other possibilities of activities together as well as acceptance of their individual differences.

Each person needs to learn the process of encouraging his partner to be himself as well as to be willing to participate in his spouse's way of experiencing life (and vice versa). The more active-social person can learn to consider and experience the quiet partner's life, and the quiet person can learn to participate in the active person's activities.

ASKING QUESTIONS

Since Trait C, Active-Social versus Quiet, is an indicator of such differences (extrovert vs. introvert), I usually bring in material such as these questions from *Type Talk*. If one of them is an introvert I make suggested comments like:

- Do you tend to rehearse things before you say them? Do you often respond with "I'll have to think about that" or "Let me tell you later"?
- Do you enjoy the peace and quiet of having time to yourself? Do you find your private time easily invaded?
- Have you been called "shy" from time to time? Whether or not you agree, do you come across to others as somewhat reserved and reflective?
- Do you like to share special occasions with just one other person or perhaps a few close friends rather than a lot of people?
- Do you wish you could get your ideas out more forcefully and tend to resent those who blurt out things you were just about to say?
- Do you like stating your thoughts or feelings without interruption?
- Do you ever need to "recharge" alone after you've spent time socializing? And the more intense the encounter, the greater the chance you feel drained afterward?[1]

If the introvert's partner is more of an extrovert, I ask, "What did you hear your fiancee say that might help you in understanding him and relating to him?" And in talking directly to an extrovert about his personality characteristics I might raise these questions (also from *Type Talk*):

- Do you tend to talk first and think later, and you don't know what you'll say until you hear yourself say it? Do you tend to think out loud or brainstorm out loud?
- Could it be that you don't mind reading or having a conversation while the TV or radio is on in the background?
- Would you say you're approachable and easily engaged in conversation by friends and strangers alike?
- Do you enjoy going to parties and prefer to talk with many people instead of just a few?
- Are you energized by being with people?

- Do you find listening more difficult than talking?
- Do you need affirmation from friends and associates about who you are, what you do, how you look, and just about everything else? You may think you're doing a good job, but until you hear someone tell you, do you truly believe it?[2]

It is necessary to clarify differences for a couple so they can understand and accept the other person. Since an introvert person doesn't share their conclusion or what they are thinking until they have thought it out completely, their extrovert partner may become frustrated over being "ignored or given the silent treatment." On the other hand, when the introvert hears the extrovert thinking and formulating ideas out loud he assumes that what he heard is what is going to occur. After all, one wouldn't share something unless it is thought through first internally and then spoken. But for the extrovert, the opposite is true. Just sharing this simple piece of clarifying information is helpful to both premarital and married couples.

THE EXPRESSIVE VERSUS INHIBITED CATEGORY

Another T-JTA trait category, Expressive-Responsive vs. Inhibited, measures a person's level of verbal expression and the expression of feelings. It is such an important trait that low scores in this area are accurate predictors of either the lack of emotional intimacy in the upcoming marital relationship or definite struggles. In reviewing results, I like to go over some of the specific questions used to make up this trait since this leads us into some very important discussions. I usually read the question, give the persons' responses, and then ask them what their reasons might be for their responses. We then discuss those occasions in which their responses might be different.

In talking with them I listen closely to their terminology to discover if they can use emotional language or phrases or if they even have an emotional vocabulary. Sometimes looking at Trait F, Subjective/Objective, will help me to determine if they respond on the emotional rather than the cognitive level. This is yet another example of the importance of the minister or counselor's being able to use the language of the counselee.

The Partner's Perception

When a person's partner is present and she sees him as being inhibited, I read the specific questions in which she rated him inhibited and ask her to again give her response. When this is done I ask her to share with her partner the following: (1) some illustrations of why you responded in that manner to the specific question; (2) how you would appreciate him learning to respond in the future; and (3) two questions: "What can I do to assist you in accomplishing this? Is there anything that I have been doing that has made it difficult for you to respond?"

Expressing Feelings

Sometimes an inhibited individual will question you concerning the value of reavealing their feelings. Your background reading will enable you to answer that question. Be sure to speak to their fears about sharing. Men tend to be more inhibited than women in displaying their inner feelings. Often I ask, "Could it be that one of the reasons you hesitate to share your inner feelings is that you would like to share the feelings or discuss them for just a couple of minutes? And you're concerned that if you open up and share, your partner will either be critical or want to talk for an hour?" Often I see and hear a more emotional response to that question than their spouse has seen in weeks. It's a common fear on the part of men.

On the other hand it will be important to stress with men that when their wives are expressing their emotions, they usually want their husbands to just listen and/or reflect back what they have heard; the husband should not attempt to fix the wife's feelings. It may help him to ask her, "Do you want me to just listen, or would you like some advice?"

The following interaction was taken from an actual premarital session of a discussion of the Expressive/Responsive trait. This discussion created an opportunity to both encourage and share information with one counselee, Jim.

NORM: Does Jim come right out and say, "I am really bothered, I am really angry," or does it show more in a nonverbal manner?

SUE: I think it is half-and-half. Sometimes if we are alone and he feels I can handle it, we can talk about it. He'll express it. Other times, if we are going somewhere and have things to do, he won't talk about it.

NORM: But you know he's angry?

SUE: Yes.

NORM: What do you prefer? What would you like from him whenever he's angry?

SUE: I would rather sit down and talk about it. But I don't always know if the circumstances are right.

NORM: Would it help if Jim would just announce it and say, "I am really upset at this time even though we can't talk about it?" It sounds like you know already that his anger is coming through non-verbally. If you can get some verbal indication such as, "I am upset and here's the reason," "I am upset and I would like to talk about this later on," would this help you?

SUE: Yes, that would help.

NORM: (*Turning toward Jim*) What are your feelings about our discussion of you, Jim?

JIM: I just reflect back to the other day, we were talking about handicapped people in our Bible study. We looked at them physically, spiritually, and emotionally, and I look at myself as an emotionally handicapped child because I feel I did not have the opportunity to express my emotions at home. I didn't develop them, I always had to be happy. My mom always is. I wasn't allowed to cry. It wasn't right to be angry at all. Now I look at my friends. I look at people. I look at people who enjoy feeling emotions. But I don't know how sometimes, and that's one of the things I am learning through Sue.

NORM: Sue, would you take Jim's hand, please? I would like you to share with Jim what you will allow him to express to you in terms of emotions.

SUE: I want you to feel free to cry in front of me, to tell me when you are angry even though it might hurt me, just to say anything you feel and not hold back because of the circumstances. If other people are there, take me aside when you are frustrated or find me if I am not there and let it out. Just verbalize it.

NORM: Jim, you are being given a gift by Sue. She is taking away the restrictions that you have had upon you for those many years on the expression of your feelings. She is saying, "The barriers are down so if you want to cry in front of me please cry; if you want to get angry, get angry; if you are hurting, share it with me even if you don't know all the right words."

        Sometimes, Jim, it helps to say, "I wish I knew more words to express this, but I want to try to express my feelings." Then try to come up with as many adjectives as possible and just work through the uncomfortableness. At first you'll feel like a stranger in a foreign land. You have a lot of cognitive ability. Your thinking ability is at an adult level. Using your own terminology, you said you are like a child in terms of knowing how to share emotions. But you're a very fast-learning child. And you can catch up in a hurry since now you have a person who says, "Be yourself." Jim, experience the emotions that God has given to you. If you find yourself holding back, let Sue know and say to her, "I want to give. I'm holding back, but I am going to try." Then just blurt it out. . . . Your relationship will have the intimacy you're seeking by sharing your emotions.

The most consistent problem that I see working with married couples is this very issue. For thirty-five years the man has been just sterile emotionally, an emotional cripple in many ways. And his wife has been dying for some type of an emotional intimacy. But it's never been there—and they go their separate ways. Your relationship doesn't have to end up that way.

It's important that whoever is conducting the premarital counseling be able to express feelings and have an extensive feeling vocabulary in order to model this process for a counselee.

Finally, remember the number of sessions needed to fully cover the T-JTA results can vary from couple to couple. If problem areas become evident, you may want to give specific assignments that must be completed during the time of the premarital counseling. Using the T-JTA can be a rich learning experience for the couple.

NOTES

1. Otto Kroeger and Janet M. Thuesen, *Type Talk* (New York: Delacorte, 1988), pp. 14-22.
2. Ibid.

10

Sessions Three and Four: Roles and Authority in Marriage

Husband-wife roles and their impact on power or influence in marriage frequently become an issue during premarital counseling. PREPARE can tell you a person's choice in wanting either an equalitarian marriage (shared roles) or a traditional (set and specific roles for husband and wife). In contrast, the T-JTA can reveal whether one or both tends to be more the dominant person (or a controller) or if one or both tend to be compliant or passive.

ROLE EXPECTATIONS

Let's consider the issue of husband-wife roles first.

I find that most couples do not go into sufficient detail in the area of roles. Though the assignment "Your Role Concepts Comparison Sheet" in the *Before You Say I Do* workbook (p. 41) is for a latter session, there may be times when you ask the couple to turn to that section and discuss some of their answers.

Note that the second item states, "The wife should not be employed outside of the home." Each statement may be answered in one of five ways: strongly agree, mildly agree, not sure, mildly disagree, or strongly disagree. The partners answer without looking at one another's copy. If you find one person who is not sure and one who strongly agrees or disagrees, it is important to stop and talk about this area. The counselor should determine why they have differences of opinion and discuss how this can affect their marriage relationship.

Whether the wife should work has become a fundamental issue. With the changing economic conditions more and more women will be employed, and some of our traditional lifestyles will be modified. A couple of items on the sheet relate to the working-woman issue, and the counselor needs to explore some of the particular problems that might arise if she works. However, the counselor also must allow the couple to make the final decision.

Consider, for instance, a man who is adamant against his wife working, yet his fiancée is a college graduate and has a profession. She has spent years training for her position and feels that it is very important for her to be able to continue in it. The wise counselor will explore some of the reasons behind each person's attitude as well as work toward some type of reconciliation of the two conflicting opinions.

Looking down the sheet, notice other statements that might bring up discussion. For example, "The husband should baby-sit one night a week so the wife can get away and do what she wants," or, "A couple should spend their recreational and leisure time together," or, "It is all right for the wife to initiate love-making with her husband." If you find differences of opinion here, then you need to discuss these.

This discussion of the dominant/submissive trait may give you the opening to focus on the issue of power in the relationship and how it may be manifested in the next few years.

WHAT IS POWER?

The word *power* has many definitions. One is "the possession of control, authority, or influence over others." The *Oxford English Dictionary* defines authority as "power or right to enforce obedience . . . the right to command or give an ultimate decision." In a premarital or marital relationship, when one partner has most of the power or authority he or she has most of the control and makes most of the decisions. The person on the other side often ends up feeling inferior, dependent, abused, neglected, or downtrodden with attitudes of dejection, anger, and resentment. Look for those indications.

Over the years we have raised shelties in our home. A sheltie looks like a miniature collie and is a very intelligent dog—until it gets into a tug-of-war with another puppy. The two shelties sit there and pull and pull on the towel and neither gets anywhere. They wear themselves out pulling, trying to get the towel away from each other. If they were really smart, they might figure out that what they're doing isn't working. In fact, if one would let up on his end of the towel, it would probably knock the other puppy off balance, dislodge the towel, and then the smart puppy could run away with it all to himself.

Sometimes Joyce and I sit there and laugh at them. Perhaps in reality we are laughing at ourselves for we are not very different from the puppies. Couples often pull, pull, pull, but nothing is resolved. Neither one is willing to risk a new approach.

Did you know that in most troubled marriages the partners are unaware of how much power each one has, and emotionally each feels the partner has far more power than he or she deserves? Ask your couple during the premarital session, "Which one of you has the greatest amount of power or influence?" Often they think the most dominant and verbal partner does, but that may not be entirely true. You may have a verbally dominant but impulsive man who is going to marry a quiet, submissive, but self-disciplined woman. She may have the edge in power and control because of her self-discipline. This is a shock to many.

In a marriage relationship, power is the ability of one spouse to influence or change the behavior of the other. The one with the greater power is usually the one who somehow controls the actions of the other person. But how? Perhaps through making most of the decisions or through having control over the finances or making more money. There may be an exception to this concept, however. When you look at a marriage in which one earns and controls the money, initially it may seem that the breadwinner has more power. But this may be offset by the wife who stays home, is very satisfied with her role, and has great influence in the areas of child-rearing, social life, directing where the finances are spent—or by having a greater knowledge about running the home than her spouse.

Unfortunately, some spouses are trapped and kept in a posture of dependency by a partner who deals out the finances when he sees fit. This type of helplessness breeds depression, resentment, and often major conflicts.

POWER AND THE JOB

Power struggles can easily emerge when both husband and wife have their own careers. A common question being raised today is, "Whose career takes precedence? Which is more important?" In previous decades there was no such question. Today economic power and status competition struggles are quite common; each spouse tends to feel that his or her career is more important and has more impact than the partner's. Many career women would like to have the same power and equality that is theirs at work extend to their homes. Many traditions have fallen away during the past fifteen years, and sometimes the debris gets in the way. Numerous marital conflicts arise because of the desire for power to be divided equally between man and woman. The conflict emerges because the marriage becomes an area of competition rather than a unified pulling together.

Since many marriages start out with both being employed outside of the home, here are a series of questions the couple needs to answer. They are taken from *So You're Getting Married.* If the couple uses this book, ask them to share what they learned from this experience. If they don't use it, reproduce the questions and give copies to them or discuss the questions with them. Another alternative is to have the contact married couple assigned to them use these with the couple.

Will you tell each other what happened during your working day?

Will you really listen and care about what has happened to your spouse on the job?

Will only one person ask or tell the other?

Will you refuse to share your concerns about your job because you think your spouse won't understand the problems you are facing at work?

Will you be too embarrassed to tell your spouse if your boss reprimanded you or that you are terrified about making a presentation at a company meeting?

Will you try to put yourself in your spouse's shoes and understand that what might prove to be no problem to you might be a great problem to your partner, requiring your helpful feedback?

Will you admire your spouse's strengths on the job as you would a colleague's, or are you even now secretly envious of those qualities?

Will you feel you are entitled to a greater say in family economic decisions and in household management because you may earn more money than your spouse?

Do you really like the fact that your spouse is going to work?

Do you secretly think you would like it better if your wife greeted you at home every evening with a clean house, refreshments, and a hot dinner?

Will you really do your full share of the housework without continual prodding from your wife or without feeling argumentative and resentful because you feel you are always getting the short end of the stick?

How will you feel if your wife makes more money than you? If she already is making more money, do you have mixed feelings about that fact? Do you talk to her about your feelings?

Will you feel that you are in competition with your husband regarding who has the best job and who makes the most money? If so, is the feeling one of healthy competitiveness as in a track race, or a feeling of guilt or anger because you are competing with him?

Will you do more than your fair share of the housework rather than hold your husband to his end of the bargain because you don't want to make waves?

If your husband makes a larger salary than you, will you feel guilty when you spend money on yourself because you believe you are spending "his" money?

Will you label the total income you and your husband make "our" joint income, or do you regard the earnings of each of you separately as a measure of the power each of you brings to your marriage?

How would you feel if you made more money than your husband? If you are making more money now, do you feel guilty or secretive about sharing that fact with friends?[1]

Remind the couple that marriage is a miniature example of the Body of Christ where each one contributes because of his or her own unique ability. Competition may be less when the husband is the primary breadwinner and the wife has a supportive role within the home. Or there could be less competition if a wife sees her employment as a job rather than a career. Then the family's life is still seen as dependent upon what the husband accomplishes.

Competition can become a major issue when a wife advances faster than her husband and eventually moves ahead of him. Anger, resentment, and distancing often occur, yet they do not have to exist. But not too many couples would admit to being in competition with one another. This competition may arise from the core of feelings of insecurity and threats to one's identity. But these are unnecessary threats if the source of our identity and security in Jesus Christ is realized. Which marriages survive when the woman earns more or achieves more than her husband? Marriages in which both individuals have a strong sense of self-esteem, respect for one another, and a willingness to support and encourage one another. Look for this in your premarital couple.

DEPENDING ON EACH OTHER

An overlooked arena for marital authority struggles is emotional power. This can be even more serious than the other problems mentioned. When a person is told what to do most of the time, when decisions are made for that person, when he or she looks to the other person as the authority, we have emotional dependency. Some couples are comfortable with this style. Many others are quite frustrated. One wife told me, "I wish I had some say in what we do or where we go. But my husband always overrides me, and I end up thinking that he is right. His ideas do make sense, and he is able to decide so quickly. It takes me longer, and I tend to waver back and forth with my decisions. But sometimes I just wish I could have some say."

Not everyone who holds the power is content with that style of relationship. One husband reflected, "I wish she wasn't so dependent on me. I would like her to make some decisions, stick with them, and carry them out. There are times I get so frustrated with having to make decisions that are so simple and ridiculous. Why can't she make up her mind? I even get phone calls at work about simple decisions. I feel like a parent!"

In a healthy marriage relationship, each person leans on the other from time to time. But because of our culture, dependency has become a problem word. We are taught to be independent and self-sufficient. We put little value on being dependent, so who wants to admit he is dependent? We all struggle with problems in our lives that we can't solve by ourselves. We need the help of another person. There are some emotional needs that cannot be satisfied alone. A marital relationship can provide the most intense and enduring support.

There are times in a marriage when each spouse parents the other by giving assistance and comfort. That's all right if the roles switch back and forth and each person maintains his or her own identity.

One husband told me, "At work, I'm seen as being strong and sometimes even tough by the others. But if they only knew. There are days when I doubt my abilities, my decisions, even if I'm in the right job. I can't share that stuff with them. But I can share it with my wife. She's safe, and she knows how to listen. Sometimes she reassures me and gives me advice, but mostly she just accepts me. Yeah, I guess I depend upon her at those times, and that's all right. I like it and I need it. Other times she sure depends on me." A healthy marriage is one in which the partners take turns leaning on one another.

DISAGREEMENTS AND POWER

When couples have disagreements, they usually are not fighting over the problem they think they are. Frequently the disagreement is over who will be in control of the relationship at that moment. Many couples compete for both power and attention. Underlying the need for attention is the desire to feel recognized or significant.

Couples argue about how long, how big, how small, what color—all seemingly insignificant facts. But are they really debating over facts? They may think so. I hear this kind of debate all the time in my office. But the real issue is not the facts or who is right or wrong—the issue is who is going to control the relationship. Power!

Some of these arguments are so intense, it's as though each is fighting for survival. If they have intense needs to be in control, it is survival and that's why the emotions become so intense.

When both couples have definite ideas and strong wills, defining "who's in charge in what area" is the best way to maintain harmony. The difficulties come when clarification or precedent has not been set for carrying out tasks. This is true in the home and just as true when couples work together outside the home. When each person is accustomed to being in charge, they have to identify the areas. The chapter on decision making in both *Before You Say I Do* and *So You're Getting Married* can help the couple in clarifying present and future decisions.

If one is more dominant than the other, and the spouse is used to being a follower, it is vital to encourage the more submissive one to enter into decisions and become more independent. You might be thinking, "But won't that encourage a power struggle?" No, power struggles do not have to occur between strong individuals. It's what you do with your strength that makes the difference.

In marriage, many power issues and conflicts are tied into the differences between what "he wants" and "she wants," what "he needs" and "she needs," what "she expects" and "he expects." Other power struggles occur not over the need to control but because of the fear of being controlled. The possession and use of power determines how and when decisions are made in a marriage.

POWER STYLES

Power is manifested in many ways. Let's consider some of the most common power styles. Perhaps you can identify your own and your spouse's even as you help the premarital couple identify theirs.

In the *passive-submissive* style, the individual usually follows his spouse's leading and decision-making. Often, he likes his partner to make the decisions and take the load off him—and he prefers being dependent. Perhaps his spouse enjoys this tendency. The balance in the marriage is maintained unless one of them begins to change. And then everything begins to fall apart. On a scale of 0-10, have the couple indicate with a check mark where they would fall on this power style. Then put an X to indicate where they feel their partner falls (see scale below).

0	5	10
Not at all	Just Average	Definitely

The *passive-aggressive* appears to be a follower but has great ability to sabotage the decisions. This person does not manifest any outward show of power but is highly proficient at manipulation. "Outwardly compliant but inwardly a rebel" is the name of the game. This person tends to be late, forgetful, makes vague put-down statements that leave his or her partner wondering what was said. He or she goes along with a decision but then does something to make it lose its value. This person might agree to take a short camping vacation but acts inept, negative, or burns every meal. The trip isn't worth the hassle.

Why are people like this? Many have never learned to come straight out with their desires. They are afraid of confrontation, rejection, and being disappointed. And they deny how much power they have. Again, using the 0-10 scale, with 0 representing "not at all" and 10 "definitely," have each partner indicate with a check mark where he or she would fall on this power style continuum. Have each put an X to indicate where he/she feels the partner falls.

The *passive sufferer* displays power a different way. He/she goes along with the partner's decisions, but suffers as a result. His suffering may be used to get back at the partner, to bring about guilt, or to display self-righteousness. Often this person lets others know in his own way how much he is suffering. Such people have gone to the college of martyrdom for their degree. Again, on a scale of 0-10, have each partner indicate with a check mark where he or she would fall on this power-style continuum. Have each use an X to indicate where he/she feels the partner falls.

The *assertive-controlling* person tends to insist that his/her demands be met. This person feels that he or she has won when the partner gives in. And the point of winning is what's important—more so than the issue. This comes at the partner's expense, however. On a scale of 0-10, have each partner indicate with a check mark where he or she would fall on this power style. Have each put an X to indicate where he/she feels the partner falls.

The *assertive-adapter* displays the ideal response. This person can openly assert his needs to his spouse but is also willing to adapt to meet his partner's demands. This unique person is comfortable using power and relinquishing power—a rare combination. In the relationship where both parties are assertive adapters, each knows the beliefs and values of his or her partner. He also knows his own needs will be taken into consideration. Opinions of others are considered. On a scale of 0-10, have each partner indicate with a check mark where he or she would fall on this power style. Have each put an X to indicate where he/she feels the partner falls.

It is not uncommon for a partner to respond one way in a particular issue or category and then shift to another pattern of power display for another issue. It sounds strange, but it occasionally happens.

A BALANCE OF POWER

To help the couple identify the balance and display of power in their future marriage, have them consider how decisions will be made in a number of common areas of marriage. This should help them identify what will occur in their future relationship. Have them complete the survey "Decision-Making Time" (on p. 199) for the next session.[2]

Later, have the couple discuss their selections and their spouse's. The counselor should help them identify both reasons for this and the potential conflicts.

Robert A. Schuller, Jr., talks about his parents and what has worked for them in *The Positive Family*. Though the Schullers do not always agree, their son reports, they have remained married for more than thirty years. These guidelines have helped many couples.

197

My mother, Arvella Schuller, . . . explains that they have a scale of nonapproval. When she and Dad disagree, they measure the depth of the intensity of nonagreement on a scale of one to ten:

1. The lowest level is, "I'm not enthusiastic, but go ahead if you want to." From there the intensity of the comments increases.

2. "I don't see it the way you do, but I may be wrong, so go ahead."

3. "I don't agree. I'm sure you're wrong. But I can live with it. Go ahead."

4. "I don't agree, but I'll be quiet and let you have your way. I can change it to my way later on. Next year I can repaint, repaper, reupholster it my way."

5. "I don't agree, and I cannot remain silent. I love you, but I will not be able to keep from expressing my disapproval. So don't be offended if you hear me expressing a contrary view."

6. "I do not approve, and I make a motion we postpone and delay action until we both are able emotionally and rationally to re-evaluate our positions. Give me more time."

7. "I strongly disapprove. This is a mistake—costly, not easily corrected—and I stand firm. I cannot and will not go along with it."

8. "My answer is no! I will be so seriously upset if you go ahead that I cannot predict what my reaction will be."

9. "No way! If you go ahead I have to tell you I quit; I'll walk out!"

10. "No—no—no! Over my dead body!"

My father maintains that in more than thirty years of marriage he and Mom never went above a six in their level of disagreement. As I think back to growing up in their home, I would say that he is correct, for the most part. They may have hit a seven or an eight once or twice, but they usually stopped at number six, which really means, "I love you very, very much. Since I can't tell you what this is going to do to our relationship, which is obviously more important than the decision, let's wait and think about it . . . give me time to see your viewpoint and what you feel."[3]

Sometimes I will give couples additional assignments, such as asking them to give me a written response to the question, "What are you bringing to this marriage that will make it work?" One woman wrote:

I am bringing a love for Jack and a desire to meet his needs. I am aware of his strengths and his weaknesses. I realize the importance of unselfish giving and feel, for the most part, I am capable of that. I have common sense, intelligence, and leadership abilities that are

Decision-Making Time

Read statements A through E.

A. I like my spouse to take the lead and make decisions in this area.
B. I let my spouse make decisions in this area, but often resent it and subtly resist it.
C. My spouse makes decisions in this area. I go along but oftentimes suffer and feel that I'm sacrificing.
D. I am pretty good at asserting my needs in this area, but I can compromise.
E. I assert my needs in this area, but have a difficult time when compromise is required.

The following is a list of decisions that commonly are made in marriages. Next to each decision, place the letter corresponding to the statement above that is most suited to how you feel about the way the decision will be made in your marriage:

____ Choosing what leisure activity to do together.
____ Deciding how often we clean our home.
____ Making major purchases for our home, like furniture, a dishwasher, etc.
____ Making major purchases for outside our home, like a car or a lawn mower.
____ Deciding who initiates sex.
____ Deciding how often to see family.
____ Deciding how much money we save.
____ Deciding how often to entertain friends and family.
____ Deciding where to live.
____ Deciding how to celebrate special occasions, like birthdays and holidays.
____ Choosing cards and gifts for family members.
____ Deciding how committed we are to our jobs.
____ Other (Please identify) _____

important in caring for a home and a family. I am not governed by emotions and I usually am willing to express and talk about problems. I have a forgiving spirit and a sense of humor.

One young man brought the following written response to the premarital counseling session:

> I believe that I am bringing much to marriage that will help it to be successful. My faith in Christ is the greatest single element that will make our marriage successful. I believe beyond all doubt that God designed for us to be joined in marriage. I have abilities in leadership that will allow me to carry out my role as head of my house. I have confidence that I can carry the responsibility of marriage. I am willing to sacrifice things that I want for the attainment of the highest good. I have an understanding of what God intended a marriage to be. I have tremendous determination to make my marriage successful above all else. I see marriage as a top priority. I have an ability to sense the needs of others, and I have strengths in being able to listen to people.

Here you have two examples of what people feel they are bringing to a marriage relationship that will make it work. Of course, people's comments are not always of this quality. Some are lacking; their reasons for marriage might be very immature. I remember one person who wrote, "He makes me feel good all the time. He causes me to laugh. I feel fun with him." Her response was superficial, and it did not include the qualities *she* would bring to marriage. When people's comments are of this nature, we need to discuss their ideas and the realities of marriage in depth. If one's reasons for marriage are superficial—looks, youth—those reasons might disappear; then what is left of the marriage relationship?

Sometimes this leads to other questions you can ask to direct the couple's thinking even deeper. The first is: "Name the personal characteristics that you possess that will build up a marriage. Name the personal characteristics your partner possesses that might tend to tear down the marriage." I have the couple write down their answers; then we share them. By this time the couple is quite perceptive, with a real freedom to discuss and share.

CHANGING THE OTHER, CHANGING ONESELF

Because of the differences I see on the T-JTA or discovered conflicts, I ask a question that elicits some surprise: "How are you going to change your mate?" Sometimes they look back as though to say, "What do you mean, 'change my mate?' He's perfect the way he is." You might have to reemphasize this by saying, "Well, most people do find some behavior or attitudes in their fiance or their spouse that irritate or bother them, and they might want to change them. Now, how are you going to go about changing this person?" Or, better yet, "What have you already done to change the person?" The man might say, "I don't want to change her. She's exactly as I like her." This might be true for now. On the other hand, some people who appear to have this attitude are actually thinking, "After I get married, I'm going to start modifying him."

It is unfortunate when we attempt to turn another person into a revised edition of ourselves. In marriage counseling, I sometimes encounter a spouse who will say, "You know, the thing that attracted me to this individual when we were dating and when we were engaged is the very thing that I'm trying so desperately to change right now. I liked it to begin with, but now I am trying to change it." I may ask, "Are you successful?" More often than not the response is, "Why, no, that's why I'm here. It isn't working."

As we look at this matter of attempting to change one's mate, we start exploring some of the attitudes and ideas that the two people might have toward each other. I want them to understand a fundamental concept: if you really want to change the person that you're married to, you change yourself. As Cecil Osborne argues in *The Art of Understanding Your Mate*, this is the way you change your spouse. The other person will change in response to the changes that he or she sees in your life. But if your goal is trying to modify or change the other person, it is not going to work. We have to begin with ourselves.

A friend told me that for many years he kept praying that God would change his wife and his children. And for some reason God did not seem to answer him in the way he wanted, and his wife and children did not change. Then one day he started praying in a very different way. He said, "Lord, change my life. Change me, mold me into the kind of man and husband and father I need to be." Then the man said, "You know, the strangest thing happened. My wife and my children changed." They changed because he changed.

If young married people would work on needed changes in their own lives, then the partner's defects and problems would not seem as large. Naturally, most couples do find areas that concern them. It is unrealistic to think that a person will be totally accepting. Some faults or behavior ought to be altered. A couple needs the freedom to express their concerns and irritations to one another, but they cannot force one another to change. All they can do is to bring problems to the other's awareness, then leave it up to the partner to respond as he or she sees fit.

Two additional principles of changing one's spouse could be pointed out to the couple. One concerns complaints. When most individuals make a complaint it is done in a negative and general manner. An example would be, "You're never affectionate." That is likely to generate a defensive response. Reversing it is more likely to bring about a positive response. Complaints should be positive and specific; in other words, point to the desired behavior that you would like to see rather than focusing upon the problem. A statement like, "I would appreciate it if you would touch me and hold me some each day" stated in a positive, loving tone of voice is more likely to bring a positive response.

The second principle in changing another person involves the method. When a person wants to eliminate an undesirable behavior in his spouse he usually goes about it in such a way that he reinforces the behavior he does not like. I ask the couple for examples or ways in which that occurs, and usually they are aware of the problem.

Change takes time, patience, and adaptability. But it begins with the individual, not the partner.

NOTES

1. H. Norman Wright. *So You're Getting Married* (Ventura, Calif.: Gospel Light, 1985), pp. 96-97. Copyright 1985, Regal Books, Ventura CA 93003. Used by permission.
2. Miriam Arond and Samuel Pauker. *The First Year of Marriage* (New York: Warner Books, 1987), pp. 106-7, adapted.
3. Robert A. Schuller, Jr., *Power to Grow Beyond Yourself* (Old Tappan, N.J.: Revell, 1987), pp. 175-76.

11

Sessions Three and Four: Expectations and Other Issues

During the fourth through the sixth sessions, the counselor should discuss the couple's responses to the homework assignments from *Before You Say I Do*, especially chapters 4 and 5, "Expectations" and "Goals." Those chapters are essential because they help eliminate some of the conflict-producing surprises from marriage and help to give direction to the marriage.

The homework project on expectations requires each partner to list twenty expectations of their mate after they are married and tell his/her fiance those expectations. Then each partner reads the other's twenty expectations for him or her. Finally, the partner marks the likelihood of fulfilling each expectation, using the letter C, S, or N for *cinch, sweat,* or *no way.* Once he/she has completed the evaluation of the other's expectations, he/she returns the list and spends some time discussing it.

EXPECTATIONS AND DEMANDS

Many surprises emerge from this exercise, and it has proved to be one of the most helpful. One of the reasons for this exercise is that unfulfilled expectations generate frustration that leads to anger. Eventually those unfulfilled expectations can evolve into demands. One spouse senses the demanding tone in the other's voice and is offended by it.

A husband's demands might be: "I demand that you get up first and cook my breakfast." "I demand that you always be home when I arrive after working all day." "I demand that you dress the way I've suggested in order to please me." Meanwhile, the wife may find her expectations changing into demands too. A wife's demands might be: "I demand that you work around the house every Saturday." "I demand that you spend time with the children." "I demand that you become the spiritual leader in the home."

Joseph Maxwell describes the negative effects of such demands:

> Most of us are unaware of the demands we make on our spouse to exhibit certain traits or behaviors. What we are aware of is the feeling of anger or annoyance we experience when we are frustrated in realizing our demands. The feeling is so strong, so dependable, so apparently autonomous that we think it is not only justified but unavoidable. We believe that the feeling is caused by our spouse's failure rather than our demand. This occurs because we are very aware of the failure but are largely unaware of the demand which designates the failure as a bad event.
>
> Demandingness is a formidable barrier to marital growth because the person doing the demanding is likely to spend most of his or her time and energy catastrophizing and pitying self, and to spend little creative energy in planning ways to develop the relationship. Since every behavior of a spouse necessarily evokes a responsive behavior from the other spouse, such personally upsetting behavior as is produced by demandingness will usually have significant effects on the actions and feelings of the partner. In most cases, when one partner reacts negatively the other one responds by behaving equally negatively, creating an endless cycle of demandingness that leads away from growth and development of the relationship.
>
> If one spouse is willing to give up his or her demandingness, the cycle can not only be stopped, but reversed toward strengthening the marriage.[1]

Here is a list of one man's expectations. Those checked (X) are the ones his fiance was unsure about her ability to fulfill.

1. Personal daily Bible study—at least five days a week.
2. I take care of finances (paying bills on time—not late); we get weekly allowances.
3. Faithful sexually.
X 4. Exercise three times a week (1/2 hour each).
5. Own a dog and allow him to roam in living room (but not on the furniture).
6. Allow me to keep guns and not sell them.
X 7. Equal participating in household chores (she assigned a house cleaner once a week).
8. Have two or three children.
9. She does not work while any of the children are under five and not in school.
X 10. Never nag.
11. Allow me to work out and go to exercise classes at least one day a week.
12. Encourage me to study.
13. Take the time to consider and listen to words and activities.
14. Have summit meetings every three months.
X 15. Spend one meal together daily if possible.
16. We buy one major thing at a time.
17. Credit cards are for emergencies only!
18. Nothing disturbs our meals together (phone off the hook).
X 19. My clothes mended within two weeks.
X 20. Dishes done daily.[2]

The next question to consider is the goals that the couple has for their marriage relationship. Here are some goals that were brought in by a young woman. These are just as she expressed them:

> First of all, to encourage the spiritual growth of each person. To encourage the physical, mental, and emotional growth of the other person. To produce an environment and relationship that reflects God's love to others. To raise children who know and love God and are equipped to live in society. To produce a relationship and home that is full of joy and excitement. To have a relationship where the basic needs of each person can be met in the other.

Now notice the difference between the above list and the next one. The goals of the following list are much more specific, time related, and measurable.[3]

1. Make the first four minutes together (morning, evening, and so on) quality time of building and affirming daily affection.
2. Pray together on our knees in a good-sized prayer session (10-15 min.) once weekly, and pray together daily (not just meals).
3. Study the Bible together once a week besides individual quiet times and/or reading Scripture at supper.
4. Refine communication patterns so that we go to sleep only after both partners are satisfied that they are understood and accepted by the other, and all is forgiven.
5. Practice hospitality. Have kids or a couple of friends over for a meal twice a month.
6. Get feedback on how marriage is going once a month. Take a two-to-three-hour block and discuss growth and satisfactions as well as dissatisfaction and "unimportant things."
7. Strive for sexual patterns that are creative, satisfying, and exciting to both partners most of the time; understanding of partner's moods, and so on.
8. Seek to use each other as our best critics; seek constructive criticism from each other and be able to give it.

One of the questions to explore at this time is: "What will you as a partner do to attain these goals?" The counselor can determine how detailed a plan the individual or the couple has worked out to achieve their mutual goals. If they need help, you can assist them.

Next you may want to spend some time getting the couple's reactions to the reading and listening materials. By now they should have completed their individual books and listened to the "Intended for Pleasure" tape series.

Sometimes when you ask, "What do you think of the material you're reading?" one person may say, "I really didn't like it. It didn't help me at all. I don't see why you asked me to read it." This is a time when you need to be careful and refrain from being defensive. Simply ask the person to elaborate: "Well, can you tell me more about that? What are some of the things you didn't like?" This leads into a discussion, and perhaps you will see that the reading was hitting too close to home. The person may have seen himself in some of the cases mentioned. Or he found some problems brought out in his life for the first time and did not know how to handle them.

It is helpful to get feedback concerning the books; it also serves as a reminder to the couple that they need to keep up on their reading. I require a couple to complete all the reading before we have finished premarital counseling.

THE SEXUAL RELATIONSHIP

On occasion, you may spend some time talking about sex, the honeymoon, and children. Attitudes expressed earlier may indicate that it is essential to spend some time talking in this area. It is helpful to talk with the couple about the way in which the Scriptures present the subject of sex. God created sex, and it is to be used for several specific purposes. Procreation is not the only purpose of sex; sex is also meant for pleasure; it is a means of relating to one another and being close to one another; it is a time of giving to each other.

The counselor also needs to talk about specific details, because sometimes couples make mistakes as they go into the sexual relationship. Quite often the woman has heard quite a bit of discussion about the question, "Do women really have orgasms?" She might have misconceptions. The series of tapes by Dr. Wheat helps reduce the time spent in counseling in this area. They answer many questions ahead of time.

Encourage the couple to be able to talk together freely about sex. One of the factors that contributes to a healthy sexual relationship is the ability to talk about what they are doing when they are doing it. If something is not pleasing to one, he or she should say so. If one is not comfortable, he or she should express it. I also point out that if one person is having difficulty adjusting sexually, it might not be just his or her own fault or responsibility, but a matter of both partners working together. There is a kind of tuning process that has to occur as each individual comes to know what the other person's body is like and how they relate together.

I tell the couple that there is no set time or set place in the house where the sexual relationship must occur. They need flexibility and freedom about time and place. They also need to be aware of the importance of cleanliness: taking a shower or a bath is very important because the nose is so sensitive to odors. Odor can either excite an individual or actually inhibit excitement.

The counselor should talk frankly and directly to the man, because men sometimes have a tendency to be insensitive to some of the little things that are important to a woman, especially the idea of showing her affection at all times during the day. A man should give his wife frequent hugs and kisses without each one having to lead to the bedroom. Some women have complained that the only time their husbands expressed affection to them was when they wanted intercourse. Affection and attention should occur every day whether intercourse is intended or not. Often couples rush around all day at a frantic pace, and then all of a sudden they arrive in the bedroom. They're exhausted, but they feel, "Well, now's the time that we have to express our love toward one another sexually," and they do not achieve the satisfaction they ought to be achieving. Timing and sensitivity are basic.

One basic procedure is for both individuals to have thorough physical exams by their medical doctor before the wedding. In most states certain blood tests have to be performed before a couple can obtain a marriage license. If neither party has a doctor or knows of one in the area, I give them a list of several names. The tape series by Dr. Wheat discusses methods of contraception; encourage the couple to continue this discussion with their doctor.

When it comes to the honeymoon, there are several suggestions to make concerning sexual behavior. Some couples seem to be convinced that intercourse is mandatory on the wedding night. But this could be the worst time if the couple has had a busy day, an eight o'clock wedding, a reception at the church, another reception at the parents' home afterwards, the get-away at one o'clock in the morning, a drive of a hundred miles, and the arrival at a strange motel at two or three in the morning. The couple is exhausted physically and emotionally, but then they feel, "We must have relations." Often it is a disappointment for both. If they will be very busy on their wedding day, including a late wedding, I suggest that they just get some sleep, and when they awake in the morning, they will have plenty of time, they will be relaxed and have their strength back, and they can have an experience that will be very beautiful. We must also caution them against expecting too much from the sexual relationship, especially if it is the first time. Most couples learn to respond to one another; the satisfaction and enjoyment they derive from the sexual relationship ten years later is generally much better than the initial encounter.

Tell them a sense of humor helps, because both of them could make some mistakes. They may feel uncomfortable, awkward, slightly embarrassed, and not know exactly what to do. We have heard of situations where the bed has collapsed or somebody has fallen out of bed, or there's a short in the wiring in the building and suddenly the lights come on. These are shocking events, but a sense of humor will help the couple work toward a healthy adjustment.

PLANNING FOR CHILDREN

Now is a good time to discuss how many children the couple would like to have, and when they plan to have children. Even though they do not have children at this point (at least most couples we see do not have children), this is an opportunity to talk with them about the importance of being united in their principles for disciplining and rearing their children. The counselor can suggest two or three books at this time.

I also suggest that when it comes time for them to consider having a family, one of the best educational experiences they could have to prepare themselves for children would be to volunteer to work in either the nursery department or the toddler department of their church. They should work as a team, teaching and helping the children for six to ten months. They will become better acquainted with what children are like and have a better idea of what to expect when their own children come along.

SPECIAL SITUATIONS

Second Marriages, Age Differences

From time to time a pastor finds himself counseling people who present an unusual set of circumstances. One such couple that I counseled arrived for the session together. The woman, we'll call her Sally, was twenty-eight years of age and had been married before. Her previous husband had been on drugs, had been involved with several other women, and had deserted the family. She had one child, who was about eight. Sally was on welfare because of the lack of support from her previous husband. She was a born-again Christian.

In contrast, Jeff was forty and had never been married. He had not had any real dating experience before meeting Sally, but they had been dating now for about a year and a half, and seemed to be very much in love. Sally was about four or five inches taller than Jeff, and other differences were apparent in terms of their personality makeup.

What would be your response to this couple? What areas of adjustment would you focus on? And what are some of the questions you might ask them?

I explored several areas with these two individuals. Sally had been living on her own for some time and had assumed the role and responsibility of both mother and father. She had been required to take responsibility for all areas of the home. Would she be willing to give up appropriate areas to her new husband? They had already discussed this and worked out a solution.

Another potential problem was that Jeff had not dated much and had waited until he was almost forty before deciding to get married. What was the reason for this? He just had not found the woman God wanted him to marry.

Another area of concern was the difference in their stature. We discussed it; both of them felt very comfortable about it.

Would Jeff be able to adjust to the woman's eight-year-old daughter? One of the positive elements in the relationship was related to his employment: Jeff had been an elementary school physical education teacher for eighteen years. He knew what elementary-age children were like and had worked with them; in fact, he had already assumed some of the role of helping to discipline within the home. This had already been worked out, and Sally's daughter felt very positively about this man. There were differences, and yet they were aware of them and were working on them.

Another factor had to be considered: Would he be aware of the added costs in caring for a family? We discussed in detail some of the new expenses he would be having in this family life. In a case like this it would be helpful for Jeff to accompany Sally to a department store and discover the cost of women's and children's clothing.

All in all, this couple was a delight to counsel. They were both genuine Christians; the Person of Christ seemed to be at the center of their relationship. They had already made a positive adjustment.

In-laws

In-laws are a topic for discussion. Unfortunately, over the years in-laws have been the brunt of so many jokes that we assume that a couple will experience difficulty with them. It is important to explore a couple's feelings about and relationships with both sets of parents. Many questions can be asked here. What is each one's attitude toward their parents and their fiance's parents? Much of this may have been discussed already.

We ask, "How close are you going to live to them?" "Do you feel that it would be possible for you to live a thousand miles away from your own parents?" If a couple or individual is incapable of living far away from their own parents, they might not be ready for marriage. A person shall "leave" his parents and "cleave" to his wife, according to Genesis 2:24. The word *leave* in the Hebrew actually means "to abandon, to forsake, to cut off, to sever a relationship before you start a new one." Those words are used in a positive sense and do not mean alienation of family members. But it is important to realize that some people may leave home physically but not emotionally. Perhaps the idea of living that far away can assist us in determining whether the person can really make that separation from the parents.

Parents and children need to say good-bye to one another when a marriage occurs. Neither child nor parents will have the same kind of access to one another after the marriage that they had before. Marriage is a developmental milestone for both of them. The marriage will change the way in which both relate to one another. Marriage has been called a passage into adulthood. Both parents and children will be experiencing a form of loss at this time although parents probably feel it more. Robert Stahmann and William Hiebert describe the difficulty in this way:

> Some families enable their children to go away, to become inde-
> pendent, and to be responsible, functioning adults. Other families
> hang on, making decisions for their children, interrupting the chil-
> dren's decision-making process, and continuing to take responsibil-
> ity for them. In the process, these families cripple the ability of
> children to become independent and responsible. Thus, children
> enter late adolescence or young adulthood physically ready and able
> to enter marriage but still not adult in terms of their own responsi-
> bility and decision-making ability. These families have made so
> many decisions for their children that even as young adults, these
> children still need somebody to help them live, to get them up in
> the morning, to see to it that they go to work, and so on. It is as if
> these families somehow do not successfully resolve the young per-
> sons' dependency needs.[4]

To initiate the discussion about in-laws and their influence upon the couple's life I ask, "How and where do you want to spend your first Thanksgiving and Christmas?" In practically all cases, the asking of this question elicits a strong response that usually is already an in-law con-flict. Often parents assume that the new couple will fit into their own family traditions without allowing the couple any voice of their own.

One couple responded by saying, "We have already worked through that problem. Her folks and mine had already made plans for us. We told them, however, that we wanted our first Thanksgiving and Christmas to be special, and so we had rented a cabin in the mountains for the two of us. The parents aren't the happiest about the decision, but they are accepting it. The next year then we can all work it out together where we will be."

Several other questions should be asked. They include, "How do you anticipate dealing with your parents after marriage? How do you anticipate dealing with your in-laws? How much time do you feel you will want to spend with your parents and in-laws in the first year of your marriage? How near do you plan to live to your parents or in-laws? If you visit one set of parents one week, do you feel that you need to visit the other set of parents another week?" These are basic questions, but they are subject areas that have not been dealt with by most couples.

The information you receive back from the parents on their forms will help you in your discussion with the couple.

Why is it so important that individuals leave home psychologically? There are several important reasons. Those who have not left home keep getting caught up in family problems. Because of the crises going on in the larger families, their own marriage tends to stay in crisis. A second factor is that individuals who have not left home psychologically tend to look for partners who might continue the parenting that they received at home. They look for a person who will take care of them rather than be an equal partner. Those who have not yet separated from their parents usually come from homes in which the parents do not want them to separate.

In-laws can be an excellent resource in terms of emotional support and advice. Young couples need to look at them as they would at other friends. Looking at them with a positive attitude builds the relationship. During the counseling session, if one individual is having difficulty with the other's parents, you could ask, "What might you have been doing to bring on this problem? What might they have been doing? What have you done to try to bring about a reconciliation?"

The counselor can present certain guidelines about in-laws to the couple. Some of these are just common sense principles. For instance, a person should treat his in-laws with the same consideration and respect that he gives to friends who are not in-laws. When in-laws take an interest in your life and give advice, do what you would do if a friend gave advice. If it is good, follow it; if it is not good, accept it graciously and then ignore it. Remember that many times when in-laws appear too concerned with your affairs, they are not trying to interfere in your life but are sincerely interested in your welfare.

Remind the individual to look for the good points in his or her in-laws. The visits should be kept short, yet the son- or daughter-in-law should act as thoughtful, courteous, and helpful as when he/she is visiting homes of other friends. That means accepting the in-laws as they are.

The individuals should go into marriage with a positive attitude toward their in-laws. They should believe it is a good family to marry into and intend to enjoy their new family. At the same time, the partner should express the faults of his spouse only to her, not to his parents. He should not quote his parents nor hold them up as models to his spouse. Remind the couple that it takes at least two people to create an in-law problem; no one person is ever solely to blame.

IMPROVING THE COMMUNICATION

Ask the individual if there is anything he/she has never shared with the partner. Sometimes I ask a couple to discuss a subject that they have not talked about much, or a controversial subject. It is healthy for the couple to disagree in your presence; it allows you to see some of the communication principles they might be employing to handle their disagreements. If they have such a discussion, ask them to sit face-to-face, to move their chairs so they are looking at one another. Many times married couples learn to communicate "from the hip," as we call it. They run past each other on the way to the other room, or the wife is in one room fixing the dinner, and the husband is in the other room reading the paper. They talk to one another but rarely have eye contact. I want the couple to experience looking into each other's face and to note some of the nonverbal communication. Once they are settled face-to-face, I sit back and let them talk for two or three minutes, or even for ten minutes.

Another method that will aid communication is to record the conversation (asking their permission to do so, and keeping the tape recorder out of their view). Then play back some of the discussion so that all of you can analyze communication. This can be a very enjoyable experience. People are surprised to hear how they express themselves to others.

As counselors we look at a couple to determine if they have the ability to share on a deep emotional and feeling level. We want them to be able to share their convictions, their ideas, their philosophies, and not only that, but how they feel about some of their ideas and beliefs. Many people communicate only on what we call the "cliché level." They talk about the weather; they talk about how they feel physically; they talk about some mundane subject, but they do not get down to serious problems and topics. They do not talk about their relationship. In premarital counseling, in a sense we are forcing people to talk about items that they have not wanted to talk about but really need to discuss.

Counseling gives us an opportunity to share some basic principles of communication with the couple. A basis for communication is an atmosphere in which people can express their ideas and their beliefs, no matter what they are. We also emphasize that they cannot really avoid controversy, so they might as well learn to face some of the difficulties. Using the silent treatment against another person is very unfair and does not solve the problem. If you have a couple who already has this tendency, you could work with the more verbal individual and ask, "When your partner retreats and becomes silent and won't communicate with you, how are you going to get him or her to communicate?"

Often people who are verbal fall into the trap of putting pressure on that nonverbal person. They will say, "Why don't you talk to me? I want to listen to you. Tell me what you're thinking." And the more pressure they put on, the more the other individual withdraws. One of the best ways to solve this problem is for the verbal person to say, "I do want to hear what you have to say, and I do want to listen. I'm also willing to wait until you find it comfortable to express yourself." Then back off and do not mention it again. It might take ten minutes; it might take an hour for the person to communicate. And when he does talk, it is imperative for the verbal one not to make value judgments such as, "Well, where did you ever get a ridiculous idea like that? That's really stupid!" If this happens the quiet one realizes that it is not worthwhile to reveal what he believes, because he will be criticized.

By now the couple should be reading *How to Speak Your Spouse's Language*. After they have completed the first five chapters, have them bring in a list of the ten most important principles that will assist them in their life together.

During the next week or so they will be completing the chapters on communication and conflict resolution in *Before You Say I Do* that will assist the couple in further growth in this area. You might want to ask them during the fourth session if they have any questions or reactions to the chapter on need fulfillment in marriage.

NEEDS FULFILLMENT

From time to time you will have a couple who is not using *Before You Say I Do*, or you believe some of the projects should be done in your presence. If the topic area of needs fulfillment is handled in the session, it is done in the following way.

The counselor asks each person to take four sheets of 8 ½- by 11-inch paper and draw a line down the middle of each one. One sheet should be titled "Social Needs." Another should be called "Physical Needs," another "Emotional Needs," and the last, "Spiritual Needs." On the left side of the page the individual should list as many of the needs as he or she can for this area of his life. On the right side of the paper he/she should list what his future spouse could do to meet those needs. The couple does not talk about the lists during the week. They bring the lists with them their session.

At the session, each page is folded in half so that the future spouse can read the list of needs but not the way he can fulfill those needs. The couple exchanges their two folded papers with each other. Then at home during the week, each one should read in detail the future spouse's list of needs. On a separate piece of paper he will write what he thinks he can do to fulfill those needs. When the couple returns the next week, they can open the other side of their papers and share their ideas of how to meet the needs with the other's list. Then they can discuss this together.

By now you have covered much of the content of the third and fourth sessions. There are occasions in which you will not cover it all in two sessions and may have to continue it into the fifth session.

Between the third and fourth sessions the couple is given several assignments that are due by the fifth session. First, they are asked to have Bible study and prayer together. Many couples have already started, but some have not. In fact, some have said, "What do we do? We've never done it before." This is an opportunity to share some basic principles with them.

You may need to remind them to remind their parents to complete their assignment and send it to you.

NOTES

1. Joseph Maxwell, "A Rational Emotive Approach to Strengthening Marriage," in Nick Stinnett, Barbara Chesser, and John DeFrain, eds., *Building Family Strengths: Blueprint for Action* (Lincoln, Neb.: U. of Nebraska, 1979), p. 112.

2. H. Norman Wright, *So You're Getting Married* (Ventura, Calif.: Regal, 1985), p. 110.

3. Ibid, pp. 115-16, adapted.

4. Robert E. Stahmann and William J. Hiebert, *Premarital Counseling* (Lexington, Mass.: Lexington Books, 1980), p. 19.

CHAPTER
12

*Sessions Five and Six:
Using PREPARE*

By now you may have discovered that there is so much material to cover that you question whether it can be done in the suggested number of sessions. You may need the opportunity to catch up on anything you have not covered so far. It is best to talk in detail about each topic so that the couple reaches a solid understanding. In addition, they need to ask questions so they can apply this material to their lives.

In sessions five and six, much of the time is devoted to a presentation of the results of PREPARE. Once you have learned how to use this tool, you will see how easy it is to make this an integral part of your premarital counseling. If there are many areas of disagreement on the questions, an additional session may be necessary. And if resolution of the issue is difficult or not occurring, postponement of the wedding plans may be in order. My own preference is to look at all the disagreement questions in every category rather than just select three categories as the manual suggests. Again, it is better to be thorough prior to marriage and avoid reconstructive work following the marriage.

Many questions have already been suggested for you to ask in connection with PREPARE. But you may cover several more with the couple. These deal with various subjects, and you can work them in where you see fit.

The first is: "Do you like sympathy and attention when you are ill?" That might sound like a strange question, but people come from different backgrounds. They have had different experiences; where one individual might like a lot of attention, the other might prefer to be left alone. If this is not discussed ahead of time, conflicts can arise. A wife, trying to care for her husband who has the flu, might give a tremendous amount of attention. But this irritates him. He does not appreciate it. She wants to know: "Why is he like this? I'm just trying to show him my love and compassion and concern." He does not see it that way: or, for some reason, because of background experiences, he reacts negatively to it.

A second question is: "As a general rule, do you enjoy the companionship of the opposite sex as much as that of your own sex?" In this particular question we are trying to see how the people relate to both sexes. Here is a young woman who enjoys spending more time with men, perhaps because she is employed in a situation with more men than women. How is her husband going to react? Is this a trusting relationship? Is there any jealousy?

You can also ask, "After you're married, do you think that either of you will look at members of the opposite sex? Do you feel that in any way you might be attracted to members of the opposite sex?" Many different answers have come. Some say, "No, oh no, we're just completely suited for one another. We'll have no interest in another individual, and that's it." Others have been quite honest and stated, "Even during our engagement we've found that there are people who come into our lives that we might admire; and in some cases we might even be attracted to them." I have talked to a number of couples who have been surprised, shocked, disappointed, and even upset because, even on their honeymoon, they've discovered they notice members of the opposite sex and are attracted to them. Honesty and realism are needed in this area.

Going into the marriage relationship with the idea that "we are never going to notice a person of the opposite sex" is unrealistic. Every man and woman will have to battle sexual temptation, particularly with the emphasis upon sex in our society, including the way people dress. We do try to clarify with the couple the fact that they will notice others and sometimes be attracted to them.

Many couples who have been married for some time have developed healthy relationships and can actually talk about others whom they admire or find very attractive. Some couples will talk about this quite openly. Often a husband will confide in his wife that he is having trouble in his thought life at work because of the behavior and dress of the women. They talk about this very openly and his wife is not threatened in any way. They discuss it, they pray about it, and they work on it together. They do not hide these things from one another.

I like to suggest that if their relationship is what it should be, and their sexual relationship and love for one another are on a high plane, the couple is going to have less difficulty with temptation. This does not mean they will not notice and admire others. That is just part of being human, and physical beauty is part of God's creation. We can, however, caution them about what they do with their thought life. It is one thing to look at a person of the opposite sex and notice that he or she is attractive. But when one indulges in sexual fantasies concerning that individual, he is guilty of lust, which is sin. It is healthy for the counselor to share honestly. You could talk about this area and tell some of the ways you have learned to deal with it.

A third question is: "How much praise do you feel you need?" Some individuals say they can exist with very little praise. However, they might need more than they realize, and it is crucial to determine how important praise is to each one.

We also talk about the area of friendship. You can ask: "Do you like the friends of the person you are going to marry? Do you have many friends? How close are you to them? After you marry, how will you choose friends? Are you going to do this as a couple, or are you going to have your individual friends and go your separate ways?" Often this contributes to conflict, because a young woman might not care for the friends of her future husband or the man dislikes friends of his future wife. Inwardly, she would like him to give them up, but has not, as yet, verbalized this. Here it is brought out, talked about, and determined what can be worked out.

BUDGET QUESTIONS

I also like to pick up any questions or topics that we have not covered previously, then talk about their proposed budget. How realistic are they in terms of what it takes to live today? That is what to look for. Often a couple has thoroughly worked this through; other times there is a tremendous amount of unrealism. I remember one couple who had gone into detail on the budget. Both of them were working, and they went through every item and had $350 to put into the bank each month. Together we worked on that budget to determine the level of realism. Yet they still came out with $250 they could put away. This couple had planned to use both paychecks, but the future needed to be explored. I asked, "What will happen if the wife becomes pregnant and you have to rely upon one paycheck? Are you going to be able to do this?" If both are working, it may be well to recommend that they try to live on one paycheck so they become accustomed to that lifestyle.

Most couples I have worked with over the past few years have not thought very much about what it takes to live. They might come in and tell me that they have put aside $200 for their rent. I may respond with "Fine. Where are you going to find a place for $200? Have you looked?" They usually say, "No, we haven't really looked, but we think we'll be able to find one." The next assignment is to send them out and ask them to look in the area where they want to live and see what they can find for $200. Perhaps they can find something, but they might not want to live in it.

We do the same with some of the other budget items. One couple, just recently, said that they could live on thirty dollars a week for food. Neither had ever done any shopping. They both lived at home, and the parents were buying the food. It was a delightful experience to have them go to a market and see what they could buy for thirty dollars. They quickly revised their budget. It is standard practice now to ask couples to shop at a market together and purchase a week's supply of food for their family. It might also be helpful if the man would accompany the woman as she shops in a department store to become aware of costs.

We go into great detail with the budget since so much marital disruption is caused by financial strain. Several excellent money management and budget outlines and resources are available. A few of the best are suggested here, all by Larry Burkett, one of which should be mandatory reading. You may want to obtain all of them and then determine which would best suit your ministry: "Your Finances in Changing Times" (set of five tapes; Moody); *Debt-Free Living* (Moody); and *The Complete Financial Guide for Young Couples* (Victor).

Other areas that need to be considered include the ways the two people have handled money in the past. Have they had a sufficient amount of money to handle? Have they had a savings account? Have they ever had a checking account?

Another question to consider is: When they are married, who is going to be responsible for handling the finances? Who will pay the bills and write the checks? And how have they arrived at this particular decision? There seems to be discussion and controversy today over the idea that this must be the husband's responsibility. Now and then you find a man who says, "Well, I don't have a head for figures. I really haven't had any experience here." Whether it is the man or the woman who has not had the financial experience, both ought to develop financial proficiency. No matter who is paying the bills, both need to be fully aware of the amount of money coming in and where it is going. If a wife is responsible for purchasing groceries each week and the husband expresses concern over the amount of money she is spending, he should go shopping with her. That way he will know what it is like to go out and pay for food; he can see for himself what food costs.

Three basic principles to develop financial unity are: (1) All money brought in should be regarded as "family" money with each person informed of its sources and destination; (2) money should be used after mutual discussion and agreement; and (3) each person should receive a small amount for his own use without having to account for it.

Another principle to follow is to consider what the money will be spent for and then classify each item as a need or a want. Too often what we may consider needs are actually wants and thus are not essential. Burkett's audio tape series "Your Finances in Changing Times" can be very helpful to both the couple and the counselor. (The counselor could buy the series and loan it to the couple.)

A prior assignment was listening to the tapes on roles and responsibilities. Time is spent talking about their feelings about and reactions to the tapes, and whether they agreed or disagreed with them. Now and then someone will say, "I really can't believe everything that that man said on the tape." That's all right. Talk about it and see in what way he or she disagreed with it. Often the couple just says, "It was tremendous. I wish I'd heard teaching like that years ago." Different reactions are given, but the discussion helps clarify points on the tape.

SPIRITUAL QUESTIONS

Another prior assignment to discuss is the couple's time of Bible study and prayer together. How did they feel as they went through it? What did they experience? Some couples say, "Oh, it was very awkward at first. I'd never prayed in the presence of my fiance before. But, you know, even though it was awkward, I really did enjoy it and it was a good experience. And when it came to Bible study, we just followed the outline that was given in that book *Two Become One*, and we filled in the questions and answers and then we talked about them and how they will apply to our marriage."

It is a valuable experience during the premarital counseling (and perhaps even earlier than I suggested) that a couple learn to pray together, to develop a time of opening the Word together, to discuss and talk about spiritual things. Often couples do feel awkward if they have not done it before. If they wait until after the marriage, they might not get into it. It's interesting to talk to some couples who say, "You know, it took us four years to pray together, because both of us were sitting back and waiting for the other one to suggest it. We didn't want to bring it up ourselves, so we just assumed the other person would." You, as the pastor-counselor, can be very helpful at this time; it would be well to tell some of your own experiences while at the same time allowing the couple to develop the type of relationship that would suit them.

A helpful devotional book that the couple can read together is *Quiet Times for Couples*, by H. Norman Wright (Harvest House).

For the rest of the session, consider the verses that the couple has selected to build their marriage relationship upon. They were asked to do this individually. Start with the young woman and ask her to read the verses and tell why she thinks these are important. This is the first time that her fiance has heard these. After the woman has presented the verses, the same process is repeated with the man.

Over the years I have gained a great deal from the insight, perception, and honesty of young couples as they have pointed out concepts that have been new to me or that I had never thought of before. We need to have a receptive attitude as we practice premarital counseling.

RELATIONSHIP TO PARENTS

After talking about communication, I read the letters their parents wrote. Most couples are very eager to hear these and to have a copy. Here are examples of two recent letters:

> We have prayed since Chuck was a young boy that the Lord would direct him in selecting his life partner. We are very pleased and excited that the Lord has led Chuck to Pattie. They met at Biola and

have had the privileges of getting to know each other these past two years. We are pleased that Pattie first of all loves the Lord and wants to serve Him and secondly loves Chuck and wants to be his mate and serve him.

Pattie has many fine qualities such as a very pleasing personality and is very loving and kind to others. She is concerned with others and above all wants to serve the Lord.

We feel that Pattie will fit into our family as if she always belonged. Chuck's two brothers love her as do his sister and grandparents. We consider her as another daughter. We are looking forward to many happy times together in the Lord and as a family.

Our prayers will be continually with them.

Why We Appreciate Charles Becoming
Our Son-in-Law

There are many reasons why we appreciate Chuck, to become our son-in-law in less than two months. Here are just a few:

He is a fine Christian, raised in a wonderful, godly family . . . .

His goals, aspirations and plans for Christian service are solid, as he plans to go on for further studies in Seminary. . .

He has so many of the character qualities described in Advanced Basic Youth Conflicts' Seminar and so complements Pattie well.

He has helped to give her stability, purpose, and new avenues of services, as he has drawn her out with his outgoing personality.

He appears to be a man of prayer and devotion to God, with a desire to serve Him, as both Chuck and Pattie have set goals for His glory, for themselves—meaningful goals in Christian life and service for their future. This pleases us very much.

Chuck is very honest, direct, disciplined, organized (as seen in his school life and whole pattern of living), humble (seen in his sports, especially), and virtuous. He has high moral standards.

We have witnessed, over the past two years, especially in the last eleven months, sufficiently to be convinced that he will take good care of Pattie, will provide for her and endeavor to make her life as much as God intends for it to be to the best of his ability. We believe he will strive for the highest and best for both of them, for God's glory. . . .

We could wish no greater joy than that they be full of Christ, His Holy Spirit and the Word, as they serve Him.

There are times when you will want to discuss significant comments from the parents' questions form, which they also filled out. The completed sheets should be given to the couple for they may want to discuss some of the responses with their parents.

Stahmann and Hiebert, in their structure of premarital counseling, have a family-of-origin (FOE) exploration. It is conducted because the degree of separation a person has from his or her family of origin can affect marital success. In order to help the process occur they have a session entitled "Saying Good-bye." This concept, as presented or with variations, appears to have significant value.

> We have added to the FOE an optional session which has to do with bringing both sets of parents into the last session with the pre-marital couple. If the counseling is being conducted by a ... member of the clergy, then the session with the parents can be the last session before part 4 (which deals with the wedding preparation); a part of the session on the wedding preparation; or the session following the one on the wedding preparation.
>
> The premarital counselor does not have a contract to work with the parents on their marriages. He or she can, however, invite the parents to join in the last session. If the counselor wishes to include parents or step-parents in the final stage of the counseling process, we suggest that he or she should inform the couple of this intention at the beginning of the process. Not only is it important for the pre-marital couples to know, but it is also important for them to be coached by the premarital counselor in how to present the invitation to the parents. They can be instructed to indicate to the parents that marriage is a very special and meaningful event in the lives of people. As young people they are making a step like the one that their parents made many years ago. The counselor's invitation to the parents, then, helps them to connect with and celebrate this event in the lives of their children, which is also a reminder of the similar event that the parents celebrated.
>
> We suggest that when the parents arrive for the session, the counselor begin by explaining why they were asked to come. In this explanation, the premarital counselor can talk about the theory of parental models. The point of this brief introduction is not to underscore any difficulty the children may have with leaving home, but rather to emphasize the concept that parents are indeed important models for children. The counselor explains that the bride and groom have observed sometimes without consciously knowing it their parents' marriages of eighteen, twenty, twenty-four, or however many years, and that these four people, as objects of such observation, have been teaching their young people about marriage and family life.

As part of the explanation to parents, the counselor also can say, in the presence of all six, that he or she has discovered that most parents have had their own struggles with trying to carve out a successful marriage, in their early years especially. He or she can add that each marriage takes adjusting; some marriages take more adjusting than others.

Last, the counselor can indicate that the parents will no longer have the same kind of access to their children after the marriage that they had before. Here one can underscore the sense that marriage is a developmental milestone. Marriage changes the way in which people relate to each other. Not only does it change the way in which a man and woman relate to each other, but it also changes the way in which parents relate to adult children. Marriage is a kind of passage into adulthood, a milestone in the maturing process of human beings. While children are single, parents frequently feel they can offer the children plentiful advice. Once a child makes the move to marriage, that child is in effect saying to parents, "I am becoming an adult; I am going to do the very same things you do." While not all people experience marriage as the passage to adulthood, it is still valuable in helping the generations to separate for the premarital counselor to stress the importance of marriage as a developmental milestone.

All of this is a way of saying that with the marriage of their children, parents are experiencing a kind of loss. Children are also experiencing a kind of loss. Marriage marks a passage of time. The focus of the session with the parents, then, is an attempt to wrap up two basic elements: the changing nature of the parent-adult child relationship and the passing on of family wisdom (last advice).

We think it well for the premarital counselor to structure the session rather than turn it over to the family. Indicate to the parents that in this setting, they are being asked to give a last piece of wisdom to their children. Each will have his or her time to talk. This is their opportunity to say good-by. The premarital counselor can aid the parents by asking or helping them to discuss two areas. First, what one piece of advice would they give their child about how to succeed in marriage—advice they learned in their own marriage? Second, how are they going to continue their own marriage now that the child is moving on? How will their relationship now be different?

It is helpful for the premarital counselor to structure the rest of the session as well. Indicate which parents should go first; if one needs more time to think, pass on to the other. The premarital counselor has the responsibility of doing the talking.

When the parents have finished with what they have to say, the premarital counselor can summarize what the parents said as a way of recapping and heightening both the happiness and the poignancy of this session.

The session with the parents will probably be experienced as somewhat strained and tense but rewarding by the premarital counselor who has not had the opportunity to experience this process before. The more of these sessions that the premarital counselor conducts, the more efficient and successful they will be. It is important, however, to underscore our idea that if the premarital counselor is enjoying the task and having fun, the couple and the parents will too—and they will benefit from the process.[1]

WEDDING ARRANGEMENTS

The arrangements for the actual wedding carry with them the potential for power struggles between the couple and their respective family members. But this can be minimized by bringing out everyone's concerns and expectations prior to making the arrangements. This is a major event in the life of the couple as well as for their families. Arond and Pauker offer eight guidelines that the premarital counselor can present to the couple.[2]

First, help the couple anticipate what their respective families may expect. When you hear them respond with "Well, I think they want this or don't want this," you have a situation where assumptions are being made, and it is important for these to be clarified. But before they do, encourage them to determine what they, as a couple, want for their wedding and what they want it to represent. Power struggles can be avoided by preplanning.

Second, help the couple empathize with other family members. They should consider other people's feelings. A parent may be experiencing a sense of sadness at the finality of the departure of a child, or fears about how the couple will make it financially. In the case of a second marriage, children may be upset over gaining new step-siblings or the fear of a new step-parent. Help the couple to consider their parents' backgrounds, previous experiences with children's weddings, finances, and so on.

Third, help the couple determine who's in charge of the wedding plans. As much as possible the counselor should include other family members in the planning, but be sure to know who is making the final decisions. The couple could ask for assistance on some of the tasks, and this could help others feel more a part of it.

Fourth, have the couple make a list of what they want their wedding to reflect and what would be pleasing to both sets of parents. Compromise will have to be a part of the process. Parents may want to invite some people the engaged couple do not even know.

Fifth, tell the couple to decide well in advance how much money is available for the wedding. Then they should decide what is most important to them. Some prefer a sit down dinner (and this could be a strong cultural factor), whereas others prefer a potluck dinner arrangement in which friends bring their favorite special dishes. I have been involved with both, and potlucks can be just as classy and dignified as a formal dinner (and much more interesting with the wide variety of food available).

Sixth, remind the couple of the purpose of the ceremony. The wedding is not an event to impress. It is the beginning of a marriage, and the spiritual dimension is the most important element. One of the most memorable wedding services I have ever attended had very simple refreshments for the reception. But the wedding itself was a two-and-a-half-hour worship service with six different quality musicians. The husband, who has multiple sclerosis, sat on the platform and sang a song he had written to his bride as she came down the aisle. The service contained tape recordings of the parents with messages to the couple, and each person present was asked to fill out a form with suggestions to the couple for their marriage. These were then collected, and the couple placed them in a book and read them over to gain insight and wisdom for their marriage.

Seventh, be sure the couple accepts the need to break fully their ties to their parents as they establish a new family identity. This may seem strange but the couple needs to be reminded of Genesis 2:24, which says, "This explains why a man leaves his father and mother and is joined to his wife in such a way that the two become one person" (TLB*). The word *leave* actually means to sever, abandon, forsake, or cut off, but not in a negative sense. In a wedding ceremony such a statement denotes the transferring of loyalties from child to parent and now to this future spouse. It is important that each of them somehow let it be known that their mate is now their highest consideration.

Finally, reassure and comfort the couple as they consider the details of their wedding day. Remind the couple that although the wedding is important, the memories of that day soon will fade. What is important is

*The Living Bible.

their marriage and what occurs during the next several decades. Not everyone will be satisfied or pleased at the wedding service. The possibility of someone's fainting, throwing up, forgetting their vows, stepping on a dress, flowers being the wrong color, the cake collapsing, and so forth, is real.

Talk with the couple about how they will handle some of these unexpected wedding adventures. Anticipation is not being pessimistic but being prepared to stay in control of whatever occurs and getting the most out of it either for growth or retrospective laughter. Two minutes prior to my daughter's wedding, a child threw up in the sanctuary and it had to be cleaned up. A potential upsetting disaster? Perhaps. Or something to handle, laugh about, and put in the storehouse of memories.

You will spend much time discussing the details of the wedding ceremony with a couple. A pastor needs to be flexible because marriage ceremonies are changing today. Couples desire to write their own ceremonies, and they want to plan in greater detail than before. Many of them might choose to be married in a place other than the church sanctuary. They might prefer a home, a hillside, or a park. I think we need to allow for the changes that are coming about. Some of the wedding ceremonies that young people have designed have been very creative and enriching, and they glorify the Lord. Many couples want more of a Christian emphasis and a time of dedication and testimony in the service.

One minister's creative approach to the wedding ceremony replaces the custom of giving the bride away with an action he calls "reaffirming family ties." Edwin Lincoln, who has conducted weddings for more than twenty years, correctly notes that "in many churches, new and revised orders for the Service of Marriage either make the giving of the bride optional, or omit it altogether," yet "most couples I talk with still want their ceremony to include some acknowledgment of family ties." He reports many couples respond positively to his innovative approach. He describes "reaffirming family ties" as follows:

> The parents of the groom and the mother of the bride are led to their seats in the traditional manner. The father escorts the bride down the aisle. But when she gets to where the groom is waiting, her father immediately sits with his wife.
>
> At the point in the ceremony where the bride is normally given in marriage, I ask both sets of parents to come forward and stand behind their son and daughter. This follows:
>
> "Mr. and Mrs. _____; Mr. and Mrs. _____; I have asked you to come forward now because your presence at this time

is a rich testimony of the importance of family ties. You have encouraged [Name] and [Name] to come to this moment in the spirit of creating a new family constellation. You are giving your children to life's adventure, and not merely away from yourselves.

"This is what you raise your children for: to let them go their way. And in their going, they come back again and again to share their discoveries and their joys with you. They confirm for you, who are parents, that you have fulfilled your task. Now, your new role is to support and encourage your son and daughter in theirs.

'It seems right, then, to ask you all, mothers and fathers, to make a vow, just as [Name] and [Name] will make theirs to each other in a moment.

"Do you support [Name] and [Name] in their choice of each other, and will you encourage them to build a home marked by openness, understanding, and mutual sharing?" (The parents will answer, "We do.") "Mr. and Mrs. _____ and Mr. and Mrs. _____: thank you for your good influence and steady ways that bring [Name] and [Name] to this day."

The parents may be seated at this point. However, I have seen some mothers and fathers pause a moment to exchange spontaneous signs of affection with the bride and groom through a brief embrace, a handshake, or a whispered word of love.

You might consider one final act in the ceremony to reinforce this reaffirmation of family ties. It is customary at the conclusion of the service to have the ushers return following the recessional and escort the mothers of the bride and groom out of the church, with the fathers walking behind. Why not have the parents leave with the wedding party, falling in step behind the last bridesmaid and usher? This visibly communicates that mothers and fathers, too, are an integral part of the ceremony, not just spectators. Also, from a practical standpoint, this eliminates that awkward pause between the time the ushers leave and return to get the mothers, who must leave before the guests can.

A word of caution. Some weddings do not have both sets of parents present. Through death or divorce, there may be only one parent on the bride's or groom's side. There are several other combinations possible. This situation does not mean you must reject the idea of reaffirming family ties. But it will require additional sensitivity to the feelings of the parents, some assurance that they are secure in their single status, and some slight revision in the service itself.

Not all couples or parents will want to try this. But enough of them will to confirm your decision to talk about it with them. The ones who choose to stay with tradition will have had an opportunity to think about marriage as a rite of passage that not only floods a new home with joy, but also flows back into the homes from which the new husband and wife both came.[3]

Many books, both secular and Christian, are now available concerning the details of the wedding ceremony.

PURPOSES OF THE WEDDING CEREMONY

Hunt and Rydman list some of the purposes for a wedding. Encourage the couple to think about this list and incorporate some of these purposes into their wedding.[4]

1. The partners' public affirmation of each other as spouses: The wedding is a public demonstration by the couple to their relatives and friends as well as to all society (in a sense, "to whom it may concern") of the couple's change in status.

2. The public affirmation of the partners' separation from their childhood homes: In anticipating a wedding, relatives and friends can express their feelings to the partners rather than keeping them hidden until after the wedding and then later berating the couple (now married) with statements such as "I wish you had never married" or "I knew it would not work out." By their attendance at the wedding, relatives and friends affirm their positive support of the couple and their intentions to assist them in creating a good marriage.

3. A religious and philosophical affirmation: If the wedding is in a religious tradition, it includes the affirmation by the partners that God is a witness to their commitment to each other. In some religious traditions, the wedding is considered to be a covenant between the partners and God.

4. A public examination of the voluntary commitment of each person to the other: The traditional phrase "Will you have this woman/man . . ." is a formal way of assuring that neither party is being forced into a marriage that she or he does not want. If someone opposes the marriage, the reasons should have been explored long before the wedding.

5. Evidence of the wedding commitment: The wedding provides for gifts that confirm the joining of two persons into the one unit of marriage. The wedding rings and other tokens that may be exchanged during the ceremony are visible symbols of the wedding pledge to each other. Handclasps, embraces, and other expressions may also demonstrate this covenant.

6. A legal confirmation: Although usually not mentioned during the wedding ceremony, the official (a minister or state-appointed official)

who solemnizes the marriage must complete the marriage license and return it to the proper court for entry as a public record of the marriage.

7. A unique real life event: The wedding actually occurs in history at a given time and place. That may seem obvious, yet it means that later, in times of difficulty, there is no way for either party to deny the reality of the commitments that were made at the wedding. For many persons, their first wedding will be their only one. For those who may marry more than once, the experiences of the first wedding ceremony cannot be repeated.

8. A statement of the conditions of the marriage: In most ceremonies the bride and groom commit themselves to each other regardless of whatever difficulties may come ("better or worse, rich or poorer, sickness or health").

When you are coming to the end of the counseling with the couple, you might make some suggestions for their honeymoon. The honeymoon can be a time of spiritual growth and development. I suggest that they read through the book of Proverbs, finding every passage that would help to build their marriage relationship, specifically those passages dealing with one's emotional life and with communication. I also recommend that they get a copy of a book that I enjoy giving to couples as their wedding present, *Quiet Times for Couples*, by H. Norman Wright (Harvest House).

THE FIRST YEAR

Helping a couple plan for their marriage involves planning the first year of their marriage. Research indicates that the patterns established during the initial year set the pattern for the following years. For that reason, the following suggestions to the couple may be in order:

1. Set aside half an hour per week for marital checkup and evaluation.
2. Set aside one evening per month for an in-depth discussion of the strengths of the relationship as well as for the areas that need work.
3. Meet together with a couple's support group to learn from them and to encourage one another.
4. Select at least two books to read together during the first year.
5. Plan at least one date per month.
6. Commit themselves to the four-month and eighth-month couples marriage evaluation.
7. See their minister or counselor for their follow-up marital session.

At the conclusion of this chapter you will find the Couples Marriage Evaluation and Growth Plan to complete at the fourth and eighth month. Reproduce as many of these as you need and give four copies to the couple at the conclusion of their last premarital session. Explain to them how to use the form and suggest they complete the form at the four-month stage of their marriage and discuss it together. During the eighth month of their marriage, they should complete the form a second time, discuss it, and compare it with the fourth month form.

Before concluding premarital counseling, I remind the couple of their postmarital visit. There are important reasons for this visit. The primary purpose is to provide them an opportunity to tell how their relationship has been developing, and what they have learned and discovered. It also gives them an opportunity to bring up questions or problems. Some couples need two or three postmarital sessions to work out problems that have arisen.

I tell them that it is their responsibility to call me. However, if I don't hear from them, then I will call and ask them to come in. Send them a copy of the first year evaluation form shown at the conclusion of this chapter. Send two copies to the couple. Ask them to complete them and return them to you prior to your session.

A last point to stress is that if they ever experience serious difficulties in their marriage relationship, they should never hesitate to seek help. Often pride, particularly on the part of the man, keeps the couple from seeking assistance. If they have tried to work out the problem and have not come to any solution, or if one is so frustrated that they just cannot see daylight, they ought to visit their pastor or a professional counselor. One of the worst problems that can develop is when a couple waits too long to go for professional help. In fact, many marriage counselors say that it takes approximately seven years from the onset of a problem before a couple seeks assistance. Such delay makes it very difficult for a counselor or pastor to be of much help.

For the last premarital visit, or the postmarital visit, some pastors have the couple over for dinner with the entire family. After a time of fellowship, the pastor and the couple can talk privately.

A time of prayer together usually concludes the premarital counseling sessions.

SHOULD THE COUPLE MARRY?

Maturity

Now we need to discuss situations in which it would be difficult to perform the wedding ceremony. Some factors have been mentioned earlier; now let's mention others. Age is one of several factors that may lead a pastor to decide against the wedding. Several states have laws prohibiting the marriage of individuals under a certain age.

However, even if a couple meet the legal requirements, you need to consider other factors. It is difficult, yet essential, to confront them with the facts about couples who marry at this age: they are more prone to divorce, they are losing out on friendships, perhaps they have not dated much, and many difficulties can arise. But, after counseling, you still might marry some of these couples because they are mature enough to make it work.

Tender age is not the only consideration. What happens if a man of thirty-five wants to marry a woman who is twenty-two? There is an age difference, but they might be very close in maturity level, in emotional stability, and in their Christian walk. How would you feel about a couple if the woman is thirty-five and the man is twenty-two? An attitude in our society implies that it is all right for the man to be much older than the woman, but not the reverse. Our culture feels that such a marriage is not proper and that there are many problems. Now and then you may run into such a couple, and you must examine your own attitudes. Such a couple might have a very good relationship.

Motivation

What about some of the other problems that we encounter? When a couple refuses or fails to complete the assignments, it is an indication that their motivation level is so low that they will probably not work on problems that will arise in their marriage. In order for them to stay in the premarital counseling, they must complete the assignments. If they fail to complete their assignments, then I talk to them. I point out that this is an indication to me that their motivation level is too low for a marriage relationship. They must be willing to work on their marriage;

they have to be willing to grow and move in their life together. I might ask them to postpone the wedding until they see the importance of making an effort. If too many differences show up on the Taylor-Johnson Temperament Analysis® test and problems on the other tests, if they have a low ability to adjust, and if they are not concerned about changing, then I would not feel comfortable marrying them.

Saying No

When you tell a couple you cannot marry them, you will find different reactions. It is helpful to formulate beforehand the words you will say and how to say them. Give them reasons and explain what you believe would be the probable consequences of their marriage at this time. Some couples might become hostile. They might say, "We can go down the street and find another church, and the pastor there will perform the ceremony. We don't have to be married here." Or somebody might say, "My father is a deacon in this church, and he's going to be very unhappy with you, Pastor." These are possibilities. You are going to have other couples who sit in stunned silence and say, "We really never thought of it that way before." Perhaps six months later this couple will come back and will be ready for marriage.

Some couples will be relieved upon hearing your decision. They have been waiting and hoping for someone to confront them and let them know that marriage would not work out. It takes boldness and sensitivity on the counselor's part. We need to pray about this decision and think it through carefully, for we are influencing not just one life, but two—not only separately, but together in a marriage relationship.

NOTES

1. Robert F. Stahmann and William J. Hiebert, *Premarital Counseling* (Lexington, Mass.,: Lexington, 1980), pp. 79-80. Reprinted with the permission of Lexington Books, an imprint of Macmillan, Inc. Copyright © 1980 by Lexington Books.

2. Miriam Arond and Samuel L. Pauker, *The First Year of Marriage* (New York: Warner, 1987), p 34-37, adapted.

3. Edwin R. Lincoln, "Reaffirming Your Family Ties," cited in *Christianity Today*, January 19, 1979, pp. 32-33. Copyright 1981 by *Christianity Today*. Used by permission.

4. Richard Hunt and Edward Rydman, *Creative Marriage* (Boston: Holbrook, 1976), pp. 132-34, adapted.

COUPLES' MARRIAGE EVALUATION AND GROWTH PLANS
(To be completed after fourth and eighth months of marriage)

Instructions: Using an X, indicate your level of satisfaction with each item using a scale of 0-10, with 0 meaning no satisfaction, 5 average, 10 meaning super, fantastic, the best, etc. Use a circle to indicate what you think your partner's level of satisfaction is at the present time.

At the conclusion of the form, there is space for you to write out the positive changes you would like to see in those areas which are low in your satisfaction level at this time. Be sure to share your suggestions with your partner.

1) Our daily social interaction with each other.

   0   1   2   3   4   5   6   7   8   9   10

2) Our affectionate romantic interaction.

   0   1   2   3   4   5   6   7   8   9   10

3) Our sexual interaction.

   0   1   2   3   4   5   6   7   8   9   10

4) The frequency of our sexual contact.

   0   1   2   3   4   5   6   7   8   9   10

5) My trust in my partner.

   0   1   2   3   4   5   6   7   8   9   10

6) My partner's trust in me.

   0   1   2   3   4   5   6   7   8   9   10

7) Our communication.

   0   1   2   3   4   5   6   7   8   9   10

8) How well we speak one another's language.

   0   1   2   3   4   5   6   7   8   9   10

9) The way we divide chores.

| 0 | 1 | 2 | 3 | 4 | 5 | 6 | 7 | 8 | 9 | 10 |

10) The way we make decisions.

| 0 | 1 | 2 | 3 | 4 | 5 | 6 | 7 | 8 | 9 | 10 |

11) The way we manage conflict.

| 0 | 1 | 2 | 3 | 4 | 5 | 6 | 7 | 8 | 9 | 10 |

12) Adjustment to one another's differences.

| 0 | 1 | 2 | 3 | 4 | 5 | 6 | 7 | 8 | 9 | 10 |

13) Amount of free time together.

| 0 | 1 | 2 | 3 | 4 | 5 | 6 | 7 | 8 | 9 | 10 |

14) Quality of time together.

| 0 | 1 | 2 | 3 | 4 | 5 | 6 | 7 | 8 | 9 | 10 |

15) Amount of time apart.

| 0 | 1 | 2 | 3 | 4 | 5 | 6 | 7 | 8 | 9 | 10 |

16) Our interaction with friends as a couple.

| 0 | 1 | 2 | 3 | 4 | 5 | 6 | 7 | 8 | 9 | 10 |

17) The way we support each other in rough times.

| 0 | 1 | 2 | 3 | 4 | 5 | 6 | 7 | 8 | 9 | 10 |

18) The way we support each other's careers.

| 0 | 1 | 2 | 3 | 4 | 5 | 6 | 7 | 8 | 9 | 10 |

19) Our spiritual interaction.

| 0 | 1 | 2 | 3 | 4 | 5 | 6 | 7 | 8 | 9 | 10 |

20) Our church involvement.

| 0 | 1 | 2 | 3 | 4 | 5 | 6 | 7 | 8 | 9 | 10 |

21) The level of our financial security.

0	1	2	3	4	5	6	7	8	9	10

22) How we manage money.

0	1	2	3	4	5	6	7	8	9	10

23) My spouse's relationship with my relatives.

0	1	2	3	4	5	6	7	8	9	10

24) My relationship with my spouse's relatives.

0	1	2	3	4	5	6	7	8	9	10

SOURCE: Christian Marriage Enrichment, Tustin, Calif.

THE FIRST YEAR MARITAL EVALUATION

I. The first year of marriage is a year of discovery. It is important to identify behaviors and responses of your spouse which are meaningful to you. Please list ten (10) items which you appreciate about your partner.

  1.
  2.
  3.
  4.
  5.
  6.
  7.
  8.
  9.
  10.

II. Please list three responses or behaviors you would like your spouse to do more often. Please explain how you have requested your spouse to do this. Be specific.

  1.
  2.
  3.

III. Please list three responses or behaviors your spouse would like from you more often. Explain how he or she has requested you to do this. Be specific.

  1.
  2.
  3.

IV. Please describe what you were most delighted with during your initial year of marriage.

V. Please describe what you have been most frustrated with or disappointed over during your initial year of marriage.

VI. 1. How often did you date during the first year of marriage? Who initiated the dates?
   2. What books or tapes on marriage did you read or listen to?

3. Did you attend any marriage classes or seminars?
4. How frequently did you pray together?
   Share Scripture or devotional books together?
5. How well on a scale of 0-10 do you feel you have learned to speak your partner's language?

0	1	2	3	4	5	6	7	8	9	10
not at all					average					outstanding

6. How well on a scale of 1- 10 do you feel your spouse has learned to speak your language?

0	1	2	3	4	5	6	7	8	9	10
not at all					average					outstanding

Thank you for completing this form. Be sure you do not share this or discuss this together, but send this to your minister or counselor before your marital follow-up session.

NOTE: This evaluation form may be reproduced for use in your ministry.
SOURCE: Christian Marriage Enrichment, Tustin, Calif.

CHAPTER
13

Intercultural Marriages

They sat in my office deadlocked. They were young, intelligent, college educated, and on their way toward successful careers. But they had just returned from a visit to his home and family; now everything seemed to be falling apart.

"I am so glad we were able to visit them before we were married," she said. "It cost a great deal financially, but I needed to know what I found out before I married him. I just assumed that everyone from his background and culture was like Jim. But his family isn't. The culture of his country is much more different than I had been led to believe. And Jim changed when we were there. He wasn't the same as he is here. He seemed to pick up the characteristics of his own culture and fit right back in again. That isn't the man I fell in love with. Nor is it the man I want to live with the rest of my life!"

June had been about to marry a man from a different culture. Fortunately, they delayed the wedding a year so that each could become more

informed about the differences. Gradually they were able to work through the issues, and June eventually married her fiance.

Any couple contemplating an interracial marriage will need a greater amount of time to learn the customs of not just their future spouse, but the land from whence they came.

As a counselor, what are your feelings about interracial marriages? Is it a concern? We have to face our own personal feelings on this issue. Are you aware of how to help couples entering into this type of union? Does the Bible have anything to say about interracial marriages for today? It doesn't appear to clarify this issue.

Are these marriages likely to increase in the next decade? Without a doubt! The population in the United States is changing and mixing much faster than anticipated. Much of the increase has occurred in the Asian population but even more so with Hispanics. Many of these changes have been concentrated in specific areas of the country, such as the western states and especially California. But in other states, such as Texas, Illinois, New York, New Jersey, and Florida, there has been a significant increase in the Asian and Hispanic population also. It is estimated that by the year 2000 more than 25 percent of all Americans will be non-white. One of every three children will be Hispanic, Asian, black, or American native. By the same year non-Hispanic whites will be minorities in New Mexico and California. These changes will impact every phase of society, including marriage. Premarital counseling will be extremely important. Certain states will become more of a melting pot than others. In the late 1970s, already about 50 percent of the marriages in the state of Hawaii were intercultural. Marriage between Chinese and Japanese became so common that not much thought was given to it. [1]

Years ago there were many more rules and sanctions concerning the selection of a life partner. The basic rule was that one marries one's own kind. This could include color, culture, family, socioeconomic status, or even profession. But along with the other changes in our society has come the loosening of these strict standards. [2]

In any kind of a love relationship couples seem to focus upon similarities to the exclusion of differences. Unfortunately, the similarities often serve as a disguise for the extreme diversity that is also present. In the beginning stages of a courtship differences are too often disregarded. They are seen as merely surface problems, challenges, or qualities that make the relationship more interesting and intriguing. But in an interracial marriage a person must discover not only what his future partner is like but a new culture as well. The new person has to be seen in light of

the culture in which he or she was raised and in many cases will return to.[3]

MOTIVES FOR MARRIAGE

Perhaps one of the greatest concerns is motivation. Why has this couple selected one another for marriage? Is it a mature, positive choice or are there other motivations that are propelling them toward one another? Later in this chapter you will find a list of important questions to consider with a couple, but let's identify the various common motivating factors that cause some interracial couples to marry. In her excellent book *Intercultural Marriage,* Dugan Romano identifies seven main motivating factors or types of people who will marry outside their race.[4]

An *outcast* person or personality type is one who doesn't fit or cannot make it in his or her society for one reason or another. Often selecting a person of another race is his attempt to find a place where he does belong or can learn to fit in. It could be he feels that his partner and new culture won't discover that he is an outcast from his own society. Color, education, or inability to relate socially are some of the reasons for a person's being an outcast. Consider this possibility as you conduct your premarital counseling with an interracial couple.

Rebels exist in any society. By marrying a person from another culture they often find freedom from what they object to in their own culture or family life. A rebel marries out of a conscious or subconscious protest against something in his own culture, which he reacts against or wants to get away from. Some rebels cross the color line, whereas others cross religious, educational, or even generational lines. But what rebels don't consider is that the decision to rebel in this way at a particular point in time in their life is really a lifelong commitment. A twenty-year-old who decides to protest in this way may not hold to the same beliefs of protest ten years later. But the evidence of his protest is still with him. As you counsel, evaluate any possibilities of rebellion through this action. How do other significant people in the couple's life look upon this match?

Another type of person who chooses a person from another culture is called the *maverick.* You may call him the nonconformist. Nonconformists usually don't care what others think and are committed to "doing their own thing regardless of other people's response." Socially they are not rejects, but they are not much concerned about what their own cultural group thinks of their decisions. They feel comfortable in not being a part of their society, and often they disagree with some of society's conventional attitudes and beliefs.

Recently I was working with a fifty-seven-year-old father whose daughter fit this category. He was concerned not so much about the interracial marriage that was about to occur but how their friends and families would handle the "unique" wedding service his daughter had planned. She was definitely a nonconformist in many ways but yet a gifted and responsible individual. Her choice of lifestyle was not wrong or deviant. It was just different, and her values of what was important to her went counter to her parents'. And the more this father spent time with his European-born fiancée, the more he could see what had attracted his daughter to him. This father was on his way to developing a healthy, positive relationship with his future son-in-law.

Compensators are persons who feel incomplete and are on the search for someone to fill the void in their lives. The motivation that propels them toward marriage is need—they choose someone whom they feel will give them what they need or what they lack in their lives. Many choose someone from their own culture, but those who choose a person from another culture believe that they can only find what they need with a person who is not from their society or culture.

Some compensators come from unstable family relationships and look for a person who has a strong family background. Some come from families in which there has been no intimacy and thus they end up being emotionally needy. The uniqueness and newness of other cultures can be very attractive to the emotionally needy. Their attitude is "If my culture can't provide me with what I need, then this other one can."

Not all *adventurers* marry cross-culturally, but many do if it provides them with the excitement that is characteristic of their life. Actually all who marry cross-culturally have a bit of the adventurer within them because they are willing to be different. But the true adventurer is bored with the stable and routine. The differences are simply challenges that add an intensity to life. But how long will the excitement last? Boredom can soon set in, and the adventurer may begin to look elsewhere.

Escapists tend to marry cross-culturally, too. They marry to improve the quality of their life or to get away from life in their own country. I have seen this occur with foreign students attending college here in the United States when they discover that life here is much better than in their homeland. But the only way to remain here is to marry a person from this country, and that becomes their goal. Many "war brides" did this during World War II, the Korean War, and the Viet Nam conflict. You may also see a person from an extremely poor background marrying someone who is quite wealthy. Most of us have heard the story of a young, attractive woman marrying an elderly, wealthy man. The financial motivation may be denied, but all too often it is real. Escapists are willing to make a trade-off by marrying in order to gain something else for their own life.

Finally, there are the people who are *unstable*. This may be an extreme group, but it happens in same-race marriages as well as intercultural. In his book *Adjustment in Intercultural Marriage,* Walter F. Char talks about this in detail and cites some who marry for neurotic, sadistic, or masochistic reasons.

Even though we have these motivations, it is important to consider the fact that an interracial couple may have some solid and healthy reasons for choosing one another. In one way or another every couple who weds is marrying a person from another culture, as discussed earlier in this book. But with an interracial couple, and especially where color differences are apparent and one comes from a different country, the adjustments will be more difficult.

Part of your task will be to help the couple seriously evaluate their motivations for marrying one another and then to consider the cultural differences in as much detail as possible. The greater the number of differences, the more extreme and intense they are, the more difficult it will be for a couple to develop their compatible level. It takes more dedication, commitment, and effort for an interracial marriage to work.

AREAS OF ADJUSTMENT

Most problems will not be solved easily just because the couple is aware of the differences and the reasons for them. Therefore, the counselor's task in working with an intercultural couple is to discover if they have the capability. Culture is something that is learned early in life, and we have strong attachments to what we have learned in the areas of values, habits, and style of life. In order to make the necessary changes and adjustments, the couple must counter the strong emotional attachments that exist.[5]

Let's consider the most common adjustment areas that have been identified by interracially married couples. Not all couples will find these as problems and some couples have more difficulty than others handling these issues. As you read through these issues you may want to consider asking the couple what they think will be the problem adjustment areas in their marriages, and then share with them the following items:

Values are very important because they tend to infuse many of the other issues involved in an interracial marriage. A value reflects what is important to the person and what may be seen as good or bad, right or wrong, important or unimportant. Values can be reflected in dress, religion, food, the way one behaves in public or when guests are entertained, and morals.

Food is an issue for many. Not only the type of food or the way it is cooked and eaten, but many other factors emerge as well. Consider these cultural differences. A Chinese wife may use her own chopsticks to pass and serve food to family members and guests. For her, this is a way of showing respect, kindness, and intimacy. But to her Japanese husband this is dirty and disrespectful. In his own culture a person uses his own chopsticks and his own bowl. In a Japanese funeral ceremony the chopsticks are used to transfer the bones of the dead from the monk to the family member. The emotional involvement in these conflicting customs overrides the intellectual understanding of the differences.[6]

The Irish drink at wakes, the Japanese have ritual tea ceremonies, and Jewish sons express love to their mother through the extent of their appetite. Food issues involve what is eaten and how it is prepared, when the main meal is served, where it is eaten, and how it is eaten. Some cultures have the main meal at noon, others in the evening. Even in our country many farm people refer to lunch as dinner and the large meal is eaten at noon. This can be an adjustment for a city person marrying a farm person.

Sex is an issue. Such things as contraception, menstruation, family honor, affection in public, hygiene, dancing, dress, and holding hands in public all could be issues.

Male-female roles will be an adjustment. Much of this will have to do with the issue of male superiority, which differs from culture to culture. In some societies male dominance is subtle, in others it is blatant. In some cultures there is a blending of roles, whereas in others there are prescribed standards.

The *use of time* is yet another concern. What is late in one culture is not late in another. Some cultures are more relaxed and unhurried than our American system. Some people are used to a large meal at noon and then a nap. If a person marries and moves to his spouse's country, he not only has to adjust to the person but to the timetable of the land as well.

The other main adjustment areas are where the couple lives, politics, friends, finances, in-laws, social class, religion, dealing with stress, illness and suffering, raising children, and language/communication.[7]

Raising Children

Let's consider the last two mentioned. The greatest problem faced by interracial couples is the difficulty of rearing offspring. The children typically are marginal to two different cultures. The adjustments faced by the couple in an interracial marriage can be insignificant in comparison to those faced by children of such a marriage. Dwight Small writes:

> Not infrequently there is a very dark child and a very light one in the same family. The colored child loves the colored parent and dislikes the other. Or the parent takes to the child of the same color but rejects the other. This is aggravated when other children make fun of the fact that two children in the same family are different in color. Our cruel and competitive culture still brands such children as "half-breeds." So the crucial question is whether parents have the right to impose upon unborn generations a radical decision of their own.[8]

Albert Gordon states:

> Persons anticipating cross-marriages, however much in love they may be, have an important obligation to unborn children. It is not enough to say that such children will have to solve their own problems "when the time comes." Intermarriage frequently produces major psychological problems that are not readily soluble for the children of the intermarried. Living as we do in a world that emphasizes the importance of family and religious affiliations, it is not likely that the child will come through the maze of road blocks without doing some damage to himself.
>
> Children may be the recipients of cruel remarks and other unpleasantness. People can be hostile and cruel, and these factors must be considered.[9]

Children are aware of color differences within their family by the age of three. Both white and black children tend to prefer the physical characteristics of white children and assign more negative attributes to black children.[10] Many interracial couples have said that they did fine until they had children. The child becomes the embodiment for the differences in values, family background, and any other issues that the couple has been unable to resolve by the time a child arrives. The naming of the child, the way a child is handled, schooling, questions of sexuality, and so forth, are involved here. Some cultures, such as the Latin, Asian, Middle

Eastern, and many European, are much more authoritarian than others. Others, such as North American, Scandinavian, and some island cultures are more lenient and permissive. If these two different orientations mix in marriage and parenthood, there will be conflict. Punishment and discipline styles are the major conflicts over child rearing in these families.[11]

Nonetheless, children can be a bonding agent in an intercultural marriage, actually strengthening it. "The birth of a child frequently solidifies black/nonblack marriages when other attempts at reconciliation have failed," writes Fred Prinzing. He argues that as God uses children in the Scriptures to illustrate the true meaning of love, so He can use children to bind together an intercultural couple.[12] And another writer disputes the argument that an interracial couple cannot bring happiness to their children.

> [People may agree in general that "like belongs to like," but] there is no authoritative evidence that an interracial home life is harmful to a child. . . "Like"is an extremely imprecise concept that covers a great deal more than skin color.[13]

Communication

Communication and language problems do not just involve the language. In the beginning of a relationship struggles to understand the other person are accepted and even intriguing, whereas later they become a major problem. In speaking different languages there is more possibility that the messages can be distorted or not fully understood. A positive word in one language may be offensive in another. A title in one language and culture may have a much different interpretation in another. The humor of one culture is not necessarily the humor of another culture. Language can affect the balance of power in a relationship. Usually, the person speaking his own language in his own country (and his partner is not) has the advantage and power. The more fluent person has more influence.

Gestures and body language can have different meanings. Silence means different things in different cultures. Even eye contact varies. For an Arab, trust is developed through eye contact whereas for a Japanese too much eye contact is rude and can become offensive. The distance that one stands in relationship to another person varies. One of my graduate students was raised in Chile and would stand about six inches away from my face when talking to me. At first, I was quite uncomfortable since my personal space had been invaded. But after he explained the difference to me and I talked to him several times, my discomfort left and I purposely would stand close to his face. I enjoyed learning to be more flexible.

In one culture characteristics of being frank, blunt, demonstrative, direct, probing, and aggressive are accepted. But in another they are offensive since that culture values being tentative, discreet, and subtle.

It is true that the differences cited by interracial couples may be the same to some degree for any couple. But that is the difference—degree. They are more pronounced, more intense, more emotionally connected, and the person living in the foreign land soon begins to feel isolated, outnumbered, and lonely.[14]

For any pastor or counselor involved in counseling interracial couples, it is imperative to become knowledgeable of the issues. I would recommend reading the book *Intercultural Marriage: Promises and Pitfalls*, by Romano, and have the couple read this as well. It is both insightful and practical. Most of the couples that I have worked with eventually understood the issues and differences facing them. But it takes more time and clarification with such a couple than with others.

PATTERNS OF ADJUSTMENT

How can the counselor help the couple work through adjusting to their cultural differences? Several adjusting patterns are available. One is the "one-way adjustment" in which one person gives up his or her patterns and takes on the pattern of the spouse. Some cultures may be so strong and dominant that they demand that anyone coming into that culture take on its religion, food, and language. For some couples this is their only alternative since it is the only way to avoid conflict. But a person will never be fully able to submit or be satisfied, because this action denies the aspect of a person's identity, or who he really is. It may work for a while, but in time it usually breeds resentment.

Some work out their difficulties through the process of compromise or alternatives. Each is willing to give to adjust to the partner's differences. The problem with compromise is that a person gives up something to get something, and often the trade-off is not satisfying. No one is fully satisfied. I prefer the word *resolve*. With resolve there are tradeoffs, but sufficient negotiation occurs so that even though each person has given up something, they are pleased with the outcome. This takes time and maturity to occur. Sometimes compromising means doing something one way this time and the other way the next time. Most couples end up learning to do this in their relationship.

One method that doesn't work well is to reject all aspects of one's culture and attempt to create your own or go to a country different from either person's culture. This produces a significant loss for both individuals, and they come to be known as "culture-poor" couples. It's as though each person is cut adrift and has given up his or her roots.

The most frequent method of adjustment is blending the two cultures. Some call this *mixing,* some *blending,* and others *consensus.*

Naturally, this is the ideal. It involves the sacrifice of the least important issues, those that are not tied into the person's identity. A sense of identity and rootedness is left intact. They may have conflict, but they return to the issue again and again until there is resolution. One of my relatives married into a Hispanic family. Their Thanksgiving holidays are unique in that they have their own turkey dinner but also eat with her family the traditional dinner of enchiladas. The husband's attitude was "This can be fun and a new learning experience." Individuals who are rigid and set in their ways will have the most difficulty adjusting. Attitude makes a great deal of difference.

Consider all of the above possibilities with your couples and let them evaluate the consequences of each and then decide whether to marry. They may not have considered all the implications of their choice, and this is where you may need to pose the possibilities.[15]

PREPARING IN ADVANCE

For healthy adjustments and understanding *before* the marriage, the couple must take certain steps for the advance preparation in interracial marriages. If one partner has parents living in another country, visiting the home country is a must, whether the couple plans to live there or not. This may be financially costly, yet experiencing the home of their future partner and capturing the flavor of the culture over a two- to-three-week period of time is a worthwhile investment. It needs to be this long for the "best behavior" period of time to diminish and reality to be experienced. This will give the person an opportunity to observe family roles, male/female role allotment, meal preparation and variety, availability of resources in the city or country, political structure, attitude toward one's own country, stability of the country, and the like. Many interracial marriages occur between people who have been reared in the same city but in different areas. This makes it easier to enter the other person's culture for a time.

Spending time with one another's friends is important to learn about the partner's taste in friends, his activities, ways of interacting with others, sense of humor, and his response to conflict.

Studying the culture of another person through books, newspapers, movies, films, and even seeking out others from that culture can certainly add much to one's awareness of the differences. If the couple is aware of any people in the community who lived in that culture for a while, it would be worth his time talking with such people as well. Sometimes missionaries from one's home church or denomination who have served in that culture can be an excellent source of information.

Sampling the other culture's food is possible without even going to their country most of the time. The wide variety of restaurants in the metropolitan area or having the potential spouse cook the standard fare for that country will be helpful.

If there is a language difference and the use of the different languages will continue throughout their life, learning each other's language will be important. I have seen situations arise in my own counseling where the couple can communicate, but one was unable to talk with the partner's friends or family members. When the other person's language is learned, then books, music, and films can become a part of learning the culture.

IMPORTANT QUESTIONS

Romano offers five questions or issues that a counselor can raise in helping the couple consider the implications of their decision to marry:[16]

1. What was it that attracted you to each other? To what extent did each other's foreign characteristics play a part in the attraction? What was intriguing about that person?
2. What needs might be propelling you toward marriage that the other person might be fulfilling? Could someone from your own culture fulfill them just as well?
3. Describe what was occurring in your life when the two of you met. When were you attracted to each other? Were there any personal or family crises occurring at that time? Were you in a school setting that was quite favorable toward mixed relationships? Was there a greater support system in that environment than you will have when you marry?

4. What are your feelings about the people from your partner's culture? Who else do you know well from this culture? Have you ever spent any time in your future mate's country or culture? What are your feelings about cultural differences? What are ten specific differences in your future mate's culture compared to your own?
5. Ask the couple to do the following during the next week. Make a list of the eight major adjustments they will each have to make during the first five years of marriage that are based upon the cultural differences. Ask them to write out a description of what their marriage and family life will be like in ten years if they lived in his culture. If they lived in her culture.

In addition, the counselor should evaluate the couple's Family History Analysis carefully for cultural differences, strained relationships, type of home, and so forth.

Interracial marriage can be a challenge, but the counselor can help an interracial couple work toward a fulfilling marriage just like any other couple. And as with any other couple, the depth of their relationship with Jesus Christ and a willingness to be led by God can assist them in making the necessary adjustments.

NOTES

1. Wen-Shing Tseng, John F. McDermott, Jr., and Thomas W. Maretzke, *Adjustment in Intercultural Marriage.* (U. of Hawaii, 1977), p. 33.
2. Ibid., p. 22.
3. Dugan Romano, *Intercultural Marriage* (Yarmouth, Maine: Intercultural, 1988), pp. xii-xiii.
4. Ibid., pp. 3-14, adapted.
5. Wen-Shing Tseng, *Adjustment in Intercultural Marriage*, pp. 96-97.
6. Ibid., p. 97.
7. Romano, *Intercultural Marriage*, pp. 28-106, adapted.
8. Dwight H. Small. *Design for Christian Marriage* (Old Tappan, N.J.: Revell, 1959), p. 149.
9. Albert I. Gordon, *Intermarriage* (Boston: Beacon, 1964), p. 354.
10. Wen-Shing Tseng, *Adjustment in Intercultural Marriage*, p. 67.
11. Romano. *Intercultural Marriage*, pp. 64-87, adapted.
12. Fred and Anita Prinzing, *Mixed Messages* (Chicago: Moody, 1991), p. 112. Chapter 12, "Mixed Identity: What About the Children?" includes several suggestions to help intercultural parents develop a healthy identity in their children.

13. "Are Interracial Homes Bad for Children?" in *Marriage Across the Color Line,* Cloyte M. Larsson, ed. (Chicago: Johnson, 1965), p. 68; as quoted in Prinzing, *Mixed Messages*, p. 111.

14. Romano, *Intercultural Marriage*, pp. 96-102, adapted.

15. Tseng, *Adjustment in Intercultural Marriage*, pp. 96-101, adapted.

16. Romano, *Intercultural Marriage*, pp. 3-5, adapted.

CHAPTER
14

*Preparing Couples
for Remarriage*

Premarital counseling has become more complex because of the increased number of divorced and subsequently remarried couples. Many of the individuals or couples that come to you will be embarking on their second or third marriage. And the statistics regarding these marriages are staggering. We already know that one of every two marriages in our country ends in divorce, and the average length of the first marriage is only eight years. The numbers get worse the second time around. Almost four of every five divorced people remarry, yet about 60 percent of those second marriages last only five years before they, too, fail. To add to this problem, when children are involved, as many as 75 percent of remarried couples do not make it.[1]

THE COUNSELOR'S POSITION

First of all, it is important that the counselor thinks through his/her own beliefs and feelings concerning divorce and remarriage. Here is the remarriage policy that one pastor shared with me.

> Malachi 2:14-16 clearly indicates God is not in favor of divorce. He wants a husband and wife to be loyal, respectful and devoted toward one another throughout their married life together. Thus, it grieves Him and the Body of Christ when a couple decides to divorce. However, while divorce falls short of God's standard, it is no greater sin than any other. It, like all sin, is forgiven at the Cross of Calvary through Jesus Christ's atoning sacrifice. Through His grace God shows His compassion for the hurts of His people.
>
> The Body of Christ is a gathering of forgiven sinners partaking of the grace and healing of God. We are not perfect people with perfect pasts. We are of the band of those who have been shown grace, mercy and forgiveness. Because of this, we are to be agents of mercy and forgiveness and not judgment. We seek to uphold God's standards of conduct with compassion and sensitivity rather than with legalism and insensitivity. Each situation of divorce is distinctive unto itself and must be approached with understanding and integrity.
>
> I affirm that remarriage is appropriate in at least the following situations:
>
> 1. When the marriage and divorce occurred prior to salvation.
> 2. When one spouse is guilty of sexual immorality and is unwilling to repent and live faithfully with the other spouse.
> 3. When one of the spouses is a non-Christian and willfully and permanently deserts the spouse who is a Christian.
> 4. When one spouse subjects the other spouse to continual emotional, physical, and/or psychological abuse.
>
> Other situations of divorce and remarriage would need to be discussed between a couple and me in order to decide whether or not I would marry the couple.

Divorcees about to be remarried are in greater need of preparation than when they married for the first time.

One would think that people would have learned something from their first marriage that would help the second one to succeed. But, unfortunately, the problems and stresses in the second marriage are so unique that what was learned in the first may not really apply or help. The reasons for the problems in the second marriage have been attributed to money, children (his or hers or both), new in-laws, ex-spouses, and so on. But the real problem may be the fact that they are so busy putting out fires, they forget the importance of their relationship as a couple. There are many forces that can undermine the couple's closeness and togetherness.

It is essential that divorced people complete a divorce recovery program before moving into a new marriage. I've also found it helpful for the divorcee's future partner who has never been married to go through the recovery program as well because it gives the person a greater understanding of what their future partner has experienced.

TOPICS FOR DISCUSSION

You may need a number of additional sessions when you work with remarriages because of the complexity of the issues. Some ministers and counselors request one or two sessions with the children and future step-children.

Group remarriage programs vary, but all should prepare the couple for the new relationship. One strong remarriage workshop program, conducted by the First Evangelical Free Church of Fullerton, California, lasts eleven sessions and includes personality tests and a self-study entitled "Is It the Will of God for Us to Be Remarried?" Topics range from the myths of remarriage to blended family living and communication skills. The final session features personal experiences from several remarried step-parents and advice on day-to-day problem solving.

As you work with couples in preparing them for their second marriage, some special areas will require attention. And you may need to bring these up since so many couples do not anticipate these problems. Comin suggests eight issues that the remarrying partner must consider.[2] The counselor can raise these topics during the sessions:

Past patterns of relating. Ask the partner these questions: How did you relate to your first spouse? What were the constructive ways and what were the destructive ways? What have you learned about yourself since your divorce? A person must realize that a destructive pattern in a first marriage will emerge in the second unless effort has been made to identify the pattern and deal with it.

Respecting one's past. Every person who remarries has a personal history that contains both hurts and quite sensitive areas. These need to be identified, and the new partner needs to listen and respond to feelings whether they seem sane or not. There will be associations occurring in the second marriage that have nothing to do with this marriage but are tied into the first.

In the first marriage couples often use their own family of origin or family backgrounds as the criterion of marital behavior they want to repeat or not repeat. But in the second marriage a person might say about his second spouse, "She is everything the first wife was not..." but then add, "But at least the first one could..." And the comparison goes on. Sometimes the second partner is chosen because he or she is totally different from the first. Or the partner might be a replica of the first spouse, but the person hopes that "it will turn out all right this time." There is security in the old type of relationship.

Realistic expectations. Each person entering a second marriage needs to have a realistic expectation of himself or herself as well as his or her new partner. The exercises in *Before You Remarry* and *So You're Getting Married* need to be broadened to include expectations regarding the former spouse and for any new step-children. The identification and evaluation of expectations will go a long way toward eliminating conflict and disappointment.

Healing past hurts. Remember that some of the hurts of the past will only be healed by this new relationship. The period of recovery for a divorce usually takes three to five years. A divorced individual has to have time to grieve and deal with the loss. Some of this healing occurs as the person has the opportunity to relate to a new person in a new way. Discover in what ways they are now relating differently and how they would like to relate differently.

Contact with the former spouse. It is vital to discuss the amount of time to be given the former spouse and/or spouse's relatives. There will be ongoing contact because of finances, children, business, and in-laws. In what way, how often, and how much time will be invested are all items that need to be identified so that both the person and the new spouse will know what to expect. If the new spouse has never been married, this could become a major issue in the new marriage.

Children from the first marriage. The children of the first marriage will occupy a major portion of time and money. If each parent deals constructively with the reorganization of his or her life, it will be an easier adjustment for the children. Two absolute guidelines to follow are: not using the children to get back at the former spouse, and avoiding criticism of the former spouse. But the new couple may need to have you reinforce this principle since they may still be carrying hurts and resentments toward a former spouse.

Making new friends. Discuss with the couple how they are going to build a world of new friends. When a divorce or even death occurs, there is often the loss of a community of friends as well. Developing new friendships together will be a major task for the new couple, and it needs to be discussed in advance. These friends can also serve as a support system as well as meeting the friendship needs.

Taking time to be together. Encourage the new couple to take time for themselves to play. They need time together each day and time to date. Ask them to identify in writing the minimum amount of time they need together just to keep their own relationship going. This should include daily time, dating time, and vacation time. Help them plan this as a part of their life together.

THE THREE R'S

Whenever you work with a couple moving into a second marriage, you need to explore what is sometimes referred to as the three "R"s: *resolve, rebuild,* and *relink.*

Resolve

Explore how the person *resolved* his or her relationship with the former spouse. What is left over from the first relationship will impede both the individual growth of the person and the growth of a new relationship.

Is the prior marriage over? Strange question? Not really. Many marriages end in court but emotionally linger on for years. If the previous marriage is alive in any way, it can be a hindrance to the new relationship.

In a remarriage there is another cast of characters in addition to the husband and wife. A person also marries his or her spouse's family and friends. People bring routines into a remarriage that were developed with a previous spouse, and the new spouse is expected to know and accept these routines.

People bring memories—both positive and negative—into a remarriage. When everything is going well with a new partner, memories of the previous relationship are negative. Shortcomings are recalled. But when things are not going well with a new partner, a person may tend to idealize the former relationship. Remarriages are fertile ground for comparison.

One may have contact with his or her previous spouse because of the children. But that relationship must be conducted as a joint-parenting venture or even as a business arrangement. Children will affect a person in his or her new marriage. And the effect will be extensive if there are unresolved issues or bitterness toward the previous spouse.

Here are some questions that need to be answered in detail by the formerly married person:

1. Describe how you tried to work through your problems in your previous marriage.
2. How did you relate to your previous spouse?
   What were the constructive ways?
   What were the destructive ways?
3. What people helped in your attempt to work through your problems? What was beneficial and what wasn't?
4. If there are children from the previous marriage, describe how you arrived at the plan of shared parenthood and how you feel about it.
5. Describe how much time you spend thinking about your previous spouse. List your specific thoughts.
6. Describe the comparisons you have already made between your former and future partner.
7. How often do you see your previous spouse and for what purpose? What feelings do you experience on these occasions?
8. Describe how you confronted and handled your feelings during the breakup of your previous marriage.

The divorced person will need to confront many feelings in order to move on. Denial keeps remarried persons and their new marriages from becoming all they could be. Denial means to avoid or reject reality. The remarrying person needs to have grieved for both the former partner as well as for the previous marriage. Grieving helps the pain of the loss to eventually go away. Denial dulls the pain of anger, which then becomes buried alive, full of energy.

Many people think they have worked through their feelings of hurt, bitterness, anger, jealousy, and fear. But these may return from time to time, and they must be faced and experienced for what they are. Denying these feelings prevents healing. Tell divorced persons that they shouldn't be surprised if some of these feelings emerge occasionally during the first few years of their new marriage. Events, dates, special occasions, and places can bring back a flood of memories. They may wonder, "What's wrong with me?" Nothing! A new relationship, with its growth and adjustments, can bring back the past. They may have to face and resolve these feelings in a new way. They need to discuss this adjustment process with their new partner without being threatened by the past relationship.

Rebuild

How has the person attempted to *rebuild* himself or herself as an individual since the divorce? Who has he counseled with? What books has he read, or classes has he taken? Here are some questions to explore:

1. How long has it been since your previous marriage ended?
2. Who were the support people you developed to help you through this time?
3. How do you feel about yourself now as compared to how you felt at the end of your previous marriage?
4. What have you learned since the end of your first marriage (skills, vocational changes, etc.)?
5. What have you learned from your past marriage that will help you in your new marriage? Please be as specific as possible. You might include what you have learned about yourself, your needs, your feelings, your goals, your flexibility, the way you handle stress, the way you handle another person's anger, or the ways in which other people differ from you.
6. In what way will you be able to be a better partner because of what you have learned? Can you think of at least six ways?

Guilt often becomes a saboteur of the second marriage. Often unrecognized, guilt sometimes appears not to have a solution. Some think they have no right to build their new life on the wreckage of the past.

Guilt can be unhealthy when it is beyond the person's awareness and when it is unwarranted. Talk individually with each person in your counseling to help them discover and express feelings which they may be aware of or which are buried beneath the surface. Flach offers four specific suggestions.[3]

First, *help the individual face and accept his/her own contributions to the failure of the first marriage.* This may be painful, but it is constructive. It is easy to project all of the blame onto the former spouse, but each person needs to assess his or her own limitations. Second, *be sure the individual does not accept too much of the blame.* It is common to hear people say "If only . . ." Ask your counselees to make a list of what they believe they did to injure the marriage. Talk with them about experiencing God's forgiveness and learning to forgive themselves. You may want to use the books *Forgive and Forget*, by Lewis Smedes, and *Making Peace with Your Past*, by this author. Third, *discuss what the person is currently doing to change patterns of response that may have contributed to the break-up*. Be thorough in your investigation of this area, and you may need to recommend some individual counseling before remarriage is ever considered.

Finally, *help the person anticipate any future arguments with the former spouse such as involvement with children, holiday hassles, and finances*. How will he handle these? What does he fear about the ongoing relationship with his former spouse?

When a person marries for a second time, he or she brings an emotional heritage that will manifest itself in the new marriage. Ask the couple you are working with if they understand the concept of an emotional heritage. They may appear puzzled until you explain.

Five emotional responses usually emerge in the second marriage, which are tied to the first marriage: fear, guilt, anger, jealousy, and resentment. Let's consider this emotional heritage in the form of questions you can use with the couple.[4]

"What are the *fears* that will emerge after you are married?" There are usually fears of the past, such as the fear of having this new relationship also end in divorce. This fear immobilizes everyone. There may be fear over the former spouse's coming back to abuse them, spread lies about them, take the children and disappear, and so forth. Help them brainstorm the possible fears and then discuss how they will deal with them.

"What might you feel *guilty* about once you are married?" Help them identify the guilt and resolve it. One man said, "My guilt came when I realized I was now loving my new wife in a way that I should have loved my first wife. If I had, perhaps it would not have failed." But perhaps he was not capable of loving his first wife in that way because growth had only now occurred in his life.

"What will you be *angry* about concerning your first marriage?" Anger could stem from previous losses, the children's schedule, or having so many demands to fulfill. Bottling up anger is destructive. It needs to be examined, expressed properly, and clearly identified in terms of what it is directed toward.

"Have you considered what you might be *jealous* about once you are married?" Usually jealousy comes because of the sharing of children and money.

"How will you handle the feelings of *resentment* that may come?" Resentments will occur because of the sharing of finances and children and holidays. And it will occur because of the memory of irresponsible behavior or an affair on the part of the former spouse. Help them develop a plan to handle the resentments.

Relink

Relinking, the third step, involves developing a new relationship. We must ask whether this relationship occurred for healthy reasons or on the rebound? Has the relinking occurred out of desperate loneliness or a positive decision?

The family of the remarried is different in many respects. In a first marriage we have a couple who usually have time to adjust to one another before complicating their life with children. They then learn their parenting roles as they raise their children from infancy through the various stages. They have an idea of what is expected of them and they know what to expect. And the parents usually share affection and responsibility for the children.

The remarriage family is different. The functions and structure are different. Now the family consists of one biological parent and a stepparent who live together with the children, and one biological parent who lives elsewhere. There is no time to build the couple relationship prior to children. In many remarried families the couple have to resort to a calendar in order to survive and have sufficient time together. But they don't anticipate this while they are planning their marriage.

When the remarriage occurs, the partners soon discover there is no such thing as instant love, or instant families. Each adult comes into this relationship having experienced a major loss and hoping to have what was formerly lacking. But they are often distracted by the demands of children living with them or with the ex-spouse. A stepparent may have just as much difficulty accepting a stepchild as the stepchild has with the new parent. Resentment can easily build as the new family struggles to accept one another and carve out a workable marriage.

NEEDS OF THE CHILDREN

Here is a sampling of what the future holds with children in the remarriage. Ask the couple to consider these issues:

1. How will you handle disagreements over the care of the children and activities in which they are involved?
2. How do you feel about the types of gifts former partners bring to the children or their former spouse?
3. What visiting privileges will you give to the relatives of your former partner who still relate to your children or stepchildren as part of their family?
4. How will you talk to your children or stepchildren about your former partner's motives and actions that you believe to be wrong?
5. What will you tell your child to say to a former partner when the child is asked about his new family relationships?
6. What will you say about your new family when you are asked by others about the new relationship?
7. What is your plan for handling holidays, birthdays, and special occasions, and for fulfilling your desires and your former partner's desires?
8. What will you share with your children about their expected response to new relatives that they have inherited?
9. Describe how you have listened to and responded to your children's concerns about your future marriage.
10. In what way have you included your children in the wedding ceremony, either by physical presence or by opinion?[5]

Should children be involved in the wedding ceremony for a second marriage couple? There are several factors to consider. For children who have experienced the pain of a difficult divorce or the loss of a parent by death, being involved may be a source of encouragement to them. They gain the perspective that life can go on again, and being a part of the happenings may assist in this process.

The enjoyment and fun factor of wedding preparations appeal to most children. When they take part in the service they have the feeling of helping their mother or father in becoming married again. Even if children are not a part of the actual service, their presence should be acknowledged so that they feel included. Often when the question is asked, "Who gives this woman to be married to this man?" the children answer in the affirmative.

I have talked to couples who have taken the honeymoon by themselves and some who included the children. Both have worked out, but in either case, proper planning and detailed preparation is necessary for it to work.[6]

Here is a list of basic questions that you can duplicate and give to the couple contemplating marriage and becoming stepparents. Usually these issues are confronted after the marriage and sometimes with unpleasant results. If the children are old enough they may need to become part of the discussion and decision process.

1. What time will meals be served?
2. Must everyone be present for mealtime?
3. Are snacks allowed between meals and, if so, what?
4. Does everyone have to clean his plate at meals?
5. Is the TV allowed during meals, or are phone calls accepted at that time?
6. Will pets be allowed and, if so, what kind? Inside or outside?
7. Who will be responsible for what chores in the house? What about the yard?
8. Who is responsible for the children's rooms, and how neat must they be?
9. What do you define as rude behavior? What happens when this occurs?
10. Are there any guidelines for the use of the TV, videos, rating of movies, and type of music allowed in the home.
11. What are the guidelines for church involvement?
12. Is it all right for some to attend a different church?
13. Is there prayer prior to meals?
14. Will there be family devotions? If so, does everyone need to participate?

These questions should create some lively discussion, but it is better prior to the marriage than after.[7]

When there are children in the new family, a couple will have to organize the use of their time very carefully. There will be times when a parent spends time with his or her biological children alone. It is important that the children know that their parent-child relationship will remain regardless of the new marriage. It will also be important that the new stepparent spends individual time with each stepchild in order to build that relationship. Naturally there will be times when everyone is interacting together including the couple and both sets of children. As the children enter adolescence it is normal for them not to want to be together with their parents as much as before.

But what is really needed for this new marriage to make it is couple time, both planned and spontaneous.[8]

ADJUSTMENTS FOR THE STEPPARENT

Both stepparents will have their own set of problems and adjustments with a remarried family. Olson and Pia-Terry cite eight possible adjustments a stepfather may confront.[9]

1. *Uncertainty about the amount of authority in his role as a father.* The transition from dating the children's mother before marriage to becoming a stepparent can be uncomfortable for the stepfather. If he tends to be a controller or quite dominant he may want to step in and assume control immediately. This can be disastrous and usually leads to alienation of both the children and his new wife as she begins to defend them. It is best to assume the role of a friend or uncle for the first five years and allow the biological parent to be the main disciplinarian.

2. *Uncertainty about the amount of affection given to stepchildren as well as how to express it.* There is an awkwardness that has to be faced.

3. *Conflicts over the rules, such as which are important and which are not.* And the enforcement of these rules may be an issue as well.

4. *A struggle to satisfy the financial demands of two families.* Unfortunately, the way money is allocated is often seen as a measure of love among spouses and the children.

5. *Guilt over leaving their children from a previous marriage.* This impedes their giving freely to their new wife and stepchildren.

6. *The question of loyalty.* It's common for stepfathers whose biological children live with their mothers to regret the time they spend with their new family. They wish they could have more time with their own.

7. *Sexual concerns.* Such concerns exist since a man may be sexually attracted to stepdaughters, stepdaughters to stepfathers, stepmothers to stepsons and step-siblings to step-siblings.

8. *Names and identity.* Even the issue of surnames can arise since some stepfathers object to sharing their name with stepchildren.

All of these issues need to be raised and faced in your counseling with the remarriage couple. If they respond with "It won't be a problem," press further to discover if they have actually discussed each issue openly.

Lillian Messinger suggests that

remarriage requires accommodating formerly established plans to present marriage plans. It also requires that both partners realistically face the fact that remarriage where there are children from the previous marriage requires preparation and anticipation of what will fit the new family life-style. The divorce does not terminate the former marriage ties. Divorce is only between the couple, not between parents and child, nor between parents and each of the extended families of the ex-spouses. As sociologist Paul Bohanner states, "My ex-wife will always be my son's mother and my ex-wife's mother will always be his grandmother."[10]

In our American culture we have many sub-cultures. One of these cultures is a group of remarried families. Blended families are not a deviant or odd group. It's been said that families have not broken up today but simply reorganized. In fact, ex-spouses are still parents to their children. The family still has the same members, the children and mother and father. It's just that they don't live together anymore.

In second marriages triangles seem to emerge. A triangle is a situation in which a remarried person is caught between the two people who have conflicting demands. And often the person involved ends up feeling torn.

It is possible for a divorced person who marries another divorced individual to have numerous conflicting relationship problems. Consider just five new relationships the divorced man must deal with when he marries a divorced woman:

1. Former wife vs. new wife
2. Children of his new marriage vs. children of his former marriage
3. Children of new marriage vs. children of current wife's former marriage
4. Former wife vs. children of his former marriage
5. Children of current wife's former marriage vs. father of those children

In first marriages, the first year of marriage is often a period of intense adjustment, conflict, disillusionment, and turmoil. In remarriages, there is usually a longer period required for minimal adjustment. This can range from two to five years. During the counseling sessions, I have seen several indicators that suggest difficulty in adjusting to remarriage. As you minister to each couple, look for these predictors of difficulty in adjustment:

1. A wide discrepancy between the life-cycles of the families (one parent has older teens and the other pre-schoolers, for instance)
2. Denial of prior loss and/or a short interval between marriages
3. Failure to resolve intense relationship issues of the first family; for example, some family members still feel intense anger or bitterness about the divorce
4. Lack of awareness of the emotional difficulties of remarriage for children

What about prenuptial agreements? Do they have any place in a Christian marriage? It's rare to find these in first marriages, but in second or third marriages they are frequently considered. Some feel that such an agreement actually limits the depth of commitment to the relationship, but because of the baggage brought from a previous marriage some believe that such a document is necessary.

Prenuptial agreements should not be used to prepare the couple for or imply divorce; yet an agreement may be helpful in certain cases, such as certain savings accounts or possessions intended for children of the first marriage. Children, homes, investments, and personal property and potential inheritance may necessitate at least some clarification and some legal agreement. Furthermore, reviewing property, assets, and obligations may bring to light other issues that had not yet been disclosed.

Items that the couple needs to discuss and clarify prior to their marriage include real estate, furniture and furnishings, stocks, money-market funds, and savings accounts. In addition, the couple may want to have separate wills. A prenuptial agreement would itemize provisions each person should make for the other in his or her will. For a fuller discussion of items and the arguments for joint or separate holdings, see "Is a Prenuptial Agreement Necessary?" by Neal Kuyper (in Belovitch, *Making Remarriage Work*).[11]

Who said life was simple! As you work with your couple, ask them to identify the potential and present triangles. Have them anticipate what triangles they will experience and what they can do to alleviate the stress that may be involved.

READY FOR REMARRIAGE?

How can the counselor know if a person is ready for remarriage? What are some of the goals that we can work toward that will let us know readiness? Besides all of the factors involved in marrying, there are some additional issues. Any individual seeking remarriage needs to have resolved his or her former marriage in relationship to all of the other individuals directly or indirectly involved. What are the indications of this?

First, persons ready for remarriage have accepted the death of the marriage relationship and the reality that they are now divorced. They have made decisions about the divorce settlement and the children that both spouses can live with, with a minimum of continuing bitterness and angry flare-ups. These decisions have been put into practice, and they are working. This can include financial arrangements, child custody, holidays, and so forth.

Second, the individual has learned how not to be "hooked" by their former spouse's responses or behavior.

You may want to ask two significant questions of the divorced person. "How much time do you spend thinking about your former marriage and partner?" "How much time do you spend talking about your former marriage and partner?"

DENIAL AND EXPECTATIONS

Help the remarried couple, as any couple, anticipate the reality of their first year. Remarried couples must deal with additional issues. For some, a fear of abandonment may contaminate their relationship. When issues arise and the relationship has some difficult adjustments, this fear frequently creeps back into a person's mind. "What if he or she leaves like my other partner did?"

Premarital behavior contains denial behavior and attitudes, but once married, a person's denial will disappear. Individuals put forth their best behavior during courtship, and the darker parts of one's personality tend to be hidden. After marriage, the counselor often will hear, "I never saw his anger . . . I never saw her moodiness . . . I never saw her act like that before."

Ask the couple what each thinks he might be denying and what he fears the partner may be denying. Your testing procedures will help to discover these areas, but they still may emerge later on. Ask how they will handle these surprises when they occur and what feelings might arise on their part.

In any marriage, expectations plague the progress of the relationship. But in second marriages they can be more extensive as well as subtle. Jim Smoke describes some that he has found over the years of counseling remarrieds. Here are a number of them:

1. My new spouse will make me far happier than my former spouse did.
2. My new spouse will be totally different from my former spouse.
3. My new spouse will always understand me.
4. My new spouse will have none of the bad habits of my former spouse.
5. My new spouse will be a better parent than my former spouse.
6. My new spouse will never disappoint me.
7. My new spouse will never handle money as poorly as my former spouse.
8. My new spouse will make me a better person and make me happy.
9. My new spouse will make all the pain and hurt from my previous marriage go away.
10. My new spouse is perfect.[12]

If any about-to-be or current second-marriage spouses knew that the above were expectations for them, they would probably leave the country.

On the other hand, the remarrying spouse needs to know there are realistic expectations. They include: "My new spouse will love me as much as I love him or her" and "My spouse will love my children as much as I love his or her children." Smoke identifies several realistic expectations in his book *Growing in Remarriage*.[13] He also clarifies some universal expectations for second marriages.

Expectations start with the person you are married to and then extend to the life you are living out with that person. The two are so closely woven together that it is hard to look at them separately. The marriage is what two persons are building together. It is the one primary thing of which they both have ownership.

The basic expectation of a new marriage is that it will be different from and better than the one that preceded it. That is especially true if the prior marriage ended in a bitter divorce. Too often I hear these sad words after a year or two of a new marriage: "Same old script!" Old patterns from the former marriage begin to reappear and discouragement sets in. At this point, some people choose to leave the relationship while others settle in and serve a sentence called marriage.

What are realistic expectations of a second marriage?

PREPARING COUPLES FOR REMARRIAGE

1. You can expect it to be tougher to build than a first marriage.
2. You can expect it to be complicated, exasperating, and tiring.
3. You can expect it to be a slow building process.
4. You can expect some "same old script" times but know that you are writing a new script each day.
5. You can expect to want to run from it every now and then—but you won't.
6. You can expect a lot of outside pressures that are new to you. They come from parents, children, families, jobs, and former spouses.
7. You can expect your second marriage to be successful if you dig in and go for the long haul instead of the overnight wonder.[14]

Your ministry with these couples can make the difference in the fulfillment of their second time around dream.

NOTES

1. Bibi Wein, "The Special Stress of Second Marriages," *Redbook,* June 1987, p. 100.
2. Paula Ripple Comin, "Love Is Not All . . . Success in Remarriage Requires Much More"; Jeanne Belovitch, gen. ed., *Making Remarriage Work* (Lexington, Mass.: Lexington, 1987), pp. 16-17, adapted.
3. Frederic F. Flach, "How Not to Let Guilt Destroy a Second Chance," in Belovitch, pp. 47-48, adapted.
4. Elizabeth Einstein, "Facing the Feelings Remarriage Brings and Letting Go," in Belovitch, pp. 57-60, adapted.
5. H. Norman Wright, *Before You Remarry* (Eugene, Ore.: Harvest House, 1988), pp. 14-15.
6. Neal A. Kuyper, "The Question of Children at the Wedding," in Belovitch, pp. 122-23, adapted.
7. Richard P. Olson and Carole Della Pia-Terry, *Help for Remarried Couples and Families* (Valley Forge, Pa.: Judson, 1984), p. 66, adapted.
8. Ibid., p. 75, adapted.
9. Frederick F. Flach, "Guidelines for Stepfathers," in Belovitch, *Making Remarriage Work,* p. 85, adapted.
10. Lillian Messenger, "More Than One Kind of Normal Family," in Belovitch, *Making Remarriage Work,* p.4
11. Jeanne Belovitch, *Making Remarriage Work* (Lexington, Mass.: Lexington 1987), pp. 28-30, adapted.
12. Jim Smoke, *Growing in Remarriage* (Old Tappan, N.J.: Revell, 1990), p. 88.
13. Ibid., p. 89.
14. Ibid., p. 90